HUMAN
MEDICINE

HUMAN MEDICINE

JAMES B. NELSON

ETHICAL PERSPECTIVES ON NEW MEDICAL ISSUES

AUGSBURG PUBLISHING HOUSE
Minneapolis, Minnesota

HUMAN MEDICINE: Ethical Perspectives on New Medical Issues

Manufactured in the United States of America

Contents

Preface 9

   I. Caring for Human Health...................... 13

  II. The Humanity in Abortion.................... 31

 III. Human Factors in Artificial Insemination......... 59

 IV. Human Experimentation 79

   V. Genetics and the Control of Human Development 97

 VI. Humanizing the Dying Process................. 123

 VII. Organ Transplants: Their Human Dimensions... 149

VIII. Medical Care for a More Human Society......... 171

Notes 191

To our parents

Inez B. Nelson

Oscar J. Nelson (1892-1952)

George H. and Mary L. Coulter

Preface

During the 1968 Senate hearings on the establishment of a National Advisory Commission on Health Science and Society some fascinating and disturbing testimonies were heard. Geneticist Arthur Kornberg, a Nobel laureate, testified that in his judgment there were no new ethical or moral problems arising from the developments in his field. Such a commission, he said, would have as its only use the education of the public on the need for more research money for scientists. A similar tack was taken by heart transplanter Christiaan Barnard, whose remarks betrayed the assumption that if nonmedical people were to influence medical or scientific policies the results could only be repressive.[1]

In the years since 1968 a great deal has happened. More people are aware that there are indeed new ethical and moral problems arising in the biomedical fields. Furthermore, there is an increasing recognition that nonmedical people not only have a great stake in what happens in the laboratory, the hospital, and the clinic, but that they also have an obligation to be informed and to enter into the processes of ethical reflection on these matters. For what is at issue is not simply technical medicine but the human dimensions and qualities of that medicine.

As a result, the literature in medical ethics is growing rapidly. Why add another introductory treatment of the issues? For one reason, most of the material of which I am aware is in anthology

9

form with different problems handled by different authors from different perspectives. I believe we also need books such as this one which attempt to view the whole gamut of issues from one perspective so that we can see, for example, how the moral problems surrounding abortion are intimately intertwined with those surrounding the care of the dying, how issues in genetics relate to those in organ transplants. In addition, the small number of medical ethics survey books written from one person's theologically-based perspective can stand another joining their number simply because "new occasions teach new duties." The rapid developments in medicine are constantly raising fresh issues, and our ethical reflections in this mobile field need repeated updating and rethinking.

While I am an ethicist by trade, I am also a medical layman, and in the course of preparing these chapters I have become convinced anew that learning is truly a communal enterprise. I have gained much from students and medical professionals participating in two classes in medical ethics at United Theological Seminary, one offered jointly with the University of Minnesota Medical School. In particular, I am grateful for the counsel of several good friends who read portions of this manuscript. None deserves to be saddled with my shortcomings, but each deserves my hearty thanks for suggestions and critical comments. These include my faculty colleagues H. Wilson Yates, Clyde J. Steckel, and Donald R. White, each of whom read portions dealing with issues in which he has special and admirable competence. These also include several whose daily involvement in the medical world has enriched me: Lloyd E. Beebe (Director of Chaplains, Hennepin County General Hospital, Minneapolis), Allen W. Delzell (family practice physician, Minneapolis), James W. Maddock (University of Minnesota Medical School faculty member and teaching partner in our joint course), Dorothea P. Nelson (science editor), and Douglas A. Nelson (pathologist at Upstate Medical Center, State University of New York, Syracuse). To each of these persons goes my special gratitude, and particular affection to the latter two, my sister-in-law and my brother.

Preparation of some of the material in this book was also encouraged by the invitations to speak on several of these subjects at local churches and at two conferences, The Pastoral Care Conference of Rochester Methodist Hospital, Rochester, Minnesota, in November 1971 and the St. Olaf Summer Theological Conference of St. Olaf College, Northfield, Minnesota, in July 1973. I am grateful to these hosts.

The Administration of United Theological Seminary of the Twin Cities has my sincere thanks for numerous ways in which it encouraged this project, and I appreciate the spirit and skillful typing of Elsie Johnson, Carolyn Jaeger, Mildred LaDoux, and Virginia Hutchison.

CHAPTER ONE

Caring for
Human Health

You go to a hospital and maybe once a day the doctor comes around and he stays there, maybe five minutes. He talks a little bit but he asks you questions. Once in a while they give you a little medicine, just a little bit of it. About the only thing they do is to put something in your mouth and see how hot you are. The rest of the time you just lie there, but the medicine men help you all the time — they give you lots of medicine and they sing all night. They do lots of things all over your body. Every bit of your body is treated.[1]

So spoke one native American about the strangeness of the white man's hospital. Another Navajo, John Dick, director of a new federally-financed training program for Indian medicine men, added this: "Navajo doctors are completely different from white anglo doctors. Some white man's hospitals don't cure the Navajos. They treat the illness, not the person. After an operation, a Navajo often goes to his medicine man to be purified, to be treated psychologically as well as physically." [2]

The Christian Faith and Health

While the technological explosion in bio-medical science has forced us to reflect with new seriousness upon the issues in this book, just as important is the related and growing concern for the wholeness of persons in medical treatment. Indeed, we might not be so perplexed by the burgeoning issues in medicine had we not become so habituated to a fragmented understanding of human nature.

Members of earlier cultures would smile at our "new" discovery that medicine and religion belong together. A cursory glance back toward ancient Samaria, Egypt, Babylonia, Greece, Persia, and Rome reveals a strikingly similar phenomenon: medicine and religion belonged together. The human being was viewed as a unity of body, mind, and spirit. Most often the priest and the physician were one person.

Similarly for the Hebrew, body and spirit could not be divorced, and hence the notion of salvation of the soul or the spirit apart from the body was foreign. Even so, early portions of the Old Testament frequently separated the notion of salvation from that of *health*. Later Old Testament writings showed a gradual convergence of the two notions, a convergence which continued through the synoptic accounts (Matthew, Mark, and Luke) of the New Testament. In other New Testament writings, however, salvation took on specialized meanings that were not directly related to health.[3]

The history of the church, in spite of a continued interest in certain forms of healing, persisted in the separation of salvation and health. The formative theological giants, each in his own way, spiritualized salvation to the consequent denigration of the physical body. In the early Middle Ages, Augustine's Neoplatonic dualism led him to see the body as the prison house of the soul. Thomas Aquinas in the high Middle Ages built upon an Aristotelian philosophy which viewed the body as significant for spiritual development but clearly inferior to the spirit. Nor did the sixteenth century Protestant Reformers overcome the divergence. Martin Luther, while not rejecting the body as evil, saw it as a realm of the devil's struggle with God and, in comparison to the soul, of relative insignificance. Even more did John Calvin disassociate physical from spiritual health. Indeed, the spiritualization of the Christian faith has continued in one form or another into the contemporary period.[4]

In spite of all this, the Christian picture is hardly one-sided. In the church of the first few centuries healing gradually became less the ministry of a few gifted people and more a ministry of the whole church. Institutionalization took place. The Order of Deaconesses, the Order of Widows, and the Order of Virgins each were established for healing purposes. By the fourth century it was common for those congregations which could maintain them to have rudimentary hospitals, "houses of lodging for strangers," including in their services attention to the strangers' ailments.

The church of the Middle Ages lacked a singular mind toward medicine. On the one hand, there were an impressive development of religious orders for the care of the sick and the emergence of numerous hospitals devoted exclusively to the ill. On the other hand, certain Christian conceptions of human nature and destiny stood in the way of medical investigation, to which the ban on dissection of bodies testifies.

While Protestant churches of the Reformation period recognized and affirmed the healing dimensions of Christian ministry, their focus was largely spiritual: care for the ill through Word and sacrament. The Reformers' rejection of monasticism also meant that the organized care for the sick diminished, and only later did Protestant churches re-institutionalize these healing ministries.

In spite of Christian concern for the ill, body-spirit dualism has persisted into the modern period. Not until the twentieth century did serious theological reassessment of the interdependence of the varied dimensions of human life and health begin to take place. For this, considerable credit is due to that secular prophet Sigmund Freud and his successors. Dynamic psychology forced us to look more seriously at the organic unity of the self, and its insights prodded the recovery of important biblical perspectives on health and wholeness.

If the church tended to fragment human nature into a body-spirit dualism, medicine did not escape its own kind of fragmentation: a mechanistic and materialistic understanding of human nature.[5] Medicine had to slough off theological rules and ecclesiastical taboos which shackled the searching mind, and in the process it declined as an art and rose as a science. As a science medicine opened up an immense range of knowledge of the biological nuts and bolts of the person. But the person tended to become a fascinating machine in need of repairs, a "case" susceptible to analysis and treatment in its dysfunctioning parts.

What Is Health?

What is health? According to a current dictionary its principal definition is "physical and mental well-being; freedom from disease, pain, or defect; normality of physical and mental functions; soundness." [6] Dictionaries reflect common cultural uses of words, and Webster's is no exception. While the negative part ("freedom from disease . . .") is relatively clear, the positive elements tell us little. What is well-being? Or normality? Or soundness?

The dictionary points to both problems and possibilities in our common attitudes about health.[7] In addition to defining health primarily in negative terms, implicit in the definition is the notion that we are speaking of the individual. While indeed we are concerned about the individual, the general thrust of the biblical understanding of health is far from individual*istic*. To the contrary, health is always a social and relational phenomenon; it concerns individuals, but it is intimately bound up with the nature and quality of their relationships with their fellows.

So also, Webster reflects the partial and functional understandings of health to which we are accustomed. I have a problem with my kidneys or with my heart; my body has a defect; certain of my functions are not normal. But beyond this functional orientation, health has to do with *my interrelated wholeness*. If I have a kidney problem, my emotions and spirit are not unaffected. And if only my kidneys are treated, my fragmentation is not overcome.

Paul Tillich assists us in understanding the various dimensions of our lives to which the notion of health refers.[8] We can think of health in a mechanical-physical sense: the adequate functioning of the parts of our bodies. Health is also chemical: an appropriate balance of chemical substances and processes within us. Health is biological: the appropriate interaction of the self as an organism with its total environment, including rest, movement, food, etc. Health is psychological: an appropriate balance between a secure sense of personal identity (finding oneself) and the ability to lose oneself in the lives of others. Health is social and historical, personal health depending in some measure upon a healthy and sane society. Health is spiritual: the awareness of and capacity of being grasped by the Spirit, that source and meaning of life which transcends us and yet is not foreign to our inmost beings.

While all of these are interrelated dimensions of our lives, particular healing therapies frequently focus upon just one of these areas. Thus, the growth of a cancer may necessitate surgery, the mechanical removal of a diseased part of the body. Nevertheless, healing in one of these dimensions does not necessarily bring healing to the others. It may actually provoke distress or disease elsewhere, as the psychological trauma of the woman who has had a cancerous breast removed often illustrates. What we yearn for is health in *all* of life's parts. The Christian understanding of the Savior, as Tillich reminds us, is that of the universal healer — one who heals life in all of its dimensions.

The "Human" in "Human Being"

If it is difficult to speak meaningfully about health without repeatedly speaking of "wholeness," it is equally difficult to talk of human wholeness without giving more content to the adjective "human." But that is no easy task. The word "human" has become one of the most-used and least-defined terms in ethical and moral discussions in recent years.

We use the word in a variety of ways. Descriptively, it is an adjective which distinguishes our race from others of the animal kingdom. Hence, anthropologists, sociologists, philosophers, and theologians have attempted to isolate those characteristics which constitute the essence of humanity. What is it that is distinctively human? Our rationality? Our capacity as symbol-makers? That we are the only animals who wear clothes, who clean themselves after defecating, who can use a face-to-face coital position, who can get drunk and take drugs? That we have the capacity to write our histories? That we can pray?

The descriptive use of "human" slips quickly into its normative uses. Negatively, we use the term to excuse our frailties: "I'm only human, what do you expect — perfection?" Or, as an old Jesuit once said, "All things human, given enough time, go badly." In another vein we use variations of the word to point to the violation of certain qualities of life: "it was an inhuman, dehumanizing thing to do," suggests both that the actor violated the essence of his own humanity and that the results of his act were destructive of the humanity of others. Contrariwise, we use the term positively to applaud the presence of certain qualities of life and action: "that person is authentically human";

"that was a humanizing thing to do." In this sense the term can take on central ethical significance. Thus, theologian Paul Lehmann combines both the descriptive and normative uses in describing God's intentions: "to make and to keep human life *human* in the world." [9]

The need for greater clarity about humanhood underlies the whole range of medical issues which face us. In a contemplated abortion, are we dealing with a bit of bodily tissue or are we dealing with a human being in the uterus? When we consider the use of extraordinary medical measures for an irretrievably brain-damaged person are we prolonging human life or are we prolonging life that somehow has ceased to be human? In our decisions about genetic manipulation and organ transplants by what standards or images do we judge that we are promoting authentically human existence?

Our need for a definition of specifically human existence is thus twofold.[10] First, we must establish negative limits to medical manipulation. It is not a question of when we should stop helping a person. Help ought not be limited. Rather, it is the question of when and under what circumstances medical intervention violates the purpose and meaning of human life. Second, we need an image of our positive goals which might be achieved by medical means. Toward what end should we allow and encourage bio-medical manipulation? Toward what kind of life are we pressing?

While we shall consider the morality of abortion in some detail in Chapter Two, it is useful to anticipate part of that debate at this point in our attempt to give more precise meaning to "human." In asking the question "when does human life begin?" Daniel Callahan discerns three basic schools of opinion: the genetic school, the developmental school, and the social consequences school.[11]

The genetic school insists that human life begins at the moment of conception or at the moment of the fixing of the genetic code. It is at this time the individual is whoever he is going to become.

The developmental position, however, holds that at least some process of development is necessary before we can speak meaningfully of the life of an individual human being. Where, precisely, the point is when the conceptus becomes human is open to debate within this school of thought. For some it may be at the time when all of the organs are rudimentarily present (between the sixth and eighth week following conception). For others, the embryo has no human status during its first two weeks, but after this it gradually attains more human status until the time of viability (about twenty-eight weeks) when the fetus should be treated as having all the rights of a new-born child. Still others wish to use some criterion of brain development.

The third school of opinion, the social consequences school, finally rejects all biological data as determinative. It is unwise, these persons argue, to equate "life" with "human life." Fully-developed adult human beings must finally decide what human is — no biological facts can decide that for us — and such decisions must take into account the kind of moral policy (e.g., as in abortion) that people want.

Callahan believes that the developmental position is most adequate for pointing to the beginning of human life. Like the genetic school, it takes biological data seriously. Like the social consequences school it realizes that part of the question is in fact a moral policy question. However, unlike the genetic school (which argues that all forms of human life must be valued equally) the developmental position leaves room for weighing the comparative values of different qualities and stages of human life which may be in competition in a given situation. Yet, unlike the social consequences position, the developmentalist will not make the meaning of human simply a matter of social utility or what is most useful to the persons who are making the decisions.

One result of the developmental position is that we are left in a more ambiguous position about the meaning of human life. It is neither simply bodily life nor is it simply what people in a given time and place choose to call human. But this perspective has advantages. First, it recognizes the ambiguity and value conflict that *will* be present in practical decisions. Second, it recognizes that bodily life is always valuable, but its value is not unchanging. Its value must be assessed in terms of its potentiality as well as in terms of its presence.

Thus, as a number of ethicists remind us, our concern is not only with *human* life but also with *personal* life.[12] We are concerned not only about human physical existence but also about that quality of existence in which the individual has some meaningful consciousness, self-awareness, and capacity for interpersonal relationship and communication. As every medical practitioner knows, there are those individuals who may well be human beings but, sadly enough, will never have the capacity or have ceased to have the capacity for personal existence.

We can and must, I believe, make some distinctions even though they are risky and relative ones and even though they shade off into one another. Human life, understood developmentally, can exist in *pre-personal* forms (as in the fetus), in *personal* forms (as in the individual with the capacity for consciousness, etc.), and in *post-personal forms* (as in the permanently comatose patient). In all of these stages it is human life and as such it deserves our profound respect and concern. Nevertheless, there are occasions in which the competition of values between lives makes choices about life's quality imperative.

Embryonic and fetal life in all stages is human life. If the fetus is reasonably "normal," it has personal existence as potentiality. As its potentiality is increasingly realized, it has increasing personal value — value as a person. Of course normally-developed, mature individuals are not always personal beings in actuality; sometimes they are drugged, sometimes they are temporarily unconscious, often they are asleep. But their capacity for reawakening to personal existence is so obvious that the ethical issue of drawing the line between potentiality and actuality hardly occurs.

But what of the seriously and permanently brain-injured individual, the comatose one? Personal existence is gone both in actuality and potentiality. Yet human existence remains so long as bodily life remains. While the individual's value is diminished when personal existence is no longer possible, deep respect is still due toward such life. Taking the argument one step further to death itself, the respect which we typically give to the bodies of the dead is significant in this regard. We sense the inappropriateness of treating the body as a person, hence our revulsion against some of the excesses of the funeral industry. On the other hand, we sense the appropriateness of treating the body with honor. This appears to come both from our gratitude and respect for the person who once lived among us, and also from our almost inchoate sense that existing personal life is endangered insofar as our respect for past personal life is diminished.

What of the *content* of personal life, of human existence in its actualization? Without attempting an exhaustive exploration of the personal, we can at least point to several major dimensions.

In the first place, to be personally human is to be *social*. We are created both physically and psychologically through the communion of human lives. Social psychologists tell us that our selfhood finds its genesis and its growth only in social relationships. We are quite literally humanized, brought into being as fully human, only in a web of personal relationships. The infant who is warped through the absence of warm, secure, and stimulating interpersonal relationships is profoundly and tragically dehumanized.

Beyond the social psychological testimony, Christian theology affirms our social selfhood. We become human through being addressed by God. In the creation stories the animals are spoken of as "they," but the human being is addressed as "you." We are created in and for community, with all that this implies. Together with self-awareness, it involves the capacity to relate interpersonally, to communicate. But communication is not limited to one's use of (or ability to use) words. There is that communication which involves a mysterious unspoken participation in the other's presence. The capacity for such interpersonal relationships thus means that value terms which describe relational qualities — love, trust, justice — are also integral to the experience of personhood.

Our human communal existence is not only interpersonal, it is also *intra*personal. Tillich, as we earlier noted, reminds us that health is expressed in not one but several interrelated dimensions. This is because the human being is a multidimensional unity. He is not just a compound of chemicals, nor just a biological existence, nor merely a psychological being, nor only a historical life, nor only a spirit. He is all of these systems and processes, seeking the creative center and the community of them all.

If social existence is fundamental to personhood, then our medical decisions ought to respect and nurture that existence. My intrapersonal community is violated when one dimension of my being is singled out for treatment and that dimension is confused with my wholeness. I am a compound of chemicals, and there are times in which I need chemical therapy; but I am not only a compound of chemicals. My interpersonal community can be violated through medical decisions, too. Decisions about my future which do not take seriously the specific relationships and responsibilities in which I stand and through which I live can dehumanize me. Decisions which do not take seriously the equitable allocation of medical resources throughout the wider community of persons also threaten my humanity — whether I am the victim of medical neglect or the recipient of medical largesse at the expense of others.

A second dimension of human personhood is the capacity to experience both *limitation and freedom*. The writer of the 8th Psalm puts it graphically in answering the question "What is man that thou art mindful of him, and the son of man that thou dost care for him?" He pictures the person as neither God nor beast, yet participating in the life of both. Unlike the animal, he is free, with the capacity and destiny for self-transcendance. He is not limited to instinctual choices. He can have a history, a remembered past. He can have a future, projecting himself into the not-yet. But unlike God, the person is finite and limited. There are boundaries to his life in time and space and capacity. Death is given to him as well as birth.

Reinhold Niebuhr has reminded us that precisely because we are both finite and free we are anxious.[13] We live on a dizzy pinnacle often trying to escape from one or the other dimensions of our personal humanity. Thus our inhumanity, our sin, comes both in the prideful ways in which we deny our finitude and play God with other lives and in the escapist ways in which we deny our own freedom and responsibility. Such is the ambiguity of our existence. But in that very ambiguity lies the possibility of our humanity. Medical practices which deny a person's freedom (through manipulating him as an object) or which deny his finitude (through endlessly sustaining a bodily existence without regard to its capacity for personal life) dehumanize.

A third major dimension of personal humanness is *the self's religiosity*.[14] It is of course true that, if religiosity is defined as the conscious worship of a supernatural reality or as a central concern with a world beyond that of daily life and ordinary sensory experience, many persons are not religious. But if our religiosity more broadly is a persisting tendency to direct our faith (our confidence, trust, and loyalty) toward centers of value which we cannot prove to be worthwhile but upon which we do depend for the worth of our own lives, then we are all incurably religious. The biblical and Christian traditions perceive this. Luther's statement is typical. Assuming that the heart does indeed need

to cling to something, he says, "Whatever your heart trusts in
and relies on, that is properly your god."

One expression of personal humanity as faith existence is in
our drive toward meaning. Victor Frankl, arguing that the "will
to meaning" is essential to man's *humanum,* recalls Freud's statement in a letter to Princess Bonapart. Freud commented that
the moment a person questions the meaning and value of life
he is sick. Frankl replies that, to the contrary, such questioning
only proves that he is truly a human being.[15] This quest for
meaning appears to emerge from the tension between our finitude and our freedom. The anxiety which inevitably accompanies this tension can be creative. It can spur us to embrace
meanings which transcend our own lives and bind us to more
inclusive communities. Or, it can be destructive anxiety when
we seize upon a partial (and hence idolatrous) source of meaning
and make that ultimate for our lives. But without meaning quite
literally we die.

Intentionality is intimately related to meaning. It too is of the
essence of our personhood and an expression of our religious
natures. It suggests that meaning and commitment go together.
According to Rollo May,

> ...*every meaning has within it a commitment....* We could
> not have one without the other. This is why commitment is so
> important. If I do not *will* something, I could never *know* it;
> and if I do not *know* something, I would never have any
> content for my willing.[16]

Like meaning and faith, intentionality is not present in equal
degrees in all persons. It is not static. In fact, it appears that
this committed thrust toward a meaningful future can be greatly
diminished by severe and neurotic anxiety. Intentionality is not
just a biological force. It is that peculiarly and personally human
vitality, that capacity for aliveness, which gives shape to our
worlds.

When these dimensions of our personhood are perceived and
expressed in Christian ways, they receive a particular shape.
Then our central faith is in the God revealed through Jesus
Christ. Then our meanings take shape around the Logos made
flesh. Then our intentionality responds to God's purposes in the
humanization of human life. These are Christian confessions. But
this does not mean that the capacity for faith, meaning, and

intentionality are any monopoly of Christians or that somehow
the market in authentic personal existence has been cornered
by Christians. The facts of Christian existence past and present
undercut any such mistaken and arrogant claims as this. But if
all individuals share these religious capacities as part of their personal *humanum,* Christians have special reasons on the grounds
of their own faith to cherish and respect deeply the humanity of
all others.

While the distinction between "human life" and "personal
human life" is important to bear in mind, for economy of expression in the following pages I shall ordinarily use the word "human" to suggest both meanings. The word will affirm that all
life which is humanly conceived is indeed human life; it is God's
gift to be valued and respected. Beyond this, however, the word
will signify the conviction that God also intends the fully personal
quality of human life and not simply its biological existence.

Ethically speaking, where does all of this leave us? Two major
questions persist. Can we agree that human life is to be valued?
If we affirm this value, is there something recognizably and distinctively human which can give us more specific guidance in the
medically-related decisions before us?

First, how do we establish and agree upon the value of human
life? Though persons of various Christian and Jewish faith
groups might have distinctive theological reasons for their concern about human life, it is important to find a wider moral
consensus, one that elicits the support of a broad range of people.
To the extent that such a consensus exists today, it is upon the
principle of "the sanctity of life." [17] The principle is a vague
one, to be sure. Some who claim no religious orientation reject
the notion of "sanctity." Others resist the indeterminate term
"life" inasmuch as it seems to exalt life without regard to its
condition or quality.

In spite of its ambiguity, the principle is important, represent-
ing as it does the attempt to find some common ground for
expressing the value of the lives of human beings. Christian
theology typically affirms that human life finds its value in the
fact that *God* values that life, not fundamentally because human
beings place value upon it. Whether this knowledge comes to us
through revelation (as most Protestants affirm) or whether it
comes through reason's ability to grasp the natural law (as Catholics traditionally have affirmed), Christians agree that God has

said Yes to life and the human response should echo the affirmation. The human being has "an alien dignity." His dignity is located outside the utility which other persons might or might not ascribe to it.

While this Christian faith affirmation gives strength to the moral protection of human life, many persons simply cannot accept the theological baggage which accompanies it. Thus, some would simply argue from common human experience. Edward Shils, for example, maintains, "The idea of sacredness is generated by the primordial experience of being alive, of experiencing the elemental sensation of vitality and the elemental fear of its extinction." [18] But this argument is open to criticisms similar to those leveled at Christian theology. Is this not, in the final analysis, unprovable? It is not at all certain that all people do in fact have this experience or would accept the sanctity-of-life principle on the basis of it.

We are driven back to the faith nature of all of our valuing. As religious beings all of us appear to live by faith, grounding our various value judgments upon some center or centers of value (God, myself, family, nation, humankind, etc.). Whatever our center of value is, it is just that — the center. It is accepted on faith. We do not prove its worth. Its worth is given and received in experience.[19] While such religious valuing experience seems universal, we cannot claim that the experience of the sanctity of human life is universal either as a general principle or (much less probably) in any specific meaning. What we *can* do is to rejoice in the fact that the general principle is widely held by persons who come to it from varying faith experiences. We can cooperate with and benefit by the insights of those who affirm the same principle but from different starting points.

The second question is this: beyond a widely-shared agreement on the value of human life, is there in "the human factor" something which gives us more specific moral content and guidance? There is a continuum of responses at this point. On the one extreme a traditionalist natural law position claims that there is a fixed and abiding human nature which can be rationally understood and which places moral claims upon us. On the other extreme are those who either deny that there is such an abiding human nature or maintain that, even if there were, knowledge of that nature would not give us any clear moral norms. Toward this latter pole gravitate those who argue that persons are their own self-creators, the only authors of their human meanings, values, and goals.

There is some truth in each of the extremes, but neither by itself is adequate. Whether in the individual or in the race, our humanity is not a fixed and static quality. As individuals it is perhaps more accurate to say that we are in the process of realizing our humanity. We are not finished products. So also as a race our human nature has a dynamic and changing quality about it. New developments in the bio-medical fields pointedly raise the question as to what humankind is yet to become, and for the first time in history we do have the technological capacities to alter in significant ways the nature of human nature. In spite of this capacity for change and modification, however, there are certain qualities which we can claim as normatively human. We have examined a range of these qualities in the preceding discussion of the personal factor. On this score there is a danger in saying too much, but there is also a danger in saying too little. Taking the latter risk, many of us would want to say that certain broad normative claims are, indeed, built into the notion and nature of the "human." If it should become possible to alter human nature so that the individual would no longer have the capacity for faith, hope, and love, then that simply should never be done! To do so would threaten the qualitative meaning of that which is distinctively human, of that affirmed in faith as the image of God.

There are varied ways of expressing the moral guidance implicit in the human factor. One is the affirmation of certain human rights and of certain rules which embody those rights. Daniel Callahan, for example, sketches five rules which, while they are not logically derived from the sanctity-of-life principle, seem to be implied by it. (1) Human beings as a species have a right to exist in all their particular racial and ethnic groups. (2) Individuals and families should be free from outside interference in determining their own procreation practices. (3) The individual must be allowed to live and must have the protection of his fellow human beings. (4) Persons should be allowed to make those choices which significantly affect their own lives and destinies. (5) The person ought not have his own body or any of its organs violated or imposed upon against his will.[20] We do need such rules to give more specificity to the value placed upon human life, even though we do not claim any particular hierarchical order for the rules or claim that they are divinely-given or infallible. Even when in a given situation such rules may conflict, they still remind us of the obligations which the humanity of others places upon us.

Instead of speaking of rights and rules, others would prefer to give moral guidance through elaborating the content of humanization as a goal to be furthered by our decisions. If to become more fully human means to live with greater self-awareness, greater capacity for faith, hope, and love, enhanced opportunities for freedom and responsibility for our futures, etc., then our specific bio-medical decisions ought to be made in ways that nourish, enhance, and enlarge these human qualities. We ought to judge our specific actions in terms of their consequences for such humanization.

In the debates over the various medical issues to follow we shall encounter some arguments which are based upon ethics of rights and duties. We shall encounter others arguing from ethics of goals and consequences. The former tends to emphasize our obligation to defend the humanity of present individuals. The latter approach is often more future-oriented and, particularly in its utilitarian forms, gives greater attention to the benefits to human society which might accrue from our acts. It is the age-old ethical debate between ethics of the right and ethics of the good. Both emphases are important, and neither should exclude the other. Sometimes we will argue that certain human rights are so primary that no calculation of foreseeable benefits to others ought to justify an action which infringes upon those rights. At other times, the good that probably would be achieved by certain actions (or the evil avoided) might require restrictions on certain individual rights. At all times, however, our decisions should be informed by a perception of responsibility. In the Christian perspective, ours is a responsibility to God for the humanity of our fellow human beings. It is an attempt to perceive through faith the meanings and intentions for humankind of the one who is our creator, our judge, and our redeemer. It is a responsibility to our fellow creatures rooted in the God beside whom there are no other absolute values, not even human life, but before whom human life in its fullest personal sense is seen as a great gift to be protected, developed, nourished, and cared for.[21]

On Caring

Our concern for human life can be expressed in the formal language of obligation. Beyond that we need to consider the meaning of caring for human life and health. Christian hospitals began with a history of *caring* more than one of *curing.*[22] The early hospitals in Europe were established principally for those considered beyond cure, the hopeless cases abandoned by society. Then, as medicine's power to conquer disease gradually developed, the church and its hospitals began to identify with this curing model, and persons in both medicine and ministry took on therapeutic self-images. Those with Christian consciousness identified themselves with Christ's healing ministry or, at least with the Good Samaritan who brought therapy to the wounded man by the roadside. There is, of course, considerable biblical justification for this perspective.

Yet, as Michael Wilson has reminded us, another biblical perspective helpfully enlarges this therapeutic model. Counterpoised with the parable of the Good Samaritan now is the parable of the Last Judgment (Matthew 25:31-46). The king (the Son of man) says, "Come, O blessed of my Father, inherit the kingdom prepared for you from the foundation of the world; for I was hungry and you gave me food, I was thirsty and you gave me drink, I was a stranger and you welcomed me, I was naked and you clothed me, I was sick and you visited me, I was in prison and you came to me." To which the incredulous listeners respond, "Lord, when did we see thee hungry . . . thirsty . . . a stranger . . . naked . . . sick . . . in prison . . . ?" Now the transformation of our model begins to appear In this parable, Christ is not the healer. He is the patient. He is the one in need. It is a stunning reversal because we see him in the wrong place. He strikes squarely at some of our usual assumptions, for we have come to think of ourselves as Christ-like therapists armed with strength, techniques, knowledge, and professional skills to cure the ill. But now it is the king himself who lies in the ditch, the crucified one who is on the hospital bed. In this parable the visitor comes not so much as a therapist as a fellow human being. *"You* visited *me."*

It is a story of caring. It does not denigrate the remarkable therapeutic achievements of medicine. It does, however, remind us that caring is a broader model that should inform all curing. As one who is ill my need is, to be sure, for therapeutic skills and techniques, but not only for that. My hunger is also for one who gives himself personally to me, in terms of myself, not just technologically in terms of my physical defects.

What, more particularly, is involved in the meaning of caring? Rollo May puts it well: "Care is a state in which something does *matter;* care is the opposite of apathy. Care is the necessary source of eros, the source of human tenderness." [23] Care is not the same as sentimentality, for sentimentality is thinking about sentiment rather than truly experiencing him who is the object of our sentiment. Care is similar to compassion, and yet the term care conveys a state of being and not only an attitude. We are constituted, in our very being, by what we care about.

Milton Mayeroff further expands our understanding of caring. "To care for another person, in the most significant sense, is to help him grow and actualize himself." [24] It is not just a momentary feeling or simply a matter of wanting to care for another; it is a process, a way of relating to another. "In the sense in which a man can ever be said to be at home in the world, he is at home not through dominating, or explaining, or appreciating, but through caring and being cared for." [25]

Caring, then, involves a profound respect for the otherness of the other. It is different than imposing my own direction upon him or her. It is grounded in the sense of worth which I experience in the other. It finds its expression in helping the other to come to care for himself or herself. It requires a sense of participation in the other, seeing the other not as I would like him or her to be but seeing that person's own particular needs for growth. Caring requires knowledge, knowledge of the other's needs and knowledge of what I can and cannot give. It requires trust in the other (and not only in my own ideas of what the other should become). It requires humility, a continuous learning about the other and an openness to the novelty of each new situation in which a mechanical application of the rules may not suffice. Caring requires hope in the possibilities which infuse the present. It requires courage because the future results of our caring cannot be neatly calculated; it is not just bodies subject to laws of physical medicine which are at stake, it is persons, for whom the future is never fully known.

But an attitude of caring is not essentially a severe and strenuous demand placed upon us in regard to others. It is, more truly, an opportunity. I find myself, my own actualization, my own growth, my place in the world in caring for others. If I aim at my self-realization, however, my caring is distorted; I then use the others as a means to my own fulfillment. My fulfillment, rather, comes indirectly and unintended, as a gift. The language and shape of care are the language and shape of love.[26]

In the last analysis, the medical issues now before us are not ones which can be *solved.* As Abraham Kaplan has wisely remarked, "We can solve some problems in human life, but they are usually the less significant ones. Those that are more significant we do not solve, but at best we only *cope* with them . . . we have no way of disposing of them; at best we learn to live with them. . . ." [27] And, we might add, in our coping with these problems, we cannot lose sight of that human quality and those relationships and persons about whom we are invited to care.

CHAPTER TWO

The Humanity
in Abortion

Cases

"A fifteen-year-old girl, self-conscious and awkward though an honor roll student, became pregnant because she felt that the way to the popularity she longed for was to do whatever the boys wanted. Her foolish and immature action (how many of us are mature at 15?) condemned her to further shame and self-hatred through the only course which seemed open to her at first: to "visit an aunt" for six months. But both she and her parents were sure that everyone would know the actual reason for such a prolonged absence...." [1]

A married, twenty-two-year-old Georgia woman was nine weeks pregnant. Her husband, a construction worker who was employed only sporadically, had recently abandoned her for a time, forcing her to live with her indigent parents and the parents' eight other children. Though now reconciled, the young woman and her husband had none of their three living children with them. The older two had been placed in a foster home because of the family's poverty and inability to care for them; the youngest was recently placed for adoption. The woman, earlier a mental patient at the state hospital, now had been advised that an abortion performed at this stage of pregnancy would be of less danger to her health than if she carried the fetus to full term and gave birth. [2]

31

A talented twenty-four-year-old woman became deeply distressed upon discovering that she was pregnant. Though she and her husband planned to have one or two children sometime later, pregnancy and motherhood responsibilities now would interrupt the interior decorating career which she was finding profitable, enjoyable, and in which she wished to continue full-time for several more years. Her husband said that he would be agreeable to an abortion if she really wanted it.

The Abortion Debate

The words "I am pregnant" usually signify excitement, pride, and fulfillment. But not always. Sometimes they point to deep embarrassment, horror, and despair in the woman who speaks them. Occasionally, the words which first signalled joy give way to anguish occasioned by the intervention of unexpected serious illness or discovery of possible fetal abnormality.

On January 22, 1973, the United States Supreme Court in two historic decisions, *Roe v. Wade* and *Doe v. Bolton*, struck down restrictive and moderate state abortion statutes, placing the public policy discussion into a new context. Among the factors influencing and intensifying the abortion debate in recent years certainly have been these:

— the claim of numerous women that restrictive abortion laws deprived them of their rights to self-determination in crucial matters of reproduction;

— the claim that restrictive laws were based upon punitive Victorian attitudes and that, in practical effect, they were socially discriminatory, the poor being their chief victims;

— the alarm at the extent of illegal abortions and their cost in life and suffering;

— with increased psychological sophistication and awareness of the fragility of our social fabric, a heightened concern about the fate and effect of unwanted children;

— an intensified ecological concern and new-found sensitivity to the world population problem;

— the growing recognition that abortion is one of the most widespread methods of fertility control in the world;

— the realization that with the combination of urbanization, female emancipation, and the small-family ideal, child-bearing is increasingly postponed and limited while sexual relations are not, and abortion becomes the answer for many persons when contraceptives fail or have not been used;

— the concern about the social effect of the wide-spread flouting of restrictive abortion laws;

— the development of medical techniques which have reduced the physical risks of properly-performed abortions in early stages of pregnancy to less than the risks of normal child-bearing;

— the acknowledged decline in the perceived influence of religious bodies upon individual moral attitudes, and the question as to whether groups have the right to impose moral attitudes about abortion on others who believe differently.

The statistics on abortion are notoriously difficult to pin down. Those arguing different sides of the case frequently use those figures which will best buttress their positions. The following, however, appear to be representative prior to the Supreme Court decisions: [3]

— Legal abortions in the U.S.: about 180,000 per year;

— Illegal abortions in the U.S.: from a low estimate of 200,000 to a high estimate of 1,200,000 annually;

— Abortion deaths: estimated as high as 6,000 per year, but more probably about 500 (mostly from illegal abortions);

— Abortion deaths by racial groups: in a recent year for every 10,000 live births in New York City, 1.0 white woman deaths, 4.7 Puerto Rican woman deaths, and 8.0 black woman deaths;

— Pregnancies as a result of rape: 750 to 800 annually.

Even given the most conservative statistics, abortion is a phenomenon of major importance. World-wide, one informed estimate places the annual number of intentionally-terminated pregnancies at some thirty million.[4]

Attitudes Toward Abortion: A Historical Sketch

References to the practice of abortion are found throughout the length of recorded human history, as far back as ancient China some forty-six hundred years ago.[5] Attitudes in early cultures varied from the most permissive (including actual encouragement) to the most prohibitive. Laws protecting the fetus are fairly common in the centuries before Christ. The Sumerian

Code of 2000 B.C., the Assyrian Code of 1500 B.C., the Ham-murabic and Hittite Codes of 1300 B.C., and the Persian Code of 600 B.C. all prohibit causing the death of an unborn child. The Assyrian Code illustrates typically harsh penalties: a woman who "causes to fall what her womb holds . . . shall be tried, convicted, and impaled upon a stake, and shall not be buried." Less puni-tive codes allowed fines, public service, and flogging to suffice.

The pro-abortion attitudes of classical Greece stand in contrast. Plato recommended abortion for eugenic reasons: it would help control population in the ideal state, and it would prevent pro-creation by persons considered above the ideal age for child-bearing. Aristotle similarly recommended abortion for population control. In Rome attitudes varied over the years. The declining years of the empire saw a callousness about human life; if infan-ticide, crucifixion, slavery, and the throwing of prisoners to the beasts were all condoned, there was little in abortion to offend the moral sensitivities of the Romans. Yet, by the end of the second century A.D., the situation had grown so desperate that harsh anti-abortion laws were passed as part of a public moral reform effort.

The virtual absence of references to abortion in the Old Tes-tament, plus the profound respect for procreation as a gift from God suggest that abortion was not practiced to any large extent among the ancient Hebrews. While the New Testament makes no explicit reference to abortion, by the late first or early second century the Apostolic Fathers were beginning to speak emphati-cally against the practice as incompatible with the basic Christian norm of love.

Two problems perplexed the early church. One was the ques-tion of "ensoulment." How and when does the fetus receive a human soul? Regarding the "how," some held, as did Tertullian, that the soul was biologically transmitted to the fetus from its immediate parents, such transmission linking all human beings back to the original Adam (a view called "traducianism" or "generationism"). Others held, as did Clement of Alexandria, that God immediately and directly created each soul ("crea-tionism").

The more crucial issue, however, was the question of *when* the fetus became ensouled. In both the Eastern and Western branches of the church theories arose about the "formed" and the "un-formed" fetus. Abortion at any stage of development was gravely condemned, but once the fetus was formed and had received its rational soul the offense became even more serious. The influential Augustine of Hippo impressed upon the Western Church the notion that the soul became present in the fetus at the time of "quickening" when the woman first felt life moving within her womb. Thomas Aquinas, the chief theologian of the Middle Ages, gave expression to the prevailing view holding that the soul was not created at the time of conception but was later "infused" into the fetus. (Inasmuch as male theologians, following Aristotle, knew that males take the lead, Aquinas maintained that such soul infusion came about the fortieth day for males and about the eightieth day for the female fetus!). The net result was that the distinction between homicide and quasi-homicide arose, depending upon whether it was a formed or an unformed fetus which was destroyed.

The first legislation applying to the entire Western Church incorporating the notion of delayed animation or ensoulment came with the *Decretals* of Pope Gregory IX (1234). In the centuries that followed, all abortion continued to be treated as sinful, but the gravity of the sin was clearly on the side of the destruction of the formed fetus. This distinction, however, was undercut by papal pronouncement in 1869 when Pius IX declared that henceforth every direct killing of a fetus at any time after fertilization would be given the same punishment. Any misunderstanding of this intent was finally eliminated in 1917 when the new *Code of Canon Law* required the baptism of *all* aborted fetuses. While spontaneous miscarriages may have been uppermost in mind in this requirement, it is clear that the Roman Catholic Church now had declared that the unborn fetus is a person at whatever stage of its development. Since then, papal pronouncements have reinforced this affirmation,[6] and Vatican II unambiguously declared, "Therefore, from the moment of its conception life must be guarded with the greatest care, while abortion and infanticide are unspeakable crimes." [7]

Protestant attitudes toward abortion have varied, though the major reformers of the sixteenth century, Luther and Calvin, were as strong in their opposition to the practice as was the Roman Church. Until recent years, strict moral censure of abortion for any purpose short of saving the mother's life was the general rule among most denominations. Increasingly in the present century, however, several important religious factors have

influenced abortion attitudes among Protestants (though the
effect of these influences has not been limited to them).[8]

For one thing, the theological certainties which once called up
firm Protestant opposition to nontherapeutic abortion have become less certain. Once it was clear that the providence of God
had given every nascent life in the womb as an expression of his
mysterious purposes. Today the presence of a fetus simply may
be an indication of human mismanagement or plain bad luck.

Furthermore, the abortion reform movement has drawn upon
themes of great importance to the Protestant tradition itself,
particularly self-determination and man's rational control over
nature. Though today's common interpretation of self-determination may be a highly individualistic, secularized, and distorted
version of the Reformation's view of the liberty of the Christian
person, it nonetheless has drawn deeply from Protestant wells of
thought and experience. Similarly, the notion of human control
over nature has significant roots in the Calvinistic Puritan's "this-
worldly asceticism," though in present belief subduing the world
to the glory of God has given way merely to subduing nature
(including the bodily processes) for the purposes people desire.

In addition, the vision of a "Protestant America" has waned
dramatically. Religious pluralism has become an inescapable
fact of our existence. The failure of the Protestant-inspired pro-
hibition law was the first death-knell for the dream of a society
where moral convictions arising out of particular religious foundations would be sanctioned by legislation. It has become a counsel of theological and practical realism for many Christians to
recognize that there is a difference between what might be considered sinful and what ought to be made criminal.

Thus, in spite of the persistence of certain notable Protestant
theologians who remained conservative on abortion, by the early
1970s the picture in the churches had changed considerably.
Some denominations had decided no longer to take formal positions on the matter, leaving decisions to the conscience of the
individual member. Other groups adopted official policy statements urging the liberalization of abortion laws. A few denominations went even further. One, for example, urged "the repeal
of all legal prohibitions on physician-performed abortions" because a responsible Christian view required judgment about the
quality of personal life and not merely an undifferentiated concern for life as such.[9]

The Bio-Medical Consensus

Biological facts alone can never produce moral judgments. Yet they are important ingredients of such judgments, and we need to bear in mind those matters about which there is general scientific consensus.[10] To the biologist there is no evident answer as to when human life begins. The process of life's creation appears to be continuous. Once the fertilization of the egg has taken place there is a continuum of development, making it difficult to justify any sharp breaks with exactness. Nevertheless, upon one fact there is unquestioned agreement: the fetal tissue is unique. Unlike any other in the woman's body, this tissue has a unique chromosome composition and genetic makeup, differing from either of the parents.

The fertilized egg (the zygote) remains in the Fallopian tube for about three days, continuously dividing. The zygote, having genetic information from both its mother and father, travels through the Fallopian tube and within five to seven days reaches the uterus. About a week after fertilization, through a continuous process of cell division, there is a cluster of cells (the blastocyst) which in about 75 to 80 percent of the cases is successful in implanting itself within another week in the wall of the uterus.

About two weeks after conception the implanted blastocyst is called the embryo. Here begins a rapid increase in organ differentiation, and by the time the sixth week of pregnancy has lapsed all of the internal organs of the human being are rudimentarily present. Within another two weeks (eight weeks of pregnancy) the embryo has matured into what is ordinarily called the fetus. The distinction between these stages is made because the embryo has produced in simple form all of the essential bodily organs and systems, whereas the fetal development produces nothing radically new. The fetus develops and matures what it already possesses.

Three stages in the fetal development are of particular note in the abortion question. The first trimester (about twelve weeks) is the time during which quite safe and simple medical techniques can be used to abort the fetus. After this there is considerably more risk to the woman. Further, it is shortly after the first trimester (often in the sixteenth to eighteenth weeks) that the woman feels fluttering and kicking movements. It is this occurrence ("quickening") that signalled ensoulment to some of the ancients.

The other two time periods of significance to this discussion are the twentieth and twenty-eighth weeks. For years spontaneous abortion (contrasted with induced abortion) was called miscarriage up to the twenty-eighth week; after that it was called a premature delivery. Though laws commonly assumed that the twenty-eighth week was the time of "viability," the time after which the fetus was able to survive outside the mother's body, medical developments by the middle of this century had moved the time of viability much earlier, to about the twentieth week.

Several medically-recognized methods of abortion are now used. It is probable that both the I.U.D. (the intrauterine device or the "loop") and the morning-after pill are both abortifacients inasmuch as they appear to prevent implantation of the blastocyst rather than preventing conception itself. This is biologically different than contraception, and as such it has different moral implications.

Most abortion situations, however, turn upon methods used once the embryo is securely implanted in the uterine wall. Most common until recently has been dilation and curettage (D & C), scraping the walls of the uterus. Lately, however, the uterine aspiration method has been preferred by many physicians. It involves a vacuum suction method which quickly empties the uterus of both fetus and placenta and involves little or no danger of perforating the uterine wall. These two reliable and effective methods are used during the first trimester. After that other methods usually must be used. Traditionally these have included the insertion of catheters into the uterus to stimulate contractions, or breaking the bag of waters (amniotic sac) which causes the fetus to die and to be expelled, or performing a type of Caesarean operation (a hysterotomy). More recently a technique has been developed for use between the tenth and twenty-fourth weeks of pregnancy: the withdrawing of some of the amniotic fluid and its replacement with a concentrated saline or glucose solution which kills the fetus and, within about 20 hours, causes contractions which expel it from the woman's body.

It is clear that abortions performed by qualified physicians in appropriate clinical or hospital settings early in pregnancy have a relatively low medical risk — demonstrably lower, in fact, than the risk in carrying the fetus to full term. After the tenth or twelfth week, however, the risks to the woman increase progressively.

The Indications for Abortion

The most commonly-cited indications which might warrant abortion can be summarized at this point, though some will be examined in greater detail later.[11] First, there is the *nonpsychiatric medical risk* of a pregnancy to the woman. Until twenty-five years ago numerous medical conditions were thought to justify abortion. Today, however, with improved prenatal care and new medical techniques, most conditions (cardiovascular, gastrointestinal, renal, pulmonary, etc.) which earlier were thought to place the life of the mother and that of the fetus in direct competition no longer do so. The same cannot be said for ectopic pregnancy and certain malignancies — but these are few.

The second indication is far more common: *threats to the mental health or psychiatric condition* of the woman. Pregnancy itself as major psychological event may also be a personal crisis. When a woman sees her pregnancy as a psychological threat, manifold reasons may be present: her age, the number and ages of her present children, whether she is married, the relationship with the father, the economic situation, the woman's personal plans, her past emotional history, etc. There is no clear agreement on the psychiatric indications that might warrant abortion. Daniel Callahan argues that nothing in the abortion literature impels the conclusion that psychological distress of the pregnant woman or the likelihood of a dangerous psychological aftermath necessarily make abortion the *only* feasible course. However, he notes, studies *do* indicate that distressed women can be brought safely through the pregnancy if there is an adoption plan in mind following birth, while they do *not* generally indicate that such distressed women can be given enough care to make them adequate mothers.[12]

Third, there is the suspected or demonstrated *abnormality of the fetus*. Fetal abnormalities are surprisingly numerous — almost 30 percent of fertilized eggs are spontaneously aborted at some stage — and anxiety about possible abnormality plagues many pregnant women. Fetal indications for an abortion usually mean "the possible birth of a child whose mental or physical handicaps or a combination of both would be such as to render the child's life insupportably unhappy, or would impose heavy burdens on the family or on the society which must support the life of this child."[13] Causes of congenital abnormality would certainly include the Rh blood factor, fetal over-exposure to radiation, serious hereditary defects, and the use of harmful drugs (e.g., thalidomide). Most common, however, is the mother's exposure to rubella (infectious German measles) during the first trimester. While the incidence of rubella is likely to drop significantly because of new vaccine, at present cases are still not uncommon. Current estimates of major fetal defects caused by rubella (mental retardation, deafness, congenital heart disease, impaired vision or blindness, bone lesions) are 30 to 35 percent overall but 40 to 60 percent if the infection occurs during the first four weeks of pregnancy.

Through the use of amniocentesis (the examination of a small sample of the amniotic fluid surrounding the fetus) chromosomal fetal abnormalities now can be known with certainty. Some other defects can be calculated in terms of probability. In either case there is no medical judgment as such which can answer the moral question of whether or not to perform an abortion. Great strides have been made in medical techniques to alleviate some birth defects, yet the geographical and financial availability of such therapy is uneven at best. Emotional factors in the family are open questions. Further, the difficult question remains as to whether or not the defect will make a reasonably satisfying life impossible for the one who is born. If we cannot predict this latter question with certainty, neither ought we routinely assume that most handicapped persons would rather not have been born.

The remaining reasons often cited as indications for abortion can be treated more briefly — not because they lack seriousness, but because they account for a much smaller number of the abortions now desired or sought. The fourth indication is the pregnancy which results from *rape*. If the fetus is hated by the woman because of her traumatic experience, is it fair either to her or to the nascent one that it be born?

Fifth, there is *incest*. It is a practice subject to severe disapproval on many grounds: deep-seated social taboos, genetic objections, and religious and moral disapproval. Condemned though it be however, its incidence is probably higher than most of us realize. While many fetuses so conceived are born and then frequently given for adoption, should they be born at all?

While the above indications are those most frequently considered by the woman or the couple, additional reasons for abortion are argued out of concern for the society at large. *Population control* is one. Given the population problem should abortion be considered morally responsible in an unwanted pregnancy even if there is no serious emotional threat to the mother or family? The *eugenic* argument is another. Ought seriously retarded women be allowed to carry their pregnancies to term if the offspring will suffer similar impairment and become wards of society?

Legal and Social Factors

In the Western world, the first significant legal restrictions upon abortion coincided with the growth of Christian political power in the Roman Empire.[14] The later development in English Common Law, that pregnancy must not be terminated after "quickening" and then only if the woman's life was in danger, set the course for most laws for centuries in Western Europe. Until the mid-nineteenth century, state laws generally became more restrictive, forbidding abortions at any time in the pregnancy with only direct threat to the life (and sometimes to the health) of the mother as allowable exceptions.

Students of abortion laws typically divide them into three broad categories: restrictive, moderate, and permissive laws. Laws of a *restrictive* nature were in effect in the majority of states in the United States prior to the Supreme Court actions of 1973. Restrictive laws are still on the books in almost all of Latin America, India, and France, though enforcement in none of these places is consistently strict and in some it is deliberately lax. The reasons usually given for restrictive laws are the legal protection of innocent human life, and the protection of the health of the pregnant woman (for the state of medicine at the time most of these laws were passed made even the abortion performed by a trained person one of considerable risk). Some would add that unspoken biases are also present: a Victorian attitude toward sex and a desire to punish women, particularly those who offend the stated sexual code.

Liberalizers argue that restrictive laws are, in fact, counterproductive. They neither preserve the sanctity of life nor protect the health of the woman, for by their very restrictiveness they drive large numbers to illegal abortion with its infinitely greater risks of death and injury. Furthermore, by openly and legally allowing those women who want or need abortions to receive them, a society, it is argued, will actually enhance respect for human life — respect for the lives of women as well as for children who will be welcomed and wanted. Finally, opponents contend with impressive statistical data that restrictive abortion laws are socially discriminatory. Affluent women who really want abortions get them; it is the poor who feel the brunt of such laws.

Moderate abortion laws are best observed in the Scandinavian countries, particularly in Sweden and Denmark. (England now has a moderate law as well, but without the inclusiveness of the Scandinavian approach to abortion.) Callahan characterizes the Scandinavian "middle way" laws as "broad in their range of permitted indications, but restrictive in their requirements that a strict legal procedure be followed . . . they have seemed to provide a way of allowing more legal abortions when reasonable grounds exist but also of stopping short of abortion on request." [15]

Scandinavian policy attempts to assist all pregnant women, both those who desire to bear the child and those who want to terminate the pregnancy. A counseling procedure is required in each case, and various social welfare measures are provided (employment protection for pregnant women, counseling centers, financial assistance) to reduce the need for abortion and to enlarge the woman's freedom of choice. Several results of these laws are apparent: abortions are, indeed, easier to get than in restrictive countries; the interpretations of the moderate laws is increasingly liberal; illegal abortions have been reduced but not entirely eradicated; and the freedom of the woman's choice about continuing as well as terminating her pregnancy has been enhanced. Nevertheless, though social assistance has enlarged the woman's choice, procedural delays increase the physical risks. Scandinavian mortality rates reflect the fact that many abortions are performed later in pregnancy than the woman desires, because of waiting lists, compulsory counseling, and the necessity of decisions by abortion panels.

Permissive legal codes have existed in the Soviet Union and in most of the Eastern European countries since the mid- and late-fifties. The provisions of these laws vary. Some, notably Hungary's, simply allow abortion on request, while others specify a very wide range of permitted abortion indications and in practice seldom refuse any woman's request. Though in recent years Japan was often viewed as having the most permissive abortion law, this is not quite accurate. Japan's law does restrict abortions to a number of permitted indications, but the interpretation and the administration of the law have in practice made it a system of abortion-on-demand. A single physician rather than a committee makes the decision, and all that is required of the woman is that she make an oral declaration that she meets one of the legal indications.

The 1973 U.S. Supreme Court decisions have placed the American abortion situation in the permissive category. "Jane Roe" (a pseudonym for a twenty-two-year-old Texas woman), single, pregnant, jobless, and with only a tenth grade education, was facing the additional stigma of bearing an illegitimate child which she feared would further jeopardize her employability. Denied a safe, legal abortion in Texas and financially unable to go elsewhere for this purpose, she took her case to court claiming that her constitutional rights to privacy in matters relating to sex and family had been abridged by the restrictive Texas statute. In its lengthy decision in *Roe v. Wade* the court ruled by a vote of seven to two that Jane Roe's privacy, protected by the Due Process Clause of the Fourteenth Amendment to the Constitution, had indeed been violated. Without directly attempting to answer the question of when the fetus becomes a person, the court affirmed that the state does have an important interest in protecting the health of the pregnant woman, and that it has yet *another* important interest in protecting the potentiality of human life. "These interests are separate and distinct. Each grows in substantiality as the woman approaches term, and at a point during pregnancy, each becomes 'compelling.' " [16] Because, in light of present medical knowledge, mortality in abortion is less than mortality in childbirth if the abortion is undertaken during approximately the first trimester, the court said this:

> For the stage prior to approximately the end of the first trimester, the abortion decision and its effectuation must be left to the medical judgment of the pregnant woman's attending physician.[17]

After this period, however, the risk of medical complications appreciably increases. Thus,

> For the stage subsequent to approximately the end of the first trimester, the State, in promoting its interests in the health of

the mother, may, if it chooses, regulate the abortion procedure
in ways that are reasonably related to maternal health.[18]

Such "reasonable ways" might include requirements concerning
qualifications and licensure of the person performing the abortion and the facility in which the procedure is performed. During
the last ten weeks of pregnancy, however, the fetus is considered viable. Hence,

> For the stage subsequent to viability the State, in promoting
> its interest in the potentiality of human life, may, if it chooses,
> regulate, and even proscribe, abortion except where it is neces-
> sary, in appropriate medical judgment, for the preservation of
> the life or health of the mother.[19]

While in *Roe v. Wade* the Supreme Court dealt with a 19th
century restrictive state abortion law (Texas), in its companion
case, *Doe v. Bolton,* the court also declared unconstitutional
Georgia's modern and relatively liberal statute. "Mary Doe,"
whose situation was described at the beginning of this chapter,
was denied an abortion request by the Abortion Committee of
Grady Memorial Hospital in Atlanta. Georgia's law closely followed the model abortion statute of the American Law Institute,
a pattern considered fairly liberal. The law allowed abortions

> ... performed by a duly licensed Georgia physician when
> necessary in "his best clinical judgment" because continued
> pregnancy would endanger a pregnant woman's life or injure
> her health; the fetus would likely be born with serious defects;
> or the pregnancy resulted from rape.[20]

These indications, to be sure, were considerably broader than
those of the Texas law which made all abortions criminal except
those done to save the life of the mother. In addition, however,
the Georgia law required that the patient be a Georgia resident,
that the abortion be performed in an accredited hospital, that
the procedure be approved by the hospital's abortion committee,
and that the performing physician's judgment be confirmed by
independent examinations of the woman by two other licensed
physicians. The court found these procedural requirements unconstitutional infringements upon the patient's rights.

Together the two decisions clearly place American abortion
policy in the permissive category. While the court emphasized
that the woman's right to abortion is not absolute, and while

permission was granted to the states to be restrictive in the last ten weeks of pregnancy, the net result up to the stage of viability is abortion-on-demand without required committee procedures — a more lenient policy than those of many countries in the permissive category. Only four state laws remained constitutional following the decisions.

Certain identifiable results have followed permissive abortion policies in other countries, results which may be duplicated in America.[21] Illegal abortions dramatically decrease (without completely disappearing), and there is a consequent reduction in deaths and injuries of women. There has been some strain on public health facilities from the increased abortion demand, but also a reduction in the need for medical resources for women suffering the complications of back-alley abortions. Social discrimination is markedly decreased. Contraceptive practices have not increased in permissive abortion areas; in fact in some places the abortion attitude has become routinized and has served as a repeated method of birth control for many women. The type of woman most commonly seeking abortion in the permissive system does not tend to be the overburdened mother, but the unmarried younger woman whose main reason for desiring the abortion is that she does not want the child. Finally, in those countries whose permissive laws have been complemented with social and financial assistance programs for the one who decides to continue her pregnancy, there is a widespread conviction that the woman's genuine freedom of choice is augmented.

Moral Arguments: I. The Right Wing

The right wing of the abortion debate is clearly expressed in the traditional Roman Catholic position. Pope Paul VI in his encyclical *Humane Vitae* (1968) says,

> We must once again declare that the direct interruption of the generative process already begun, and above all, directly willed and procured abortion, even if for therapeutic reasons, are to be absolutely excluded as licit means of regulating birth.

Here the central issue is the sanctity of human life, and the genetic interpretation (see Chapter One) is affirmed: the conceptus at whatever stage of development is fully human life and is to be accorded all human rights and protections.

This general argument, however, is not reserved to the official Catholic voices. Three respected Protestant ethicists are cases in point. Helmut Thielicke declares, "The fetus has its own circulatory system and its own brain. These elementary biological facts should be sufficient to establish its status as a human being." [22] Similarly, Dietrich Bonhoeffer says, "Destruction of the embryo in the mother's womb is a violation of the right to live which God has bestowed upon this nascent life." [23] Paul Ramsey, arguing that human dignity is an "alien dignity" given by God, maintains, "A life's sanctity consists not in its worth *to* anybody. . . . No one is ever much more than a fellow fetus; and in order not to become confused about life's primary value, it is best not to concentrate on degrees of relative worth we may later acquire." [24]

Whereas the God-given inviolability of the conceptus at every stage is the central affirmation of the right wing, several related arguments usually are put forward. One is the contention that a principal mark of a just and compassionate society is its defense of the defenseless, its special concern for the weak and the powerless — in this case surely the fetus. Of all living beings involved in a contemplated abortion it is only the fetus that cannot speak for itself and that thus needs to be surrounded by special legal and moral protection.

Further, it is argued, both the physical and the mental health of the mother actually are best guarded by serious restrictions on abortion. The main threat to the woman's physical health is from self-induced attempts and bungled operations by illegal, incompetent abortionists. But, says one physician, "In an atmosphere of permissiveness toward abortion the criminal abortionist seems to flourish and is rarely prosecuted. Women will go to him because of the secrecy and expediency involved and the reluctance to face an inquiring physician with their problem." [25]

The mental health of the woman also is at stake, and advocates of the right wing position often maintain that it is, in fact, permissiveness which is the real emotional and spiritual threat to the woman. The persistence of guilt as a common experience of women undergoing abortion is a sign of health and not a legacy from an unenlightened past. Guilt signals the violation of the natural order of things, and subtle personality damage afflicts the woman who directly wills the abortion of the fetus.

If social discrimination is decried by others, this position replies that two wrongs do not make a right. If the manner in which existing laws are enforced permits abortion for the affluent, ought we therefore to sanction readily-available abortion for others? "It is somewhat like saying that if a man is wealthy enough to move to a Moslem country and marry four wives, we must change our bigamy laws here because the poor are being discriminated against." [26]

Finally and crucially, the moral health of the entire society is at stake. This contention is argued in varied ways. Some maintain with considerable passion that permissiveness about abortion simply and decisively opens the door to an unimaginable range of moral horrors. If the denigration of human life which takes place in abortions is given legal and social sanction, in the end what is to prevent us from repeating the Nazi experience in which gross sacrifices of the "unfit" were commanded for the purported welfare of others? If we are to make judgments about the "quality" of life rather than committing ourselves firmly to the protection of all life, what is to prevent the quality from being decided by those in political power?

Others argue if we cannot prove that permissiveness in abortion would lead to a wholesale disregard for human rights, there may still be a more subtle threat. Abortion implies a rejection of a world view advocated by the Christian gospel for two thousand years. It is a world view which puts before us the high vision of selfless sacrifice, concern for the weak and defenseless, and willingness to undergo redemptive suffering. Even though societies which are dominated by visions of self-realization and self-satisfaction can and do function, they are the poorer for it. [27]

The right wing, however, is not opposed to abortion under all circumstances. Rather, it is opposed to the direct and willful taking of *innocent* life. (Many persons of this persuasion would consent to the necessity of a "just war" or to the use of capital punishment.) The "principle of double effect" is called upon in those rare instances in which abortion might be permitted. David Granfield, a Catholic ethicist, summarizes the principle: "When from a licit act there immediately follow two effects, one good and the other bad, and the good outweighs the bad, it is licit to intend the good and permit the evil." [28] Four conditions must be fulfilled if the act is to be morally justified: (1) the act itself must be morally good or at least indifferent; (2) the evil effect cannot be a means to the good result; (3) the foreseen evil effect must not be intended or approved but only tolerated; (4) the good effect must outweigh the bad; there must be serious reason for the act if the evil result is to be permitted at all. Protestant ethicist Paul Ramsey defends the same principle but puts it in somewhat different language: the distinction between an indirect abortion (morally permitted) and a direct abortion (not morally permitted) is the distinction between an action whose "primary thrust" is to save the mother's life even though the "secondary thrust" is to kill the fetus, and an action whose primary thrust is to kill the fetus.[29]

Thus, the principle of double effect permits the removal of a cancer of the cervix even though the fetus dies in the process; its death was foreseen but unintended. Likewise it permits the removal of a section of the Fallopian tube containing an ectopic pregnancy, for again the sacrifice of the fetus is only indirect. However, the woman who has a serious lung, heart, or kidney condition and would die in pregnancy or childbirth constitutes a different situation. "Although such a case would be a medical rarity nowadays, if it did occur, no abortion of the child could be permitted, since the killing would be direct." [30]

The *form* of the right wing arguments as well as their substance is worth noting. Simply put, the argument is a syllogism: human life is sacred and must never be directly and intentionally killed; the conceptus in all stages of development is human life; therefore, the conceptus must never be directly and intentionally killed. James M. Gustafson helpfully (and I think fairly) characterizes the style of argumentation.[31] The arguments are made from an external viewpoint by persons who claim the right to judge the actions of others. They use a basically juridical model, determining right or wrong by whether or not the action conforms to a rule or law. They confine the data of the arguments largely to physical (and not emotional or spiritual) factors. They tend to deal almost exclusively with the patient and physician at the time of that pregnancy, omitting other relationships and a longer view of time. The arguments tend to be rationalist ones, based upon natural law which is assumed to be binding upon all persons regardless of particular religious persuasion.

Moral Arguments: II. The Left Wing

The other end of the spectrum is abortion-on-demand. While some suggest that abortion-on-request is a better term, I shall use "demand." "Request" is a softer word implying that some requests might rightly be refused. But it is the force of left wing arguments that *no* woman sincerely desiring an abortion ought ever to be refused. "Demand" suggests precisely this.

If the right wing finally reduces all related arguments to one central conviction, the inviolable sanctity of the fetus, the left wing argues in a very similar fashion. All related arguments converge upon one paramount affirmation: the woman's absolute right to control of her body and its reproductive processes. While the Supreme Court found reason to modify that right in the last weeks of pregnancy, it clearly affirmed it in the earlier stages:

> As recently as last Term ... we recognized "the right of the *individual,* married or single, to be free from unwarranted governmental intrusion into matters so fundamentally affecting a person as the decision whether to bear or beget a child." That right necessarily includes the right of a woman to decide whether or not to terminate her pregnancy.[32]

Understandably, the literature of the left wing is less fully-developed than that of the right, for only in recent years has it become socially acceptable to make a public and vigorous defense of abortion-on-demand. Nevertheless, in the decade prior to the court's decision, articles and essays proliferated. For example, Rachel Conrad Wahlberg writes,

> Impersonally — medically, morally, legally — there may seem to be two entities, the woman and the fetus. But for the woman there is one entity, her body — me. *To her, the fetus seems to be a part of her own body....* The crucial point for the woman is: she feels that if she does not have power of decision over the contents of her uterus, then the fetus has a certain power over her. She is at the mercy of her reproductive system.[33]

Tilda Norberg maintains,

> Because society has for so long refused to face up to this tragic situation, I say that women are angry. We protest being victimized by lawmakers and doctors who say we have no voice in what happens in our bodies.... We protest the way we are taught to please men.... We protest the double standard.... But our anger is not just "against." We believe it has helped us to see more clearly that woman too is destined to live in

responsible freedom according to the Christian view and to act to achieve that destiny.[34]

According to Garrett Hardin,

> The question "How can we justify an abortion?" plainly leads to great difficulties. It is operationally unmanageable: it leads to inconsistencies in practice and inequities by any moral standard. All these can be completely avoided if we ask the right question, namely: *"How can we justify compulsory pregnancy?"* [35]

While the woman's right to reproductive self-determination is the central assertion, a number of additional arguments are made.[36] First, a permissive abortion system is necessary *to protect women's lives and health* by making medically-safe abortion available to anyone who chooses it. Only when abortion-on-demand is socially recognized, legally accepted, and medically facilitated, will the tragedies of coat hangers, knitting needles, back-alley practitioners, and extortioners be minimized.

Second, abortion-on-demand will *preserve the autonomy of the medical profession*. It is not assumed that all physicians, hospitals, and supporting medical staffs are professionally or morally obligated to perform abortions. If a physician conscientiously refuses, the patient has every right to seek the services of another. However, in a restrictive situation physicians are prevented by law from performing those abortions which, in their professional judgments, are needed.

Third, *to ensure that only those children who are wanted will be born* abortion-on-demand is necessary. The tragedy of rejected children is one which affects not only the child, its parents and its immediate family; the tragedy is society's as well. All of us must pay the human and financial costs of social deviance which spring from emotional and financial impoverishment. And everyone must pay the costs of population pressures needlessly augmented by unwanted children.

Fourth, such abortion policy is necessary *if women are to attain equal status in society,* be accorded their full civil liberties, and be freer from male domination. Compulsory pregnancy is a form of slavery. Its unfairness to the individual woman is matched by the toll it takes upon the fabric of society, for when anyone's freedom is diminished that of everyone is lessened.

Fifth, only a permissive abortion policy will *avoid the social and racial discrimination* which flourishes in every restrictive system. Not only has it been established that affluent women commonly travel to places where they can receive medically-safe abortions; it is also clear that far more abortions are performed in private than in public hospitals in areas which have restrictive legislation.

To be sure, there are varieties of emphases and convictions within the left wing. Prior to 1973 some were willing to accept the liberalization of restrictive laws, the expansion of the range of indications for which abortion would be legally permitted. Thomas S. Szasz spoke for a larger number, however. Such "liberalization" would still restrict human freedom and hence be anti-liberal. Why? Such laws "would only increase the number of times *other* people could provide abortions for women; they would not increase the number of occasions on which women could make this decision for *themselves*." [37]

Moral Arguments: III. The Justifiable Abortion

A third general approach lies somewhere between the right and left wings, affirming some of the arguments of each but differing from either. It is, I believe, a more responsible moral position. Let us look at several of the major issues to see how the justifiable abortion stance responds to the other positions.

Ethical style. Each wing of the abortion argument focuses upon a very significant value or right: the sanctity of the life of the fetus in one instance and the woman's right to self-determination in the other. The ethical problem which arises in each case, however, stems from absolutizing one value at the expense of all others. In effect, this removes the ambiguity of any particular decision. If the rights of the fetus are absolute, there is no question about what we should (or should not) do. Even in the rare cases when the principle of double effect must be invoked, the outcome of the decision is clear in advance. Or, once we assume that the woman's right to control her own body is inviolable, if she should opt for an abortion there remains no moral ambiguity about the decision.

But this is to oversimplify our moral experience. Sensitive persons in the midst of making abortion decisions usually experience considerable conflict, the conflict and competition of *relative* rights. Theologically, the relativity of all values and rights (even those of great importance) is part of the radically monotheistic affirmation that only God is Lord. Only he is absolute, and there are no other gods (or absolute values) beside him.

This ethical stance thus finds the style of reasoning used by both extremes in the abortion debate unacceptable. The rationalistic, syllogistic, physically-oriented, truncated-context approach is more obvious in the right wing, but it is present in its counterpart as well. More realistically, abortion decisions need to be seen as ones which involve living beings immersed in widely varying patterns of social relationships. While two particular decisions may be identical in the sense that the fetus is destroyed in each case, the moral meanings of those two decisions may differ considerably because of different intentions, different personal and family situations, and different social conditions.

In short, any social policy should recognize that, in spite of certain commonalities among abortion decisions, there is both *uniqueness* and *moral tragedy* in each one. If we gloss over either we do violence to reality. To say that each situation has its own uniqueness does not mean that general principles are useless. It does mean, however, that no absolute right or principle automatically can resolve complex human dilemmas. It is no more obvious that desire for an abortion constitutes its adequate moral justification than that the rights of the fetus should always prevail. Further, to affirm that every abortion decision is interlaced with moral tragedy does not mean there are no good and responsible abortion decisions. Rather, it is to recognize that we find ourselves caught between important and competing human values which we cannot always equally affirm in practice.

The humanity of the fetus remains a difficult but crucial question. In Chapter One we looked at three major ways of assigning humanity: the genetic (the fixing of the genetic code renders the conceptus human and hence inviolable), the developmental (the conceptus rightly is considered human life, but is of increasing capacity for *personal* human existence), and the social consequences school (decisions about the humanity of the fetus must rest upon the consequences of that decision for the moral policy that is desired). Our affirmation of the developmental position actually reflects a certain underlying value theory. It is a relational theory which understands values and rights neither as objective (things that exist quite independently of the concrete

situation) nor as subjective (our preferences and desires). Both
elements are present in the sense that value arises in the particular relationships and genuine needs of the beings who are
involved — including the fetus, the woman, the man, others
immediately and more remotely related, and God the ultimate
Valuer.[38] The developmental view affirms that there is something
unique and given in conception and ever thereafter. It is *human*
life and as such deserves our profound respect. But it is not
personal human life until it gradually develops the capacities
for personal interaction and response.

The truth of the right wing position lies in that "pro-life bias"
which ought to inform every abortion decision. Any destruction
of fetal life is tragic, and we ought not to hide behind sterile
clinical language ("emptying the uterine contents") to disguise
that moral affirmation. However the woman may *feel* about the
contents of her uterus, it is not just another piece of her tissue.
It is a human being, potentially but not yet personal. Potter
summarizes the tension well: "Abortion is not just another surgical procedure. Nor is it murder. Abortion is abortion. It is a
peculiar moral problem that can be neither 'solved' by clumsy
analogies nor dissolved by some rhetorical sleight of hand." [39]

The woman's right of self-determination is the central emphasis of the left wing. While this ought not be absolutized any more
than fetal rights, we ought surely to affirm that God values the
woman's personhood and fulfillment just as God values nascent
life. Moreover, we should remember that history's cards have
been stacked against recognition of the woman's rights. In the
centuries of abortion discussion only very recently has this side
been given vigorous public affirmation, and only very belatedly
have many recognized the extent to which male sexism has
shaped abortion policies.

Two related matters need consideration. First, granting the
high value of the woman's rights, if she is to have genuine freedom for decision about a problem pregnancy there must be a
range of options open to her. Callahan has argued this per-
suasively:

> If the goal is perfect freedom for women, then it is hard to see
> how it could be fulfilled without taking account of the pos-
> sibility that, given some genuine options (money, therapy,
> support), many women who *say,* at first, that they do not want

a child might well change their minds and feel all the freer
for having some real choices presented to them.[40]

The strength of permissive legal arrangements in Eastern Europe
is evident at this point. While not denying abortion to any
woman who seriously requests it, these systems make counseling
a regular feature of the abortion process, and various forms of
socially-acceptable support are readily available for the woman
who decides to bear her child (pregnancy and maternity leave
without jeopardizing her job, financial assistance, adequate day-
care centers, etc.). That these features in practice are not just
another disguised way of stacking the cards against the woman's
freedom is indicated by the high number of legal abortions in
these countries.

A second related consideration is too frequently overlooked:
the rights of the man, the father of the fetus. While some fathers
(married as well as unmarried) may care little about the woman's
situation and some appear untouched by the agonies of an abortion decision, it is hardly fair to generalize from this. Many do
care. Abortion counselors find that often the man has greater
difficulty in working through the experience of abortion than
does the woman.[41] And as a general moral policy, the affirmation
that those who will be significantly affected by the decisions of
others ought to have some voice in them has good grounding in
both Christian ethics and in the philosophy of free societies.

That the woman's rights in abortion questions have been dis-
valued more than honored in most of human history is rather
clear. For the Christian conscience, however, the ambiguity about
abortion must remain. Freedom is not simply unencumbered
autonomy. The vision of self-giving love, sacrifice, and care for
the defenseless ought not be lost in favor of a simple bias toward
solutions which are more personally convenient and immediately
rewarding. Yet this part of the vision must not be used as
a thinly-disguised reason for violating the freedom of women,
for such human freedom is equally important to a Christian
humanism.

The issue of the unwanted child deserves further comment.[42]
It is, next to the woman's right to self-determination, that argument most frequently raised by the left wing. Whose interests are
at stake? Those who maintain that in such situations abortion
is always in the prospective child's own interest (if he is unwanted

he ought not to be born) have a difficult case to make. If we argue the right of self-determination for the woman, ought not this have some weight for the prospective child as well? Can we rightly make that decision for him and claim that it is in *his* interests? No available evidence shows a clear causal connection between the unwanted child and the battered child.

The interest of the mother, the father, and others in the immediate family are at stake, too. Here the question, particularly as it concerns the mother, is best seen in terms of a range of available options. Does the mother feel this way because of factors which might be alleviated through various types of assistance — therapy, financial aid, and the like?

Society's interests must be considered. There is ample evidence that severely-rejected children frequently develop destructive behavioral patterns. But *frequently* does not mean *always,* and rejection by the mother or by both parents does not mean that accepting environments for the child's growth are out of the question. Yet, society does have interests at stake, including the right to protect its internal order and peace.

Ethically, the nub of the question is whether the fetus receives its *value* exclusively from being *wanted* by other human beings. Even on a purely human level it is hard to establish this, but when the issue is seen in light of God's valuing of nascent life the answer is clear: the fetus *has* value quite apart from the attitudes of other human beings, even those most immediately involved.

Where are we left concerning the unwanted child? Once more we are in the midst of an inescapable moral tension and ambiguity. A humanly-unwanted fetus does have value, but the desires of the mother or of both parents are also of importance. God values the fetus, but God also values other relationships and persons in that particular situation. Hence, the not-wanting of the child is always a serious but never an automatically-decisive element in the abortion decision.

Public abortion policy raises additional moral factors. Stable families able to provide good child nurture and population control are two requisites of a society's health. If these were the only considerations, outright abortion-on-demand would be wise public policy. But society also has important stakes in other values. An abortion policy which legitimates the oppression of women diminishes the humanness of a society just as does one which denigrates nascent life, or sees abortion in utilitarian terms as a matter of personal convenience, or suggests that technological capacity to do safe abortions equals a blanket moral sanction for them.

The implementation of the Supreme Court's decision in *Roe v. Wade* and *Doe v. Bolton* presently is unclear. Efforts to evade or to nullify the decisions may well continue for some time. Yet, the dramatic shift of public opinion in recent years toward the position which the court finally took would suggest that these rulings will prevail.

While the court's decisions did not and could not fully answer our public policy needs regarding abortion, they deserve support as morally-responsible actions. There are a number of reasons for this: [43]

1. The decisions will mitigate the undesirable consequences of restrictive abortion policies which we have already discussed.

2. While denying that the Constitution intends that the full rights of persons are applicable to the fetus, the court wisely refused to legislate an opinion on when human life begins.[44]

3. The court gave recognition to the competing rights that are, indeed, involved in any abortion decision. It attempted to balance the woman's right to private decision with the society's concern for protecting fetal life in its later stages. It saw individual rights gradually giving way to social rights as the pregnancy progresses.

4. The decisions recognized it important for the woman's health that states be able to regulate the licensure of persons and facilities performing abortions.

5. The court's ruling allows all persons to follow their consciences in abortion matters without allowing those of one particular persuasion to restrain others from abortion under penalty of law.

What is at stake is not the rights of anti-abortion groups to espouse their theological and moral convictions, educate their members, and seek to influence others. These rights are constitutionally guaranteed. Neither is the freedom *of* religious practice jeopardized, as would be the case were the state to compel a woman under certain circumstances to have an abortion. Rather, what is at stake is the freedom of sizeable numbers of citizens *from* the religious views of others with whom they sincerely disagree. Surely there are moral issues on which a broad consensus does exist, convictions which for many persons are based upon religious beliefs, and for which the power of civil law is appropriate. Racial segregation is a case in point. The case of abortion differs, however. Here the moral position is tied much more directly with the theological convictions of *particular* groups. Here a broad public consensus is lacking. In matters of abortion choice in the early months of pregnancy, what many consider a sin ought not to be made a crime, and the court was right in insisting upon the religious neutrality of the state at this point.[45]

A responsible public abortion policy, however, must go beyond the freedoms and protections of privacy afforded by the court. It must also respect the rights of conscience of those medical personnel who cannot with integrity participate in abortion procedures. Beyond this, public policy must attempt to minimize the felt necessity for abortion. If the measure of a good society is the willingness to live with that delicate tension between respecting the rights of personal conscience and defending the defenseless, so also the good society is marked by the willingness to take vigorous steps to alleviate those conditions which give rise to these decisions involving tragic moral conflict. The experience of those countries whose moderate and permissive abortion laws are combined with a broad range of supportive services (counseling, job protection, day care centers, financial assistance, etc.) strongly indicates that it is in these situations that the woman's genuine freedom of choice is enhanced and she is not forced into abortion as the only hope.

The role of Christian churches is augmented by the new abortion situation in this country. On the first level, its role is theological and ethical. Though the fetus prior to its final weeks has no legal rights, it demands our respect as human life and potentially personal life. The church needs to keep alive a Christian vision which always goes beyond the secular law, a vision which reminds us of the ultimate basis for life's sanctity. The church needs to affirm the gracious and justifying acceptance of God which helps us face the abortion ambiguity squarely, with less proneness to pathological self-justification and its inevitable dulling of our moral sensitivity.

The church's roles in education and counselling are potentially of great importance. The change to permissive abortion policies in other countries has increased the demand for abortion (presumably in part by women who would not otherwise have felt the need for such procedures). Sex education and family planning assistance on a vastly more effective scale are now needed if the number of unwanted pregnancies is to be kept within bounds. The churches have a role in this effort. Furthermore, whereas prior to the Supreme Court's decisions, clergy abortion counseling services frequently accented technical information and referral channels, now counseling surely needs to take a broader focus. It means helping persons through a process of serious self-examination so that abortion does not become routine, even when widespread availability of chemical abortifacients becomes a future reality. Such counseling means helping women to see the full range of options before them. And it means furnishing a community of support for persons in whatever decisions they finally make.

Abortion is one crucial life (and death) experience which the church has not yet included in its liturgical assistance to persons.[46] Yet, there are great Christian resources upon which we might draw in symbolizing the human meanings of the decision to have an abortion. A pre- or post-abortion rite would most likely be private, including only those specifically invited to participate. It could incorporate acts of confession, conscious acknowledgment that it is human life which is being ended, and assurances of God's strengthening forgiveness. For every decision to abort involves an inescapable moral ambiguity, even when that decision in a given situation is the better and humanly more responsible thing to do.

CHAPTER THREE

Human Factors
in Artificial
Insemination

Cases

When bad timing faded as the probable cause for their failure to conceive, Evelyn sought medical counsel. The gynecologist saw no impediment. Harry, slow to believe that he might be the source of the problem, finally went to a specialist who soon diagnosed a very low sperm count — he was effectively sterile. With the extremely long wait for adoptable infants and with Evelyn's strong desire to experience pregnancy and childbirth they began to talk about artificial insemination with sperm from an anonymous donor. Yet Harry honestly wondered if he would always feel differently toward the child than his wife would.

In spite of the usual precautions taken in such work, Frank's new job in nuclear research exposed him to some radiation dangers. While the risks of sterility were not high, they were there. He and his wife had a one-year-old daughter. Though they wanted at least one more, they had agreed to wait a few years so that Carol could return to her career. Active Catholics, they also practiced birth control regularly. Now Frank began to consider depositing semen in a local sperm bank as insurance against the possibility of sterility. The couple knew that their church frowned upon artificial insemination even with the husband's sperm. They were not at all convinced that this would violate anything fundamental to their Christian understanding of sex and marriage. But they wondered.

Lord Wheatley, a Scottish judge, was confronted by an unusual case in 1958: a suit for divorce by a Mr. MacLennan. The husband was charging his wife with adultery. Evidence? She had given birth to a baby girl in spite of the fact that both admitted they had not had sexual intercourse for over a year. In contesting the divorce, Mrs. MacLennan argued that the conception was not adulterous. She had not had intercourse with the child's biological father; she had procured the semen of a donor and had introduced it into her own body with a syringe. Admittedly, she said, it was without the knowledge of her husband though her intent was not to commit adultery but to have a baby.[1]

The Past and Present of Artificial Insemination

Artificial human insemination (or therapeutic insemination, as some prefer to call it) is the introduction of semen in the woman's vagina, cervical canal, or uterus by means of instruments. Its purpose is to produce pregnancy when the wish to have a child apparently cannot be satisfied through normal sexual intercourse. This procedure is of two general types. When the semen is obtained from the husband it is called homologous or, more simply, AIH (artificial-insemination-husband). When the semen comes from a man other than the husband the procedure is heterologous, AID (artificial-insemination-donor). On occasions, the husband's semen is mixed with that of the donor (AIHD). This is done largely for psychological reasons, though it remains possible (however improbable) that the husband with a low sperm count could be the source of the fertilizing sperm. In both theory and practice, though, AIHD should be treated as AID, donor insemination. Couples usually turn to artificial insemination because of impotence, sterility, or hereditary disease on the part of the husband, genital malformation of either husband or wife, or dyspareunia (painful intercourse).

Historically, human artificial insemination does not have a long clinical past, though interest in the subject is legendary. According to a story in the Midrash which was repeated in a number of medieval works, Ben Sirah was conceived accidentally because of

some contaminated bath water his mother had used.[2] Use of AI
in animals is said to have been done as early as the fourteenth
century, though successful experiments were not documented
until four centuries later. By 1790 a well-known English physician had performed the first effective human insemination. Successful experiments in France were followed by the report of an
American doctor in 1866 that he had performed fifty-five inseminations on six women and had obtained the first AI baby in this
country.[3] While all of these cases appear to have been AIH, one
report of AID dates that event around 1885.[4]

Because of both moral and scientific uncertainties, artificial
human insemination was not widely practiced for a number of
years after the first successful experiments. Following World
War I, however, the practice again surfaced into public view,
and since that time an increasing number of inseminations have
been done, particularly in the United States and Israel but also
in countries of Northern Europe. The understandable secrecy
surrounding both infertility problems and the practice of artificial insemination makes accurate statistics difficult to obtain.
Perhaps three and one-half million couples in the U.S. are involuntarily childless, and in well over one-third of these the husband is the source of the problem. While only a small fraction of
such couples have attempted artificial insemination, recent estimates suggest that there are 150,000 living Americans whose
conception came through AID or AIH. Annual figures range
from the conservative estimate of 10,000 AI pregnancies to the
liberal figure of 25,000 in recent years. The world-wide total of
donor insemination births may be as high as one million.[5]

Freezing and storage of semen for future use is a relatively
recent achievement in human insemination.[6] Christopher Polge,
an English scientist, developed the method about a quarter of a
century ago by adding the chemical glycerol to the semen before
the freezing process. Since his discovery, the use of frozen semen
in veterinary medicine has produced over one hundred million
calves. R. G. Bunge, a urologist at the University of Iowa,
reported the first human birth resulting from frozen semen in
1953. In 1970 Bunge wrote that the boy was then "16 years old,
six feet tall, in excellent health, an 'A' student, musically inclined and a promising athlete." [7] In the last two decades several
hundred normal babies have been born through the use of frozen
semen.

The first reports of semen storage facilities came from Iowa City and Tokyo in decade of the 1950s. Since then a number of sperm banks have sprung up, particularly in the United States. The length of time during which frozen semen remains viable is open to dispute. Bull semen thawed after twenty years has been successfully used. Human semen stored for ten years has produced one child, and some proponents argue that no limit has been found for the effective length of storage.[8] On the other hand, critics hold that most births have been produced from semen frozen for only sixteen months or less and that deterioration apparently sets in after that time. The genetic adequacy of long-stored semen is also unclear. Conservative medical people urge extreme caution in using old semen. Others, however, argue that out of four hundred reported frozen semen births only two had minor congenital abnormalities and that frozen semen probably improves in genetic quality inasmuch as weaker, malformed sperm die with age.[9]

In addition to the storage of donor semen, sperm banks are used for a number of potential AIH purposes. Men planning vasectomies bank sperm as insurance against the possibility of a future change of mind. Patients about to undergo potentially sterilizing cancer therapy have used sperm storage, as have men in high sterility-risk occupations such as professional athletes, police, firemen, and men occupationally exposed to radiation. Occasionally sperm storage facilities are used for more unusual purposes. A prominent midwestern man banked some of his sperm so that if his pre-puberty son should later prove sterile the father's semen could impregnate the son's future wife in order that the family blood line might be preserved! [10]

The Legal Status of Artificial Insemination

When the semen donor is the husband (AIH), legal problems rarely arise. After all, the child is the genetic offspring of both husband and wife, and had they not earnestly wanted the child they presumably would not have resorted to medical assistance in conceiving. In a few AIH cases one type of problem has arisen, however: the later attempt of either husband or wife to dissolve the marriage on grounds of non-consummation. It is still possible that such dissolutions might be granted. Yet, as one legal authority observes, "At one time such a decree would have bastardized the child, but statute has now prevented this result both in England and in many American jurisdictions." [11]

Even if Christian opinion is divided about the morality of AIH, it is not a matter for regulation by civil law. Such impregnation with the husband's semen threatens neither marriage nor the common good even though couples will come to differing decisions concerning the appropriateness of using artificial means. These are personal decisions of conscience which are hardly matters for the state's jurisdiction.

Thorny legal problems do arise with donor insemination. [12] Legal uncertainty surrounds two questions. First, does AID constitute adultery under civil law? Second, is the child conceived through AID legitimate? Before examining these issues directly, we must recognize that both statute law and case law on AID are at present exceedingly sparse. The picture is very fluid and clear precedents simply have not yet emerged. A legal scholar studying the situation in 1971 found that only five states had AID laws: New York, California, Georgia, Oklahoma, and Kansas, and only the last three laws attempt to be comprehensive. He also found only six American court cases dealing directly with AID, and in these there emerged no consensus on either main legal issue, adultery or the child's legitimacy. [13]

What about adultery? The practice of adultery itself is a statutory crime in most American states, though the law is very rarely enforced. The legal issue for AI usually arises in connection with divorce suits, and in the case of AID it surfaces when a husband sues for divorce on the grounds that such impregnation of his wife was an adulterous act. In the Scottish court case mentioned at the beginning of this chapter, Lord Wheatley distinguished between the moral and the legal issues at stake: "just as artificial insemination extracts procreation from the nexus of human relationships in or outside of marriage, so does the extraction of the nexus of human relationship from the act of procreation remove artificial insemination from the classification of sexual intercourse." [14] Thus, in his view, while a woman who engaged in AID without the consent of her husband had certainly committed a serious breach of the marriage contract, she had not legally committed adultery. Adultery so-defined involves actual contact of the genitals. While judicial opinions have varied, most attorneys in the United States would agree with Lord Wheatley: AID, even without the husband's consent (a practice in which very few physicians would cooperate), does not constitute adulterous grounds for divorce. The moral issue, however, is quite another matter.

Regarding the AID child's legitimacy, the legal situation is no more definitive. By the time of the 1971 survey, three American courts had considered the question, all hearing cases in which the husband had given his consent to the impregnation. One of the courts held the child to be legitimate, but the two others did not. Several matters hinge upon this question: the child's inheritance rights and (in divorce actions) child support, custody, and visitation privileges. On only one thing did all three courts agree: the husband was liable for child support.

The child's legal status could be cleared up if all states passed AID legislation such as Oklahoma's law of 1966. It says in part, "Any child or children born as the result of AID shall be considered at law in all respects the same as a naturally conceived legitimate child of the husband and wife so requesting and consenting to the use of such technique." [15] In those states (currently the great majority) which have no AID legislation, it is particularly important that couples draw up documents of written consent with attorneys' assistance prior to the operation. But written consent alone will not create a clear legal context. Inasmuch as AID will probably increase in our society, creative law-making is urgently needed. In addition to the cardinal issues of adultery and legitimacy a number of others clamor for clarification, including the legal responsibilities of physicians and donors and the use of a dead donor's frozen semen. But how these questions are answered in law depends in no small measure upon the community's moral consensus. [16]

Current legal cloudiness in most states presents an important question of practical moral wisdom about the use of AID. Even if the couple is persuaded on all other grounds that AID is right for their situation, does the risk of legal confusion about the AID child warrant proceeding with the operation?

Weighing the Psychological Factors

The feelings any husband might have in deciding about AID are described by one who went through the process:

> I burned at the idea of another man's sperm in my wife's womb, another man's child growing inside her. . . . How would

I react to watching my wife's body respond and change to a strange man's seed? ... Would Jo secretly feel the baby was more hers than ours? ... Although frightened and confused by all this, I eventually was able to admit to myself that there was a child in me: a wounded ego. ... Could I deprive Jo of the experience of carrying and delivering a child? [17]

Undoubtedly the husband usually has the greater psychological adjustment to make. He is the "deficient" one, a difficult role for many in a society with exaggerated masculine virility images.

Two studies of emotional issues for the husband are illuminating. Herbert D. Lamson, a sociologist, and William J. Pinard, a psychologist, classify prospective AID husbands into three groups. First, there are the neurotic types who oppose the procedure violently when it is suggested. For them AID would probably invite strong rejection of the child and jealousy toward the unknown donor, courting psychological and family disaster. In contrast, there is the relaxed husband for whom AID comes as a welcome solution to the problem of childlessness which both he and his wife share. Adjustment is minimal. In the third group are those who feel ambivalent but desire to make an adjustment to AID. These men may weigh the issues, may fear legal complications, may be uncertain about the moral dimensions, and may resent their sterility. But they also yearn for fatherhood, and they strongly desire to see fulfillment for their wives.[18]

Assessing a number of other studies of AID families, clinical psychologist Karl Ostrom observes that the masculinity threat to the AID husband may be a double one. First, he has the usual male adjustment to make to fatherhood: he must moderate his own self-assertiveness and become a nurturing parent along with his wife. But, unique to AID fathers, he also must cope with the recognition of his sterility which "threatens to evoke very deep seated feelings of helpless dependence in relationship to women and also feelings of inadequacy in relation to other men." [19] If he cannot resolve these feelings, he might overcompensate in his work; if he cannot produce a child, at least he can produce more income. Or he might experience homosexual panic. Or he might reject his child, particularly when the child moves into the stage of his own self-assertion.

Inasmuch as the typical woman entering into AID is strongly motivated to do so — she wants to bear her own children — the wife usually adjusts to the process with greater ease than does her husband. Nevertheless, the road for the woman is not always smooth. Somehow she must cope both with her husband's deficiency and with the potential guilt of carrying "another man's baby" in her womb.

In her extensive studies of the psychological reactions of women, Helene Deutsch finds three types.[20] One is the masculine-aggressive woman who refuses to accept the verdict of her childlessness. She might intimidate her husband emotionally, threaten conception by another man, or demand that the marriage be terminated. In spite of the strong desire for her own children, she is obviously a very poor AID risk. Another type of woman seems to accept her husband's sterility in terms of her own childlessness, but she needs other proofs of his masculinity — perhaps constant professional and financial success. Frequently such women made good adjustments to AID, and the experience of bearing their own children eases their concern about their husbands' masculinity to the great benefit of both partners. Deutsch describes her third type as the truly "motherly woman." In childlessness she has transferred her maternal love to others, and in child-bearing after AID she finds a natural fulfillment. She is the ideal AID candidate.

If there are serious problems for either of the parents, undoubtedly there will be problems for the AID child. Over-solicitousness toward the child may signal parental conflicts. The child may be dimly aware of a "big secret" about his origins. The male child who is told of the AID procedure may experience difficulty in his psycho-sexual identification if he feels significantly less bound to his father than to his mother. Nevertheless, many of the potential psychological quandaries for AID children are not significantly different from those of adopted children and of children in re-marriage situations.

While discussions of AID usually omit the psychological issues affecting the semen donor, these also deserve consideration. If a medical student (the most typical donor) frequently responds to the semen requests which come from physicians and laboratories, and if the sperm contained in one ejaculate can be divided for several different inseminations, the mathematical possibilities for his siring numerous children are great. If his donations are all used within one local community, he might be prone to fantasizing about "his" children whom he sees on the streets. But, as Joseph Fletcher wisely says, "The children he helped to bring into the world would be 'his' only in a most materialistic and naturalistic sense. . . . Once more, in dealing with a question like this, we come face to face with the problem of deciding just what kinship is: whether it is a matter of blood or of loyalty and love." [21] In addition, the capacity for freezing and shipping semen now makes possible a considerable geographic distance between donor and recipient, a factor which is of no small importance to the donor's psychological objectivity. Suffice to say, the donor's mental health as much as his physical health ought to be the concern of the physician or laboratory using his services.

The foregoing recitation of AID psychological hazards may sound gloomy indeed. Yet, it is well to remember that the available psychological studies of AID participants involve only a small fraction of the total number and, at that, tend to focus upon those who have come for therapy. We should be wary of the generalization syndrome seen frequently in other situations: for example, the psychiatrist who argues that all homosexuals are emotionally disturbed because all those homosexuals who come to him for treatment are emotionally disturbed. There is in fact no evidence at present that the majority of AID participants experience serious psychological difficulty. A recent Duke University study of thirty-eight AID couples indicated that 76 percent of them "definitely" would repeat the use of AID if they decided to have another child.[22] The point of raising these psychological issues is to recognize them as one of several important types of moral ingredients in any AID decision, whether that decision be one by prospective participants in the process or whether it be one concerning social policy. One thing, however, seems clear: AID is no magic potion for a shaky childless marriage. Its soundness depends upon the prior soundness of the relationship.

Social Policy Questions

Social policy questions arise with donor rather than with husband insemination. This does not mean, as we shall see, that AIH is morally neutral. It simply means that AIH decisions are hardly ones in which society has a compelling stake. But the picture is far less clear with AID. At least four broad questions should be raised: does AID threaten marriage in such a way that the social fabric of the larger community is threatened? are there

socially-adverse genetic implications in AID? in light of population pressures should AID be sanctioned or discouraged? is the
use of adoption (which is socially accepted, legally protected, and
institutionally supported) a better answer for society as well as
for childless couples?

First, granting that society has a large stake in the moral and
emotional health of its families, how can we answer the social
policy questions about AID? While widespread use of AID is
still rather new, and while, as we have seen, current studies do
not show adverse effects on the emotional health of most families,
we need to remember that our empirical data are not numerous.
Perhaps we need to hold this question in abeyance until in the
following section we probe more deeply into additional factors
which affect the morality of AID. There is, after all, a close
relationship between what is morally responsible and what is
socially and emotionally healthful in such questions as these.

What of the genetic implications? Some persons have strongly
urged that AID be used eugenically, as a measure to improve the
human species. It could be a device of negative eugenics (to
breed out certain undesirable genes such as those carrying hereditary diseases) or, as some maintain, of positive eugenics (to breed
in desirable genes such as those bearing on intelligence and
physique). In fact, negative eugenics of a sort is now being practiced in AID. The selection of semen donors by reputable physicians and sperm banks includes screening for histories of disease
and transmissible defects. In a limited way positive eugenics is
also present. At least one commercial sperm bank has developed
a genetic registry in which are recorded the various characteristics of semen donors and to which the physician requesting
semen for patients can refer. To be sure, in the present AID
practice the conscious attempt to improve the genetic characteristics of the race is far subordinate to the effort to make a good
genetic "fit" for the particular couple. The net result, however,
is that society's rightful genetic interests are protected in the
present practice of donor selection. The broader, more ambitious
eugenic proposals for AID's use in improving the race must
await our consideration in Chapter Five.

Still, there remains another genetic question: the increased
possibilities of unintentional incest through the use of AID. One
calculation has it that "a fecund donor who submitted two donations a week could produce four hundred children weekly, or

more than 20,000 annually." [23] Though mathematically possible, it is highly improbable that one donor would be used to such an extent or that his sperm would be parcelled out so economically. Even so, reasonably frequent donations from one man statistically do increase the chances for two AID children of the same biological father (but unaware of that fact) marrying. While, biologically speaking, in-breeding is probably seldom harmful except among eugenically poor genetic stocks, the possibility of unintentional incest should be kept deliberately remote. This means that the number of donations accepted from any one man ought to be severely limited. It also is part of moral wisdom that donor semen from localities distant from one's own community be used.

A third social question links AID with the population issue. In light of a serious population problem on this overcrowded planet (including our own society in spite of recent drops in our birth rate), ought not childless couples be steered to adoption agencies for the satisfaction of their parenting desires? Can society responsibly encourage or even allow AID? One problem with this argument is simply the shortage of adoptable infants. The advent of the pill, the increased acceptance of abortion, the increasing social acceptability of the unwed mother, and minority group pressures against interracial adoptions all have resulted in a supply of adoptable infants far exceeded by the demand for them. But even beyond this, the argument is a poor one. It implicitly invokes a double standard. It suggests that we say one thing to the childless couple plagued by involuntary infertility ("you ought not bring any additional children into the world") without saying the same thing to the childless-but-fertile couple. Given the population and ecological facts, on some future day strong social discouragements against being more than a certain number of children may well be necessary. Such might be necessary to safeguard one of the cardinal implications of the sanctity of life: the right to the survival of the species. But when and if such judgments are made, common justice dictates that they be applied equitably, to fertile and non-fertile alike.

Finally, there is the question of the institutional support (or lack thereof) for AID. One professional adoption supervisor argues that AID suffers mightily compared to adoption.[24] In AID most states lack legal regulation and protection. The counseling and screening procedures for prospective AID parents are haphazard at best. The atmosphere of secrecy (because of the absence of strong legal and social sanctions) may be subversive to the welfare of those using it. And, in the present state of AID practice the information on paternal heritage is usually unavailable to the parents, a fact that can be detrimental to the child's developing personal identity and a fact which can raise medical complications. All of these comparisons may, indeed, show that adoption has far more social and institutional supports than AID presently has. These may be good reasons for a particular couple choosing to adopt (assuming an adoptable child to be available) rather than to use AID. These reasons do not, however, point to an inherent weakness in AID as a socially-sanctioned practice. Rather, the arguments merely highlight the need for social, legal, and institutional supports if AID is to become a more viable option for the childless.

Theological Questions and Moral Decisions

The official Roman Catholic position is unequivocally opposed to artificial insemination, particularly by donor but by husband as well. Pope Pius XII made his church's position patently clear in a 1949 statement to Catholic physicians.[25] First, he said, AID runs counter to God's plan for marriage which decrees that the husband and wife have exclusive, nontransferable rights to each other's bodies and their generative powers. In short, AID is adultery. Second, artificial insemination emerges out of a false philosophy of life. It assumes that happiness is a right and if a couple needs a child for their happiness then that child, too, is their right. Third, both AID and AIH usually rely upon masturbation to procure the semen, and as an act against nature masturbation is inherently evil. Fourth, the social consequences stemming from AID in particular would be disastrous.

Jewish opinion is divided on AID. According to Wilfred J. Finegold three fundamental Hebraic decrees are pertinent: "1. consanguinity is sinful; 2. the 'wasting of the seed' is sinful; and 3. it is a sin for a married woman to conceive by the spermatozoa of a man not her husband." [26] Nevertheless, many other Jewish scholars do not feel that AID is adulterous inasmuch as there is no physical contact of the sex organs of the donor and the woman. Moreover, many feel that consanguinity or marriages between blood relatives is improbable enough to make AID permissible.

Protestant theologians, typically, are also divided on the issue. Two noted ethicists who have written widely on medical issues illustrate the contrasting extremes. Paul Ramsey argues that the separation of procreation from the husband-wife covenant of faithfulness is a violation of the divinely-created order of marriage:

> Human parenthood is . . . a basic form of humanity. To violate this is already dehumanizing, even if spiritualistic or personalistic or mentalistic categories are invoked to justify it. . . . The parameters of human life, which science and medicine should serve and not violate, are grounded in the man of flesh and in the nature of human parenthood.[27]

Furthermore, contends Ramsey, the breach in the structure of human parenthood represented by AID is critical. Once we allow this, we must be prepared for even more socially and personally destructive evils:

> . . . to assault the nature of human parentage by putting the bodily transmission of life completely asunder from bodily love-making (as in AID) is already essentially to have warranted many of these other procedures as well — perhaps the hatcheries, too.[28]

From a more personalistic and situational stance, Joseph Fletcher responds:

> . . . the fidelity of marriage is a *personal* bond between husband and wife, not primarily a legal contract, and . . . parenthood is a *moral* relationship with children, not a material or merely physical relationship. The claim that A.I.D. is immoral rests upon the view that marriage is an absolute generative, as well as sexual, monopoly; and that parenthood is an essentially, if not solely, physiological partnership.[29]

In favor of AID, maintains Fletcher, is that kind of Christian ethics which does not rest in the determinisms of nature or in the rigidities of law, but which rather rests fundamentally upon love, a personal bond, which is the only principle which is always relevant and without exception. And, for many childless couples,

AID may well be the loving and hence Christianly appropriate act.

To clarify our own moral positions on artificial insemination we need to look again at a number of issues. They can be put as six questions:

1. *Is AID adultery?* The question itself presupposes the judgment that adultery, from a Christian perspective, is wrong and irresponsibly (though not necessarily irreparably) damaging to persons and families. With that judgment I concur. But before answering the question about AID we need to ask, just what *is* adultery? The usual definition is voluntary sexual intercourse between a married person and one who is other than the spouse. A strictly legal and physically-oriented definition does not apply to AID; there is no sexual intercourse.

Yet, theologians opposing AID on adulterous grounds are virtually unanimous (and perfectly right in their intent) in going beyond the letter of the law to its spirit and inner purpose. If, strictly speaking, AID is not adultery because there is no bodily contact, does it yet participate in the malicious spirit of adultery in violating the exclusive sexual bond of marriage? Does it violate the bond between procreation and love-making, a bond essential to the covenant of marriage? The answer, I believe, is "Not necessarily. It all depends."

In the Sermon on the Mount, Jesus assumed the physical act of adultery to be wrong. But he went beyond the physical description to the intentions, the inner thoughts, and desires of the persons involved implying that here is the origin of the moral offense. Marriage is essentially a personal covenant. Sexual fidelity is an essential ingredient of that covenant. But to define sexual fidelity in dominantly physical terms (such as the exclusive monopoly upon the sexual and reproductive organs of the partner) falls far short of an ethics which takes with even greater seriousness the whole contextual meaning of the act to the persons involved. What is their intent? What is the desire here being expressed? Does the act of AID constitute a gross act of unfaithfulness and covenant violation toward one's spouse?

If these questions are ethically significant, then it is quite clear that when AID is undertaken out of freely-given mutual consent, when it is decided upon as an act of love which expresses the inner meaning of the marriage covenant, when it expresses the desire for a child of the wife's own flesh who will be the child

of the parenthood covenant of the husband as well as the wife —
then AID hardly constitutes adultery. To the contrary, it may
well express the very opposite: fidelity in the richest sense of the
term.

But if the meaning of adultery depends in large measure upon
the meaning of the act to the persons, a given instance of AID
certainly *can* be adulterous. It can, for example, express a wife's
revenge against her sterile husband. However, far from condemning AID as intrinsically adulterous, a more adequate Christian response will welcome its possibilities for expressing marital
faithfulness and fulfillment in situations of involuntary sterility.

2. *Is masturbation for purposes of artificial insemination to
be condemned?* The censure of masturbation as inherently wrong
and a grave sin, the traditional Roman Catholic position, hinges
upon the separation of the act from the procreative intent which
should be normative for every sex act. (Also in the background
of this position on masturbation there frequently are residues
of unproven and disproven ideas about the physiological harm-
fulness of the act and mistaken ideas about "life-containing"
qualities of semen.) To the contrary, many of us believe that
sexual acts are divinely intended always to be acts of love and
only occasionally to be acts of procreation. (And, we should add,
masturbation brings no physiological harm whatever and is
emotionally and relationally damaging only if and when personal
intentions and attitudes make it so.)

The curious twist ushered in by medical technology now is
this: what about masturbation *for* a procreative purpose *and* as
an expression of covenant love in marriage? This is the usual
AIH situation in which the husband masturbates in order to
inseminate his wife. Some contemporary Catholic theologians,
eschewing the older physiological and external definition of
masturbation, find this quite permissible. Charles Curran, for
example, concludes, "It is true that insemination must take place
within the context of a relationship of marital love; but the
physical act of natural intercourse does not seem to be of absolute
and determining moral necessity." [30]

What of the donor's masturbation in AID? It may well be that
many sperm donors are primarily motivated by the fees they
receive. To that extent, the donor is prostituting his sex functions. Yet, the result of such prostitution (unlike the usual result
of ordinary postitution) is not the damaging of the marital union

of others but, more likely, the strengthening of such unions. And it is not beyond the realm of possibility that some donors might even be principally motivated by this latter intention.

The tortuous reasoning which makes masturbation a ground for condemning artificial insemination has led some to advocate other methods for procuring the semen: aspiration of semen after intercourse, rectal massage, intercourse with a condom, and coitus interruptus. If such methods are personally preferred and medically adequate, well and good. But it makes little moral sense, Christianly and humanly speaking, to reject AI on the grounds of rejecting a masturbatory component of the procedure.

3. *Is the right to bear a child a woman's inherent right?* In the first place, if we affirm that God alone is absolute, it is difficult to affirm any *absolute* human rights at all. Seriously important and significant human rights there are indeed. But inherent and absolute rights are difficult to defend from a radically monotheistic position.

In light of this theological affirmation, can we yet affirm every woman's important right to pregnancy? We could hardly do so without taking lightly marriage as the context within which child-rearing is intended. Children have rights, too — to be reared within these human relational networks which afford the nurture they need — and the Christian faith places high premium upon the marriage covenant as affording the appropriate context.

But is it the right of every *married* woman to bear her own child? Here again the answer cannot be absolute or an unqualified yes. Much depends upon the marital relationship itself, upon the psychological factors (involving husband as well as wife), and upon the social and legal situations which will affect the child's well-being. A case for artificial insemination by either donor or husband cannot rest upon any assumption of a wife's absolute rights to pregnancy.

4. *Do psychological factors significantly affect the morality of a decision to inseminate artificially?* Before speaking directly to this question, I must make a brief ethical comment. Moralists frequently make a distinction between "intrinsic" reasons and "extrinsic" reasons. Intrinsic reasons are usually considered the moral ones, while extrinsic factors are considered the practical issues. Thus, some conclude that while there may be nothing intrinsically or morally wrong with an AI decision, certain psychological factors, for example, would make it imprudent.

But this is an uncomfortable and misleading distinction. In regard to artificial insemination, surely the theological issues surrounding the nature of marriage and sexuality are of central importance for Christian reflection, but they do not exhaust the moral issues. Psychological, sociological, and legal factors are also crucial moral data. Hence, a decision to proceed with AID even when there are grave psychological risks is not "moral but imprudent," it is simply irresponsible and immoral.

That there are frequent psychological hazards in potential AI situations is evident from the earlier discussion. We have looked primarily at psychological factors which might intrude upon donor insemination. Yet, artificial insemination by the husband's semen may be rendered morally irresponsible in certain cases, too. For example, AIH has been used for husbands who are not sterile but who are impotent, unable to maintain an erection. But impotence is often psychologically based, and it may very well be morally irresponsible to bring a child into a marital situation in which there are serious and unresolved psychological difficulties.

Our answer to the general question is, of course, yes. *If* there are serious and unresolved psychological difficulties about artificial insemination itself or difficulties that probably would threaten the child, the morality of a decision to proceed is in grave jeopardy. Yet, it is impossible to generalize. Helmut Thielicke, an eminent German Protestant theologian, unfortunately does just that. He approves of AIH, reasoning that it does not depersonalize but rather enhances the marriage relationship. But he fears that the child born of AID will be a constant symbol of the woman's achievement of motherhood and her husband's failure in fatherhood. And this rupture, argues Thielicke, is psychological but not only that. "We are against [AID], therefore, not primarily because we fear the symptoms, but rather because the possible symptoms betray the violation of the far deeper *mysterium* of marital fellowship." [31] Thielicke's psychological warnings are perceptive and must be taken seriously. But such psychological warnings are translated into moral absolutes only at the risk of making the marriage relationship rest essentially upon the normal procreative method. It is one thing to warn that some men will be unable to cope psychologically with the presence of the child. It is quite another to suggest that the essence of fatherhood is biological procreation. As the thoughtful adoptive parent knows, the reality of parenthood lies in the creative *covenant* with the child, a covenant which also importantly includes God, the spouse, and the community.

5. *Does the present legal situation regarding AID affect the morality of a couple's decision?* Given the present state of legal confusion surrounding AID in most states of this country such uncertainties clearly *must* be an important moral consideration. The dangers of legal uncertainty are not likely to affect the stable AID family. The problems usually come in connection with divorce actions. Thus, the current situation must be counted as an additional important warning flag for any couple with psychological difficulties and relational instability. Physicians, clergy, and others who have opportunity for AID counseling need to bear this in mind. Any couple seeking AID as medicine for a sick marriage puts the prospective AID child in double jeopardy: experiencing his parents' divorce and being declared illegitimate in the process.

If AID does not threaten the institution of marriage and does not constitute any clear and present danger to the public good, the present state of legal irrationality and ambiguity over AID is scandalous. It is not impossible for states to adopt legislation consistent with each other on important medical-moral matters. The Uniform Anatomical Gift Act is a case in point. A Uniform Artificial Insemination Act, carefully prepared, interpreted, and lobbied for, would go far toward facilitating the institutional and social supports that AID now sorely needs. Henry Clark rightly sees that legal reform is crucial if other aspects of AID are to shrink to their proper proportions:

> When this has been done, the childless couple can accept relatively inexpensive counseling without qualms, physicians will have no compelling excuse for their reluctance to give A.I.D. services to couples requesting them, and lawyers will presumably have little opportunity to stir up trouble over situations involving A.I.D. youngsters. Then individuals will be free to follow their consciences, as these have been formed by their moral tradition, and as they are instructed by the counseling they receive, in whatever direction they feel drawn.[32]

6. *Are the consequences for society from the use of AID likely to be dangerous or even disastrous?* Both Pope Pius XII and Paul Ramsey have answered yes and many would agree. Their argu-

ments center on two propositions. First, AID violates the divinely-given nature of marriage by cutting asunder the procreative act from the act of love, and such violation of marriage constitutes a threat to the stability and health of society. This argument fails, however, because it is based upon an interpretation of the basic constitution of marriage that is far too physical and external. It is no denial of the fleshly and embodied nature of our humanity to insist that the essence of a procreative act is located in the relationship of wife and husband and in the meanings which they give to that act, not in the physical form which the act takes. Indeed, the evidence we presently have says that AID can make basically healthy marriages more fulfilled, thus enhancing the social fabric.

The second argument against AID because of social consequences is more difficult to assess: the acceptance of AID amounts to an acceptance of the principle that any technologically feasible separation of procreation from the marriage union can also be morally acceptable. For example, if the wife of a sterile husband ought to be given the opportunity for biological motherhood, should the same right be extended to the husband of a barren woman? Harmon Smith makes the point: "If it is so self-evident that AID is no invasion of marital chastity owing to consent, impersonality of procedure, and all the rest, one might reasonably ask why no one . . . has seriously advocated anonymous egg and womb donors who would (for a fee, of course) receive a husband's sperm, be hostess to this nascent life until delivery, and thereby provide the same *technical* service as the sperm donor." [33] As I shall argue in Chapter Five, there *are* reasons for moral comparisons between the *egg graft* and AID. In this case an egg is donated by an anonymous woman and implanted in the barren wife whose husband then fertilizes the egg through normal intercourse. But this is certainly far different from the *womb donor* who would actually carry the fetus and bear the child.

Yet, the point is that we cannot utterly separate the meanings of "personal" and "human" from our physical and bodily processes. Though AID does not intrinsically breach the meaning of human parenthood, surely some other technically feasible processes (the womb donor among them) would make that breach. Can we count on ourselves and our society to make the crucial distinctions? Or must we assume that if the camel's nose is allowed under the flap of the tent he will come in all the way?

Two things must be said. First, surely human technological pride *may* become an uncontrollable monster and prove the fearful right. It is a possibility. But, second, there is no necessary and fated reason why this must be so. God gives us the awesome human freedom to use our technology both to destroy and to enrich human life. In the process of using medical technology responsibly, we are called upon to make particular decisions about particular techniques. The case of AID is not morally comparable (and ought not be considered such) to a multitude of personal-life-threatening scientific technologies which may be within our powers to employ.

Our conclusions? In the absence of unresolved and threatening psychological problems, artificial insemination by the husband's semen would appear to be a Christianly and humanly viable moral alternative for a couple. Donor insemination raises a whole variety of additional and morally-relevant complications. The presence of socially and legally sanctioned supports for the adoption process make the adoption route to overcoming childlessness preferable for many couples and, perhaps, more responsible. But the lack of adoptable babies and the understandable worries about such factors as drug use and inadequate prenatal care in the unmarried mother make adoption highly problematic for many a couple. For such a couple, when their relationship is strong, their motivations are responsibly sorted out, and the risks are carefully weighed, AID may be a responsible use of medical technology toward divinely-intended human ends. And when our social wisdom sees fit to give AID the legal and institutional supports it needs, the procedure will become a still stronger moral possibility.

CHAPTER FOUR

Human
Experimentation

Cases

The patient was dying of cancer — malignant melanoma, one of the most feared and fast-spreading forms. The doctors suggested that tumor cells be transplanted from the patient's body to her mother's in the hope that she would form antibodies which could be used to combat her daughter's disease. The process might also help the medical staff to understand cancer immunity. The mother agreed, and the cells were transplanted. But the patient died on the following day. About three weeks later the implanted cancer cells were removed from the mother's body, but she herself died of the same cancer fourteen months later. "It had spread widely through her body, evidently from the original transplanted cells." [1]

Dr. Saul Krugman of Willowbrook Hospital on New York's Staten Island, with the knowledge and consent of the children's parents, deliberately induced hepatitis (a serious liver disease) into a group of institutionalized, mentally-retarded children. Commenting on this case, a nationally-known surgeon said, "There was a tremendous uproar over the ethical approach, but the [end results] were fantastic, and couldn't have been obtained any other way." [2]

A San Antonio clinic was the site of a recent experiment with birth control pills, funded by Syntex Labs (a manufacturer of oral contraceptives) and the federal government's Agency for International Development. Subjects for the experiment were mostly poor Mexican-American women who had already borne at least two children and were coming to the clinic for contraceptive assistance. The experiment's purpose was to determine whether the reported side effects of the pill were mainly psychological or whether they were actually physiological. Some of the women received hormone contraceptives while others received placebos (dummy pills), though all were instructed to use a vaginal cream as well in case the pill might not be completely effective. Ten of the seventy-six women given placebos became pregnant during the course of the experiment. None of those involved had been told about the research. None knew she might be receiving a dummy pill. All of them, however, had come to the clinic to prevent additional pregnancies.[3]

The Question and Its Context

What is human experimentation? The question which at first appears so obvious is not easy to define with precision.[4] One can argue that all medical treatment is experimental: the physician never knows exactly what the results of his prescription of bed rest and cough syrup will be. But most people would say this is far too broad. We do know the highly probable results of certain courses of treatment, and these are appropriately labeled "therapeutic." Experimentation occurs when a researcher deliberately induces or alters a person's physical or mental functions either (1) in ways which he hopes might prove therapeutic to the patient but for which there is as yet insufficient evidence to make this reasonably certain, or (2) in ways which will not be of any conceivable benefit to the particular patient but which hopefully may advance scientific knowledge and human welfare.

Human experimentation in medicine goes on all the time, not only in formally-designed research projects funded by foundations but also informally in countless doctors' offices. As one microbiologist says,

> If a physician gives a patient a new drug because he believes (even if only on the basis of advertising) that the drug will do the patient good, then he is acting as a physician. On the other hand, if he has doubts about the adequacy of the information furnished to him, wants to resolve these doubts himself,

and therefore gives the drug to alternate patients with the disease in question, the others receiving the standard drug, then he is experimenting on his patients.[5]

Thus, in an important sense, what is experimental depends upon the knowledge and purposes of the one who initiates the action.

Though experimentation during the course of therapy is not unusual, the central moral question emerges when therapy either is subordinated or entirely absent in the experimental situation: when may a researcher (or a society) either by conscious decision or by default expose some individuals to potential harm in order to seek benefits for larger numbers in the future? The same issue can be put in slightly different ways. It is the question of the one and the many: the benefit of this particular patient or the benefit of larger numbers of yet unknown sufferers? It is the present in tension with the future: the one before us now or those who will benefit from new therapies in the months and years ahead? It is the question of *right* in tension with *good:* does the possibility of a greater social good make it right to undertake this kind of experiment?

The central question is as old as medicine itself. Yet it is new in at least two respects: the intensity of public discussion and the sheer quantity of human experimentation now in process. With the Nuremberg Trials of the late 1940s came the sordid revelations of experimental medicine under Hitler. It is difficult to overestimate the impetus these gave to professional and public moral reflection. Further, in post-war America public funds for medical research multiplied many times over, and human experimentation was under way on a hitherto unknown scale. The two decades following 1945 saw research money from the National Institutes of Health climb from $700 thousand to well over $436 million, and total medical research expanded from $161 million in 1950 to $2.5 billion less than twenty years later.[6] University hospitals and medical schools increasingly came under the dominance of the research ethos, leading Dr. Henry K. Beecher to say, "Every young man knows that he will never be promoted to a tenure post, to a professorship in a major medical school, unless he has proved himself as an investigator. If the ready availability of money for conducting research is added to this fact, one can see how great the pressures are on ambitious young physicians." [7]

Medical science has proved its point dramatically: human subjects are crucial in much of the experimentation which has led to unprecedented breakthroughs in solving problems of disease. At the same time that the public has enthusiastically applauded these medical triumphs it has also awakened to the potential human risks for research subjects. A recent patients' rights booklet written for low-income people pointedly says, "You have a right to understand whether the treatment is necessary ... [whether] there are alternatives ... [whether] the treatment is experimental." [8] And such medical leaders as Dr. Beecher in the U.S. and England's M. H. Pappworth have forcefully opened the subject for fuller discussion. It is evident, they conclude, that "unethical or questionably ethical procedures are not uncommon." [9]

Research: Its Need, Its Design, Its Investigator

The emerging moral norms for human experimentation can be seen through three clusters of questions:

1. *The research and the investigator.* Is the research genuinely needed? Is its design carefully and competently drawn? Is the researcher a person of integrity, intelligence, and compassion?

2. *Consent.* Is the consent of the subjects freely given? Have they been adequately informed about the purposes, procedures, and potential risks? To what extent is free, informed consent really possible? Under what conditions, if any, is it morally responsible to experiment upon minors? upon captive groups?

3. *Professional supervision and public review.* What kind of supervision is provided by professionals not immediately engaged in the research? What criteria should be insisted upon in the publication of research results? Is there peer and public review not only of the results but also of the manner in which those results were obtained?

First, what about the research need? The Declaration of Helsinki, adopted by the World Medical Association in 1964, says, "Clinical research cannot legitimately be carried out unless the importance of the objective is in proportion to the inherent risk to the subject. Every clinical research project should be preceded by careful assessment of inherent risks in comparison to foreseeable benefits to the subject or to others." [10] The "Ethical Guidelines for Clinical Investigation," accepted by the American Medical Association in 1966, adds that the research must be designed "to produce data which is scientifically valid and significant."

Hence, not only the needs must be justifiable, but the design must be carefully drawn. Both codes speak to this concern. The experiment must be "part of a systematic program competently designed, under accepted standards of scientific research" (A.M.A.), and it should "conform to the moral and scientific principles that justify medical research and should be based on laboratory and animal experiments or other scientifically established facts" (Helsinki).

Beyond legitimacy of research need and the competence of experimental design, there is no substitute for researchers of integrity, intelligence, and compassion. The same concern toward the patient required of a physician engaged in purely therapeutic treatment ought to mark the researcher's concern for the lives and health of his subjects. Peculiar problems arise in both general types of experimentation — that in which experimentation is conducted in the course of therapy and that in which the experiment holds no hopes of therapeutic value to the person.

In the former situation the patient can be surprisingly vulnerable. The British Medical Research Council recognizes this: "Owing to the special relationship of trust that exists between a patient and his doctor, most patients will consent to any proposal that is made. Further, the considerations involved in a novel procedure are nearly always so technical as to prevent their being adequately understood by one who is not himself an expert." [11] Because the patient will almost always accept professional medical judgment about the course of treatment, an inescapable moral responsibility rests with the physician.

When the doctor is not treating a person's ailments but only using him as part of an experiment, additional problems arise. In such cases the subject is usually a virtual stranger who has not been in a therapeutic relationship with the physician. Furthermore, the physician has strong drives to pursue his experiment — visions of the benefits for mankind, his own scientific curiosity, and, not to be forgotten, his ego and status needs (occasionally even the dream of a Nobel prize). In such situations the investigator surely needs the important checks provided by the subject's full consent and by the ongoing review of his medical peers.

Beyond these checks and balances, the responsible investigator is bound by a covenant of partnership with the research subject.

Dr. Otto E. Guttentag speaks to the meaning of such partnership: "In experimentation on human beings, experimenter and experimental subject are *fellow beings:* the veterinarian and his animal, the engineer and his machine, are not." [12] Although this affirmation may seem trite, it is profoundly important. The subject is always subject, never merely object. Through eyes of Christian faith he is seen as one gifted by his Creator with "an alien dignity."

The responsible researcher remembers not only the humanity of his subject but also his own. His own humanity is marked by finitude and sin as well as by freedom and dignity. Hence he does well to remember that even his highest idealism is eminently corruptible into a veil for his own ego needs. While even the Golden Rule and its varied formulations can be misused, they provide a helpful check for the investigator: are these experimental procedures ones to which I would willingly subject myself, my spouse, my children, my closest friends?

Treating human research subjects as ends in themselves does not mean that persons cannot be used for the purposes of scientific advance. One can use another and still respect him as a person to whom dignity is owed. Misuse comes when the subject is seen as an object of the investigator's control, when the subject is a means to an end in which he cannot have a voluntary share but for which he may be called upon to pay heavily.[13]

The Ethics of Free, Informed Consent

Inextricably tied to the researcher's responsibility is the crucial matter of insuring that the potential subject gives free and informed consent. This means that the nature, the purpose, and the risk of the experiment must be explained to the prospective participant. It means that he must be of such mental, physical, and legal state that he can exercise fully his power of choice. (If such is not the case his legal representative must consent on his behalf.) These conditions are all emphasized in the Helsinki and A.M.A. codes as well as in the earlier Nuremberg Code of 1949. As presented in the codes it might appear as if meaningful consent in experimentation procedures is a rather simple matter. Nothing could be further from the truth. Consent problems are numerous and often subtle.

Before turning to these problems themselves, recall once again why consent is so crucial. Seen in Christian focus, the principle of consent expresses our recognition of both the grandeur and misery of human nature. The subject's human grandeur is affirmed when scrupulous attention to the principle of consent is given so that he can participate fully in those decisions which will significantly affect him. But insistence upon meaningful consent also speaks of human sin. We do well to remember that the Nazi physicians whose experiments were unsurpassed in their brutality did not recognize, even at the very end, that they had done any wrong.[14] Paul Ramsey fittingly observes that Lincoln's statement about political covenants ("no man is good enough to govern another without his consent") applies here: "no man is good enough to experiment upon another without his consent." [15]

Voluntary and informed consent is the most commonly mentioned difficulty in human experimentation according to the researchers themselves. It is the primary factor of legal significance in the experimental procedure. It is, in the continuum of steps taken in a typical experiment, one of the last steps before the experiment actually begins. Furthermore, most public challenges to medical experimenters have centered upon the inadequacy of the consent obtained in particular projects. Difficult though some of the issues in the ethics of consent may be, it is heartening to know this: while experimentation on human subjects is as old as medicine itself, the routine practice of obtaining consent from subjects is a uniquely modern development.[16]

Free, informed consent — the two adjectives are interdependent in the actual process of giving consent, though we can separate them for analysis. What are the issues which surround *free consent?* It is helpful to divide them into issues of internal and external constraints. Internally the subject must be an authentic volunteer. He must have a sense of meaningful inner freedom about his choice. Those who step forward upon hearing the call for experimental subjects need careful screening to insure that this freedom is present. One study at Harvard Medical School revealed that over 60 percent of the experimental volunteers were diagnosed as seriously maladjusted in adapting to their social environments. Other studies underscore the warning: "such volunteers may, from a psychological point of view, differ considerably from the rest of the population." [17] Granted, "maladjustment" is a very relative and culture-bound definition. Some individuals judged abnormal by current psychological criteria may, indeed, be acting out of authentic internal freedom and concern for humankind. The point is simply this: the experimenter's respect for personhood must caution him against taking advantage of any whose volunteering for science appears less a matter of genuine choice than a matter of being driven to this as escape or self-punishment.

The issue of external constraints raises the varied problems regarding captive populations. Indeed, most research subjects do not arrive on the experimenter's doorstep because they answered the newspaper ad or the note on the university bulletin board. Rather, the experimenter has found them, has invited their involvement, and has requested their permission. Members of various controlled groups—prisoners, institutionalized persons, members of armed forces units—are frequently sought as subjects since the uniformity of their life styles can make the experiment more productive. Inasmuch as one of the barriers to meaningfully free consent is the feeling of dependence upon the experimenter to satisfy the subject's needs, such groups pose their own problems.

Because armed service regulations now prevent military personnel from consenting to any medical experimentation which might interfere with their proper discharge of duties, problems here are minimal.[18] More complex is the prisoner question. Prisoners have long made important contributions to medical research. During World War II, for example, the advances in malaria treatment and in the uses of blood plasma owed much to these subjects.[19] But various inducements offered to prisoners, from special privileges to reductions in sentences, easily jeopardize their freedom of decision and amount to undue influence. On the other hand, if sentences are reduced for good behavior and if volunteering for medical experiments is an act of benefit to humanity, some argue that such rewards are not out of place. If prisoners are used, however, moral prudence dictates that any proffered rewards be very modest and that the principal appeal be to the opportunity to render service to society and, as a practical matter, the opportunity to relieve the monotony of prison life. Beecher's conclusion in his thoughtful study deserves attention: "The exigencies of national peril may excuse the careful use of prisoners in medical experimentation, as may other pressing needs. The ice is thin. In weighing the pros and cons of

such use, one must face the fact that the *bonum communum* was
precisely the rationalization claimed by the Nazis." [20]

The combination of internal and external constraints upon
the freedom of consent is particularly striking in the case of
children. Experimentation connected with therapy for a sick
child of normal capacities is far easier to evaluate. If the experimental procedure (the insufficiently-tested drug or operation)
seems crucial as a possible means for the child's recovery when
standard methods have failed, then that is one thing. In spite
of the fact that the child cannot give mature or legally-valid
consent, his parents or guardians have every right to give permission for what is in his best interests, according to the best
available medical advice.

It is quite another thing to consider consent when the experiment is not directly for the child's benefit, but for society's. The
question becomes particularly poignant when the potential
subjects are institutionalized children or mentally incompetent
adults. If the covenant of faithfulness to the humanity of persons
means anything, it is unthinkable that these captive groups be
seen as happy hunting grounds for medical research.

Perhaps two positions on this issue are feasible. One is Paul
Ramsey's definitive "No!" No parent is morally competent to
consent to experiments which have no therapeutic significance
for the child himself. No parent ought to consent, and no parent
ought to be asked. Even in the case of the normal child, argues
Ramsey, it makes no difference that the parent thinks the child
would probably approve when he grows older. The child must
be treated as he is now — a child.[21]

The other feasible position is that of cautious permission. It
is not totally out of the question that non-therapeutic experiments might responsibly be performed upon minors and adult
incompetents. But extreme caution is warranted. Beecher insists
that several conditions must be met: there must be no risk,
screening and approval must be handled by a review board, the
goals of the experimentation must be demonstrably useful, and
there must be no coercion or deception of the parents.[22] Guttentag, as a medical researcher, concludes his judgment on a
theological note. The answer about such non-therapeutic experimentation might logically and usually be no. "But in the
sense of the mutual trust that lies at the base of interhuman

relations the answer is at least equivocal. True enough, selfishness intrudes itself into every human action, but to view these actions exclusively in the light of man's finiteness is as erroneous as viewing them exclusively in the light of his freedom." [23] Perhaps Jonas Salk's development of poliomyelitis vaccine in the 1950s is a case in point. His use of children (including his own) was clearly non-therapeutic; he was not treating a disease with which they were afflicted. Yet the care with which he respected the canons of consent and the medical need for which the research was conducted led to results which have placed us all in his debt.

An absolutely negative answer to experimentation upon minors or the mentally retarded might well forestall the development of those therapies needed for diseases which are peculiar to persons of those ages and conditions. At least, however, we can insist upon extreme caution. Experiments entailing substantial risk to the subject are not justified even if the parents give consent. Consent is a necessary but not sufficient condition of moral validation.

Hans Jonas wisely proposes "the rule of descending order." "The poorer in knowledge, motivation, and freedom of decision (and that, alas, means the more readily available in terms of numbers and possible manipulation), the more sparingly and indeed reluctantly should the reservoir be used, and the more compelling must therefore become the countervailing justification." [24] This scale of descending permissibility is quite the opposite of a social utility standard. It suggests that the *least* expendable persons in society's view ought to be the first candidates for experimental risk — the standard of *noblesse oblige*. The rule is eminently humane. It means that scientists should consider themselves at the top of the list of available subjects (which, in fact, many do), and that children and the mentally-retarded ought to be the least permissible subjects, to be used only when no other subjects are appropriate for the disease in question, and then only with reluctance and great care.

What about using the sick as research subjects? If medical progress on certain diseases is to occur, it is inevitable that some experimentation be done upon those who are already suffering. In certain instances, the research might be upon the disease a particular subject has, and yet not be research which holds therapeutic hope for that patient. Even this is more defensible than that which has neither therapeutic promise nor any relationship to the patient's own illness. Yet, the covenant of partnership with the subject raises several important cautions.

First, illness may drastically reduce a person's energy and conscious determination. It may increase his tendency toward dependency. Hospitalization itself may greatly augment the anxiety. In such a situation the patient frequently has a difficult time distinguishing between what is research and what is treatment. Even though told that a certain research proceure cannot benefit their condition, many seem willing to submit to any medical process in the hidden hope that somehow this might help them recover.[25]

The situation becomes particularly complicated since much of our medical research goes on in teaching hospitals which are the charity wards of the city. Welfare recipients arrive with low ego strength. Socially and educationally deprived, they are frequently willing to submit to anything suggested. They may understand little of the doctor's communication about the proposed research. The staff physician himself all too often has a paternalistic bearing: sympathetic, kindly, and concerned, but markedly different than if he were treating one of his own socioeconomic (or racial) kind. And the public assistance patient may well cooperate in this paternalism. Through long conditioning he may simply want to be taken care of. Or he may fear that disappointing any of the medical staff (even those not assigned to his own therapy) may mean jeopardizing interest in his case and threatening his chances for speedy recovery.[26] The rule of descending order has obvious applicability to such situations as these.

What about the desperately ill, the dying? Here the researcher might violate the principle of partnership in two ways. Since the patient is dying anyway, the physician might feel entitled to greater experimental boldness. Indeed "he may consider himself particularly noble since he restricts these bolder experiments only to this group of patients." [27] Such attitudes can be highly presumptuous and exploitive. Surely, there is the occasional dying person who earnestly wishes to make one last gift to human life — the use of his body for experimentation while he is yet alive. It would be far safer, however, for the researcher to wait for clear indications from the patient than to approach him with any overture — a request which he may not be able to handle emotionally and which may be highly unfair to lay upon him in his final days. To die in dignity means that one has conscious control over his own personal responses to the dying process. An experiment which intrudes upon this hour can be inhumanly exploitive.

Thus far we have focused particularly upon voluntary and free consent. What about *informed* consent? The Nuremberg Code is most explicit, requiring that "before the acceptance of an affirmative decision by the experimental subject there should be made known to him the nature, duration, and purpose of the experiment; the method and means by which it is to be conducted; all inconveniences and hazards reasonably to be expected; and the effects upon his health or person which may possibly come from his participation in the experiment." [28] The Helsinki Declaration and the A.M.A. Guidelines speak more briefly. The former simply says that "the nature, the purpose, and the risk of clinical research must be explained to the subject by the doctor," and the latter stipulates that "a reasonable explanation of the nature of the procedure to be used and the risks to be expected" must be given.

Obviously, any consent that is truly voluntary and free must also be informed. But when is a patient reasonably informed? What kind of information and what manner of informing fulfills the partnership of researcher and subject, this covenant of human care? Since we are aware of enough experiments in which adequate, honest information was not given and in which consent was subtly engineered, we have a right to insist upon exceptional concern at this point. Credibility gaps, whether in politics or in medicine, are humanly destructive.

The information issue is often complex, and in experimentation procedures at least three problems arise. First, how much information constitutes a reasonable explanation? Surely, the purpose, the methods to be used, the duration of the experiment, and the possible risks all must be shared honestly and openly with a potential participant. Beyond these (though the codes neglect to mention this), true partnership compels the investigator to share frankly his own personal stake in the project. This is an important ingredient which the subject has a right to know. In all of this, how much information is responsibly enough? No precise lines can be laid down. The simple recital of every conceivable risk or implication of the experiment may violate the spirit of partnership as much as withholding important data.

Truth-telling is not a mechanical process; it is a matter of integrity within the relationship. Perhaps the best we can say is to affirm with Guttentag that "informed consent implies that the experimenter has made the most honest effort he can to say everything that will enhance the experimental subject's freedom, so that the subject can make the most adequate choice of which he is capable in agreeing or refusing to become a volunteer." [29]

Communication involves more than simply telling the facts, as honest as the investigator's intent may be. This is the second problem: can the subject be told about the experiment in non-technical language that he, given the level of his education and scientific sophistication, can readily understand? Can he be told in a manner which does not threaten his grasp of the situation but rather enhances it? The problem is not insurmountable, but it is often considerable particularly since most medical researchers are very well trained in understanding physiological processes and in manipulating scientific data, but they have virtually no training in evaluating interpersonal relationships.

A third problem arises when the nature of the experiment itself requires some form of deception. Here, for example, are those experiments in which one group of subjects is given an actual medication while a comparison group is given harmless but neutral placebos in order to test the extent to which the patient's psychological state determines his physiological responses. Frequently, the attempt to account for the psychological variables involves not simply one deliberate deception but two, hence "the double blind" experiment. Here only the experimenter knows which is the true medication and which is the placebo, but another medical person (who does not know) actually administers the substances so that no unconscious signals are given the subject.

The moral considerations in such situations rest heavily on at least two questions. Does the nature of the experiment and its deception involve any appreciable risk for the subject? (That it did for those San Antonio women who were given placebos instead of contraceptive pills is tragically clear.) And, is deception really necessary for the experiment? Some experienced investigators now maintain that its use has been far overrated as an experimental necessity.[30] In this area, as in others relating to consent, clear moral pronouncements and strict legal regulations will not solve the problem. It is reasonable, however, to insist that whenever anything short of full and honest disclosure of the experimental method characterizes the procedure, the burden of proof fall heavily upon the investigator; he must prove to his colleagues both why such deception is necessary and why there will be no significant risks to the subjects.

Genuinely and meaningfully free and informed consent is crucial to the morality of any experimentation, as two of the deans of medical investigation remind us. Beecher would have us all remember that the medical researcher does not have the right to choose martyrs for science.[31] And Pappworth insists, "An experiment is ethical or not at its inception, and does not become so *post hoc* because it achieved some measure of success." [32]

Professional Supervision and Public Policy

A third cluster of issues in the morality of human experimentation pertains to professional supervision and public policy. The researcher should show a decent respect for the judgment of the scientific community and for that of the wider human community. What are the limits on human research? Who should formulate those limits? By what means should they be imposed upon researchers?

The Nuremberg trials of 1946 to 1949 brought these questions to the attention of a worldwide public. Professor Paul A. Freund observes that "the most striking thing about the Nazi episodes is the high standing of a number of the doctors involved and of the medical science they represented." [33] But repulsive experiments tacitly or officially sanctioned by public authority were not limited to Hitler's Germany. In 1972, public revelation was made of a study begun in 1932 and continued for the next forty years under the sponsorship of the U.S. Public Health Service. Four hundred black men were denied treatment for syphilis and were used without their knowledge or consent in a study of the ultimate effects of the untreated disease. Even though therapy was available, our government physicians deliberately refrained from giving the men any form of treatment. Recent reports indicate that at least twenty-eight of the men died from causes directly related to syphilis and that the number may be far higher.[34]

Since the inception of the above experiments a great deal has happened within both the medical community and the larger commonwealth. Peer review has increased. One form of medical review comes through professional journals. Beecher has taken the lead in insisting that such journals refuse to publish even the valuable data of medical research if it is not accompanied by strong evidence that it has been obtained with adequate protection of the rights of the subjects. "There is," he writes, "a practical aspect to the matter: failure to obtain publication would discourage unethical experimentation. How many would carry out such experimentation if they *knew* its results would never be published? [35]

Prior to 1960 there was little American law dealing with medical research. No specific federal or state statutes regulated research methods, and experimenters were guided as far as law was concerned by hypotheses drawn from a small number of appellate court decisions involving liability suits. In the late 1950s however, considerable medical discussion was generated around the principles of the Nuremberg Code. By the early 1960s the thalidomide tragedy in Western Europe and Senator Kefauver's committee in this country prompted new congressional legislation and the first efforts of the Food and Drug Administration to regulate clinical testing procedures. By 1966 the F.D.A. had incorporated in its regulations the principles of the Declaration of Helsinki along with those of Nuremberg. In that same year the Surgeon General promulgated an extensive revision of the rules governing federal research money granted through the Public Health Service and the National Institutes of Health. These regulations required the functioning of decentralized, institutional review committees in all schools and agencies receiving grants. The committees must establish procedures for review of research designs, provide surveillance over the conduct of the research, and advise investigators about safeguarding the rights of their subjects.[36]

In an age of highly specialized research, such regulations and review committees alone cannot guarantee protection of the subject. If the investigator sees codes and committees as external, unnecessary, and resented restrictions, they will be less than effective. Important as these checks upon human sin and finitude are, they are not a substitute for moral sensitivity and keenly-felt responsibility within the medical scientist. Professor Freund concludes his review of the legal situation by saying that inner checks even more than external constraints of the law may have to be our hope.[37] Further, law faces an inherent difficulty in this area. It appeals to accepted standards of practice of the medical community. But, as Dr. Beecher notes, "research, if new and valuable, can hardly be in such accord. If it is truly useful, it goes beyond standard practices. It is new. It is different." [38]

By the early 1970s proposals were being made in congress to establish national commissions on science policies, including human experimentation standards. Though worthy, these proposals have not yet come to fruition. When and if they do, they will not replace the need for medical self-discipline. They will, however, give recognition to the fact that human experimentation is a concern of the entire civil community. And they will provide one more pressure toward vigilance about human rights, one more reminder that all of us are prone to misjudge our finiteness in our enthusiasm for the ends we pursue.

Further Ethical Reflections

One of the theological-ethical issues lurking behind the whole area of human experimentation is that of freedom and determinism.[39] In this scientific age we are tempted to assume that scientific progress is an inexorable forward movement and that our frameworks of ultimate meanings and values simply must adjust to this reality. But if we are serious about the ethics of experimentation, we must take seriously the freedom of the person lying on the table as well as that of the person in the white coat. If the experimenter is free as a human being, free to explore the scientific and medical future, then the subject of his experimentation is also free.

Ethics of human experimentation, as we have seen, revolve around several interrelated basic questions.[40] One way of putting the matter is in terms of ends and means. Is the morality of an experiment to be decided primarily upon the results of that research, upon whether its outcome is truly productive of benefits for the wider society? Or does its morality rest more heavily upon the rightness of the means which are used to obtain those results? Similarly, it is a matter of the present versus the future. Are we obligated primarily to the present generation (especially the research subjects now before us) or are we more obligated to generations yet unborn? Again, the ethical issue can be posed in terms of the rights of the individual in tension with the good of the larger society.

We distort the larger issues of human research when we absolutize either side of the question — means *or* ends, present *or* future, individual *or* society. There is undeniable truth on both sides. We are on better ground if we pose the question in terms of responsibility. The researcher is responsible to the welfare of the subjects of his experiment. He cannot violate their free humanity without impunity. He is also responsible for the welfare of the larger society. He is aware of the potential harm of *not* doing his research as well as of the risks in doing it. Beyond these affirmations, we who attempt to perceive the world through Christian lenses, affirm our common responsibility to God — the one who values each human being beyond all human valuing, and the one who also calls us into the risks of moral ambiguity in our decisions for the future. With this perspective we recognize that medical progress which violates individual rights is not moral progress. We also recognize that the claims of those now suffering diseases for which therapy is inadequate are also claims upon us. We admit we cannot eliminate the ethical tensions between means and ends, individual and society, present and future — but we can try to live responsibly and faithfully with them.

CHAPTER FIVE

Genetics and the
Control of Human
Development

Cases

A couple contacted a genetic counsellor. They had a daughter of twenty, two sons in their teens, and twins aged five. The twins were born afflicted with microcephaly, resulting in heads about two-thirds the normal size. Both were born blind, one was deaf, the other had a rare and difficult blood disorder, and both were prone to epileptic seizures. At age five, one of the twins continued to cry from sixteen to eighteen hours a day and weighed only seventeen pounds. The parents, devout and conservative Roman Catholics, indicated that their daughter was about to become engaged. If she married and had children, they asked, would this strike again? [1]

In 1961 an Italian biologist, Daniele Petrucci, fertilized a human egg in his laboratory and kept it alive *in vitro* (in the glass) for twenty-nine days. Although by that time it had a noticeable heartbeat, he let it die because it was monstrously deformed. Another of his test-tube embryos lived for fifty-nine days before a laboratory mistake caused its death. The Vatican sternly condemned Petrucci for his experiments, and he agreed to curtail this type of research. [2]

97

In addition to these two factual cases, consider the following imaginary situation which could take place in the not-too-distant future. Mrs. Smith and her husband, married for eight years, desperately desire children of their own but have none because of her chronic heart disease. Her physician has indicated that she can, indeed, conceive, and, if she does not overwork herself there is no reason why she could not raise children quite normally. However, the pregnancy and childbirth process would be far too risky for her. The doctor now advises that a new embryo-implantation procedure would make it possible for the couple to have their own child. They proceed with the plan. She conceives in the normal manner, and three days after conception the doctor flushes from her body the tiny speck of life which is already rapidly developing. He implants the embryo into the uterus of a volunteer mother, Mrs. Smith's sister, who carries the pregnancy. During the following nine months the two sisters are inseparable, with Mrs. Smith delighting in every development her sister feels. Both Smiths are present in the delivery room when their baby is born. With effusive thanks to the sister, they then take possession of their child.[3]

The Situation and the Possibilities

We are faced with a genetic dilemma.[4] Geneticist Theodosius Dobzhansky puts it in these words: "If we enable the weak and the deformed to live and to propagate their kind, we face the prospect of a genetic twilight. But if we let them die or suffer when we can save or help them, we face the certainty of a moral twilight."[5] How has this come about?

About 1910 medical science turned a corner. From that time on a person's chances of coming out of a hospital with a better physical prognosis than when he entered improved to greater than 50-50. In this sense the law of the survival of the fittest was repealed. Though it was long before we realized it, conventional medicine emerged as one of the greatest threats to the human race. It enabled numerous persons carrying genetic defects, who earlier would have died before the age of reproduction, to produce children and pass on that inheritance. For this reason scientists speak of the increasing pollution or degeneration of the genetic pool.

An obvious case in point is the discovery of insulin. It has insured that the number of people with genes for diabetes has increased and will continue to do so. Even so simple a matter as serious nearsightedness is another illustration. In the past accidents before the reproductive age took their toll; now that we have glasses the numbers of babies being born with serious eye defects is increasing. To be sure, natural processes take care of many of the worst genetic defects. At least 25 percent of all conceptions fail to reach the stage of viability and are naturally aborted. Of these at least one-third have identifiable chromosomal abnormalities. Nevertheless, the cells of each living individual carry between three to ten *potentially* harmful genes, and one out of every five persons has a genetic defect that will be passed on to or through the offspring. Furthermore, most persons are quite unaware that they have defective genes until deformed, diseased, or retarded children are born to them. Thus the dilemma is posed. What benefits the living individual and the present generation is bad for the human race as a whole and bad for future generations. Geneticists agree upon the trend; they disagree only about its rapidity. "They are pessimistic or optimistic within an ultimate genetic pessimism." [6]

We have several types of choices. First, we can make no conscious attempts to modify the condition of the genetic pool. We can continue with our present medical practice of treating individual ailments without regard to the wider genetic picture. The more pessimistic scientists hold that within five to ten generations one out of every ten children will be born seriously defective if this course is pursued. Others are less certain of the rapidity of decline. Nevertheless, medical business as usual without regard to the individual and social implications of genetic defects is not a live option for those concerned about the *humanum* of persons.

Two other groups of choices remain the viable alternatives. Various forms of negative eugenics, some already being used. constitute one range of options. Eugenics as a science is concerned with the improvement of hereditary qualities. Negative eugenics is the attempt to eliminate hereditary defects that have already occurred in individuals or to prevent those who carry defective genes from passing them on to their offspring. Genetic counseling, genetic screening programs, and genetic therapy are its major forms.

The other option takes us into positive eugenics. Rather than eliminating present defects, positive eugenics is concerned about improving the race through various forms of controlled reproduction. Positive eugenics has been practiced with farm animals for years, and its advocates for human beings are increasing with the advent of new possibilities in genetic technology. Some recommend genetic improvement through the controlled and widespread use of artificial insemination by donor. Artificial inovulation, *in vitro* fertilization, and selected cloning are urged by others.

Genetic Counseling

While the popular press has given far more attention to the more exotic possibilities and predictions in genetic engineering, the relatively quiet movement of genetic counseling presently has a much greater impact upon parenthood and the family. In 1947 Dr. Sheldon Reed of the University of Minnesota pioneered the establishment of genetic counseling in this country. Reed broke with the prevailing European counseling philosophy, which was heavily concerned with positive eugenics, and advocated that genetic counselors restrict their concerns to the individual family and its prospective offspring. About six hundred counseling units are now scattered throughout the world, perhaps most of them operating with a negative eugenic policy.

At least a thousand possible genetic defects are now known. Prior to the late 1960s, most couples coming to the counselor had already produced one genetically defective child and wanted to know the likelihood of having another. Some came because of their ages or because of genetic diseases in their family histories. In such cases, the counselor's role was largely one of medical mathematics: taking a detailed medical history of the family, and, after applying the known genetic principles, quoting a risk figure to the couple. Their decision whether to have another child (or even their first) would then be based upon mathematical probabilities, betting on the odds.

Today such probability assessments are still widely used and, of course, can be the only method when the woman is not pregnant. In recent years, however, the use of amniocentesis for definitive genetic testing has changed the picture for the pregnant woman. The technique of withdrawing amniotic fluid is hardly new. It had been done for many decades for other purposes, but only in 1955 was it discovered that the fluid contained sex chromosomes of the fetal cells, and not until 1966 was the method of photographing and systematic cataloging of the chromosomes developed.[7] About seventy genetic disorders, most of them serious ones, now can be detected with great accuracy by amniocentesis between the thirteenth and eighteenth weeks of the woman's pregnancy.

Some genetic counselors maintain that there are no moral issues involved in their task. It is simply their job to make an adequate assessment of the risk or an accurate medical diagnosis and then to provide the couple with that information. The counselor is strictly the neutral information-provider.

Others, however, see a host of moral and ethical issues interlacing the whole genetic counseling procedure and its implications.[8] One issue involves the counselor's responsibility to deal with the effects of genetic counseling upon the couple. Frequently the genetic diagnostic process is accompanied by considerable anxiety, marital stress, and sexual maladjustment. If the counselor restricts his role merely to that of the information-provider, he will bracket these emotional and interpersonal factors as being beyond his concern. To the extent that he does this, however, he treats his counselees as medical cases more than as human persons.

While the issue of privacy affects genetic screening programs even more than genetic counseling of the type we are now considering, it is also at stake here. Who owns the information obtained by the doctor? Is it the possession of the couple alone, or does the doctor have the duty to inform relatives who may also be affected? Does the genetic counselor have a right to furnish such information to the family doctor? to an insurance company? to an employer? to a government agency? Particularly since the rights of informational privacy are increasingly under assault in our society, it is important to affirm the genetic counselor's responsibility for confidentiality. Only if there is a serious and foreseeable danger to others ought this rule be set aside, and then only after the counselor has failed in his attempts to persuade the parents that they themselves ought to share the information, and only after he has indicated to them why he must disclose certain facts and to whom.

A number of moral issues cluster around the central question of genetic counseling: is its aim strictly therapeutic (for the immediate family) or is its aim also positively eugenic (concerned about the wider society)? This question, like that of human experimentation, frequently finds expression in the ethics of the *right* in tension with the ethics of the *good,* the ethics of known present obligations versus possible future benefits. Two scientists articulate the different emphases. According to Dr. Marc Lappé, "To maintain that we are adding to the public good by conscientious genetic guidance and screening may be both fallacious and ethically dangerous. The genetic counselor's obligation, I will maintain, never should extend beyond the family within his purview." [9] On the other hand, concern over the increasing pollution of the gene pool led Dr. Philip Handler while president of the National Academy of Sciences to suggest "that some people are dispensable" and should be aborted.[10]

The strictly-therapeutic school of genetic counseling advocated by Reed and Lappé mounts two major arguments. First, it is scientifically erroneous to think that even if all of the genetic counseling presently going on were to proceed with a positively eugenic purpose any appreciable affect on the gene pool would take place. Spontaneous mutations and admixture continually reintroduce bad genes into the breeding population, and the scattered "individual sifters" (counselors) can hardly affect this situation. Only a positive eugenic policy on a massive scale would make any impact. Secondly, the physician's prime responsibility is always to the welfare of his immediate patients. The couple has a right to know that the counselor has their welfare uppermost in his mind, that their immediate interests will not be sacrificed for some long-term social interests. Upon such trust the medical profession crucially depends.

The alternative approach does not simply reverse the picture by putting society's interests above those of the parents. Rather, the counselor attempts to bear both in mind. The counselor's aims are therapeutic for his patients, but he sees their welfare and that of society related. If their decision, through his help, is informed by grasping the social implications and costs as well as the personal, it will be more responsible.

Child-bearing is not the inalienable or absolute right of parents. Even though a couple, having received the prediction of high probability in bearing a seriously diseased child, still is willing to take the risks and to face the personal costs, their responsibilities to society and to others yet unborn ought to weigh equally with their own desires.[11] When the woman is already pregnant and the fetus is diagnosed as seriously defective, all of the moral issues surrounding possible abortion come into the picture (see Chapter Two). Abortion may well be the responsible decision in many cases, though it is never without its morally tragic element. In any event, a whole host of factors need weighing: the nature of the disease and its probable physical and psychological costs to the child, the parents' ability to cope creatively, and the parents' responsibilities to the wider community of the present and the future. In the midst of sorting out these elements, let it not be forgotten that the fetus is still human. It does make a difference to say "the fetus *has* Down's syndrome" rather than saying "the fetus *is* a Down's." [12]

Does society have a right to require couples to refrain from producing genetically-defective children? [13] Answering in the affirmative, some persons invoke the time-honored principle of society's right to self-defense. In this instance it is defense against increasing genetic deterioration and against the rapidly-rising financial and social costs of caring for the genetically-diseased. At least one country, Denmark, has decided that in some such instances society's rights transcend those of the individual: marriage licenses are refused to persons carrying certain genetic defects until one of the couple has been sterilized.

Opponents of such social control argue that we risk more by entrusting those decisions to an omnicompetent state than we do by leaving the judgment in the hands of its private citizens. What, after all, is "normal"? Will we begin to destroy before birth all those fetuses considered "abnormal"? And what will this do to our attitudes toward the handicapped living? Daniel Callahan maintains that "society has taken many centuries to develop a sensitive, receptive response to the defective person; that gain should not be jeopardized by new-found powers to ameliorate defectiveness." [14]

Thus the issue is posed, and responsible social policy must take into account both the rights of individual couples and the larger social good without absolutizing either of them. Even with the most zealous measures we could not eliminate genetic diseases from our society. The regular rate of spontaneous genetic mutations would see to that. Furthermore, since all of us carry several potentially harmful genes in our cells, a stringent policy aimed at preventing transmission of bad genes logically could preclude any human reproduction whatever! Nevertheless, the question of social control ought not to be dismissed by pressing it to its absurd extremes. The real question is whether society has the right to attempt to prevent *the most seriously-crippling* genetic diseases from being transmitted.

In one sense the question is not all that new. Virtually all cultures prohibit certain marriages — those with close relatives — for reasons at least partly genetic. Further, we admit the propriety of blood tests prior to marriage for the control of venereal disease. Granted, failing a pre-marital genetic test would have more permanent consequences than failing the V.D. exam. But the implications of certain genetic diseases are far more serious, too. It is not, finally, a matter of preventing certain *marriages* from taking place. It is rather the question whether the right of couples *to reproduce* is absolute and of greater importance than the avoidance of producing more children who are gravely and permanently incapacitated.[15]

Judicious compromises between parental rights and the rights of future children and society will have to be made. Social attitudes will require reassessment. For example, the increasing availability of amniocentesis and abortion will mean that couples will have the choice of whether or not to bear a mongoloid child; when such a child is born the neighbors will know that the parents made that deliberate choice, and it is difficult now to predict the consequences in attitudes which might ensue.[16] The place for moral education in these matters is large indeed. Christian churches in past ages were able to promote celibacy to the glory of God. "These same Christian churches should be able to promote voluntary or 'vocational' childlessness, or policies of restricted reproduction, for the sake of children of generations to come." [17] Of such ingredients we might yet forge an ethics of genetic responsibility for counselors, their counselees, and the wider society.

Genetic Screening

In genetic screening programs the focus shifts from the individual couple to the testing of whole groups of persons to determine carriers or actual presence of genetic disease. Recent screening programs to detect the sickle-cell trait and sickle-cell anemia among blacks, Tay-Sachs disease among Jewish groups, and phenylketonuria (PKU) in infants have raised important new questions in medical ethics.[18]

A blue-ribbon interdisciplinary research group on ethical, social and legal issues in genetic screening recently concluded that the most important goals of such programs "are those that either contribute to improving the health of persons who suffer from genetic disorders, or allow carriers for a given variant gene to make informed choices regarding reproduction, or move toward alleviating the anxieties of families and communities faced with the prospect of serious genetic disease." [19] These are, indeed, important goals. Let us look at them briefly in turn.

First, certain genetic diseases for which there exist effective therapy can be discovered early, and the afflicted person can be steered to medical help. The problem lies, however, in the discovery of those diseases (for example, a certain type of muscular dystrophy or sickle cell disease) for which there is no effective therapy now available. What then? If the patient or the parents are informed about the disease before its slow debilitating course has begun, anxiety may well be created without the offer of any positive reassurance. On the other hand, early knowledge of the disease for some families might give them time to adjust emotionally to the problem so that the diseased person might be treated with helpful human support rather than dehumanizing pity.

Second, by detecting persons who are carriers for a disease they can be assisted in making informed choices about having children. However, genetic diseases vary in their detectability as well as their treatability. Some potential diseases can be detected in pregnant women who then can be offered therapeutic abortion. Tay-Sachs disease is a case in point. But at present there is no reliable method of intra-uterine diagnosis for sickle cell anemia, hence the woman concerned about this has no means of obtaining definite knowledge.

As a third important goal, many anxieties can be alleviated. The relatively high incidence of sickle cell disease among blacks and of Tay-Sachs disease among certain Jewish groups is general knowledge, but the great majority in any tested group can be given meaningful peace of mind with the knowledge that they are neither carriers nor afflicted.

Beyond clarity about the goals there must be careful attention to the means by which genetic screening is done.[20] The program ought not promise any benefits it cannot actually deliver. The community in which screening is to be done should be involved in the planning and educated about the program so that every interested person has access to it. Trained genetic counselors must provide adequate information about types, availability, and costs of therapy for diseases which are uncovered in the screening.

The subjects of a screening program need various forms of protection. In the present state of genetic knowledge, it is wise to make mass screening programs voluntary and to insist upon written expression of free consent by each participant. Further, the privacy rights of each subject should be jealously guarded. Since most states do not have laws enforcing the confidentiality of public health information, those in charge of genetic screening programs need to be unusually careful that medical information is given only to the subject or, with that person's permission, to a specific doctor or hospital. The information does not belong to insurance companies. Nor ought those discovered as carriers of a genetic disease be publicly identified in any way. Being stigmatized by others would be a dehumanizing outcome of a program designed to enhance human care!

Genetic screening is a new and promising tool. Consider the problem of Tay-Sachs disease. Here is the tragedy of the afflicted baby, doomed to die of brain deterioration before the age of four. Screening for Tay-Sachs is practicable because almost all cases are found among one ethnic group, Jews of Eastern European (Ashkenazi) descent, and because a simple new blood test is available for identifying carriers. In the early 1970s the first mass screening for Tay-Sachs was conducted in the Baltimore-Washington area where sixty thousand couples of childbearing age belonging to this Jewish group live. In perhaps one to two hundred of these couples both man and woman are carriers. In these cases their offspring have a one-in-four peril of being diseased. When screening detects mated carriers, and when such a couple is expecting a child, amniocentesis can detect with accuracy whether the fetus is afflicted. At that point the parents can make a decision whether or not to have a therapeutic abortion. And while no abortion is without its own moral ambiguity, the opportunity for numerous families to avoid the larger Tay-Sachs tragedy is now available.

The dangers of genetic screening, however, are illustrated by the phenylketonuria (PKU) programs.[21] In the mid-1960s a relatively small group of dedicated parents of retarded children and a small group of physicians were able to persuade forty-one states — within a period of less than three years — to pass laws requiring the testing of newborn children for PKU. PKU is a rare form of mental retardation which is only partially understood in present medicine. While the disease affects no more than one person in ten thousand, the detection of those cases which do exist would be a valuable human gain. The problem lies, however, in the inadequacy of available testing procedures. The tests can miss actual cases of PKU and give falsely positive reactions in an even larger number of children tested. When a child who does *not* have the disease is put on the special therapeutic diet for PKU, he will suffer physical deterioration at the least, and quite possibly even death.

Here, then, was a well-intended but ill-informed rush into genetic screening legislation, legislation now in effect in the majority of our states. As this program is now operating, some PKU-afflicted children are being diagnosed and treated early with beneficial results. On the other hand, false diagnoses are endangering the health of other children. Furthermore, records of the test results are being filed in various places in the state health departments, accessible to nonprofessional, nonmedical personnel. This practice in itself can endanger the privacy and future careers of those who are stigmatized as having this genetic disease (whether they in fact have it or not). Thus, in addition to the beneficial possibilities of genetic screening programs, there are dehumanizing possibilities in those which are ill-advised.

Genetic and Fetal Therapy

Genetic diseases include cystic fibrosis, diabetes, hemophilia, sickle-cell anemia, PKU, Down's syndrome, and some forms of mental retardation and illness. Further, there are genetic factors in some forms of cancer, arthritis, high blood pressure, stomach ulcers, and gout. As one geneticist says, "mistakes in the genetic information carried in the cells are responsible for an enormous amount of human suffering and death." [22] In light of all this it is easy to understand the enthusiasm for effective gene therapy, the treatment of specific diseases by directly influencing a person's genes.

Dramatic advances in genetic knowledge, including the deciphering of the language of the cell, have led some geneticists to speculate that shortly it will be possible to alter portions of chromosomes (chemically with anti-mutagent substances or surgically with radiation beams) thus attacking specific defects. Other scientists are less optimistic that this will be done *safely* in the near future. But few doubt that it will come. Sickle cell anemia may be one of the first diseases to be prevented by gene therapy, followed by the detection and treatment of prediabetic and precancerous individuals.[23]

A related but different area is fetal therapy. The stillbirths and babies who die within the first month after birth number three times the children up to age fourteen who die from all other causes each year. To attack fetal diseases medicine has created fetology as a new subspecialty. Intrauterine transfusions on fetuses suffering from Rh disease are now commonly performed. Chemical treatment of fetal diseases is under way. Fetal surgery already has been performed by cutting through the uterine wall, but in the experimental stage are instruments which will be able to perform certain surgical procedures without cutting the womb at all.[24]

While most of the moral considerations surrounding any experimental therapy apply to both fetal and gene therapy, there are some important differences particularly in the treatment of genes. Gene therapy is incredibly complex and the consequences of errors would be incredibly serious.[25] It may be some years before scientists know enough to treat genes with the reasonable assurance that not only will the patient be done "more good than harm" but also that *future* offspring of the patient will not suffer genetic repercussions. Leroy Augenstein points out this problem. We might develop a virus with the necessary DNA for correcting diabetes, and because of the commonness of diabetes the pressures for both testing and using that therapeutic virus would be immense. But, even if the treatment were to cure the diabetes problem, it is possible that the offspring of those treated might be afflicted with schizophrenia. Thus, even before the trouble was suspected, a whole generation of persons would have been produced with extensive genetic changes.[26]

Doubtless the manipulation of human genes for therapeutic purposes will be undertaken. In fact, in one case this has been attempted already. However, in the present state of the art moral wisdom lies with those who insist upon a moratorium on any further human use until such time as the risks are much more fully known and controlled. In the future these techniques could also be used for large scale genetic engineering. Were that the case a significant moral shift would have occurred, from negative to positive eugenics, from therapy for individuals to attempts to improve the race.

Germinal Choice: Artificial Insemination for Genetic Improvement

Earlier we examined artificial insemination by donor (AID) as a therapeutic procedure for childless couples. The late Nobel laureate Dr. Hermann J. Muller took a long step beyond this, proposing its use as a positive eugenic device.[27] Muller had a deep concern about the deterioration of the gene pool coupled with the increasing need for more persons of intelligence and cooperation in our time. The trouble, he argued, is that the very kinds of persons whom we need most are those most inclined to restrict their reproduction, while at the same time the numbers of genetically defective persons are steadily rising.

Muller envisioned a program of germinal choice. Sperm banks could be stocked with frozen sperm from outstanding men. The sperm would be carefully catalogued for its genetic traits and retained for at least twenty years and until the donor was dead so that additional assessments of his quality could be made. Prospective parents could then select the traits that they wanted in their offspring. "The idealistic vanguard, and those following them, will foster sound genetic progress by their general agreement on the overriding values of health, intelligence, and brotherliness." [28]

In addition to the psychological, social, legal, and moral problems we have already examined with therapeutic AID, Muller's proposal raises a host of others. Though sharing his concern for the quality of future life, both scientists and ethicists have entered these objections: unknown but injurious recessive genes might become widespread throughout the population; present-day children of geniuses do not seem to validate the idea; temperamental compatibility and the psychological adjustments of the father could be acute; and the mutation rate of frozen semen is still unknown.[29] Furthermore, it is seriously debated whether the types of character traits which Muller wished to foster are all that inheritable. James F. Crow contends that "many of the traits of greatest importance have a low heritability"; J. P. Scott maintains that experimental evidence shows "the lack of congruence between genes and complex behavioral character" and Hudson Hoagland argues, "We know too little about the human genotype to feel confidence in our ability to do anything to modify it in favor of desirable traits." [30]

Beyond the questions of scientific viability lie those of moral and social viability. Even if we were to assume that behavioral and moral traits were significantly inheritable, do we have the wisdom to determine what qualities are best for future human generations? (In his earlier proposal in the mid-thirties, Muller argued that Lenin's sperm would be of valuable use; in later versions he dropped Lenin's name and nominated men such as Leonardo, Descartes, Lincoln, Pasteur, and Einstein.) [31] While AID might be warranted in some cases of involuntary childlessness, are we prepared to use it as a general practice when couples have no natural barrier to procreation — thus radically sundering baby-making from the act of love-making? And what of the moral questions surrounding social policy? Theodosius Dobzhansky asks, "Are we to have, in place of Plato's philosopher-king a geneticist-king? And who will be president of the National Sperm Bank? What checks and balances are to be imposed on the genetic legislature and the genetic executive powers? Who will guard the guardians?" [32]

To raise these serious questions is not to take lightly Muller's concerns about the quality of present and future life. Rather, it is to question his solution. It is one thing to see AID as therapy for the involuntarily childless; it is quite another to encourage the fertile to forego that part of the covenant of intimacy to improve the human race. At this point we have neither the scientific knowledge nor the moral wisdom to embark on such positive eugenics. Given these doubts, Paul Ramsey's concern for present rights becomes persuasive: such a plan must be rejected "because of its massive assaults upon human freedom and its grave violation of the respect due to men and women now alive and to human parenthood as such." [33]

Cloning: Carbon Copy People

Another Nobel laureate, Dr. Joshua Lederberg, advocates the future possibility and desirability of cloning human beings.

"Clone" comes from the Greek word for "cutting" and refers to a method of asexual reproduction. *Sexual* reproduction, whether in the forest, bed, or laboratory, requires the cooperation of both female and male, and the resulting offspring is genetically different from either parent. *Asexual* reproduction requires only one parent and produces a genetically-identical offspring.

While asexual reproduction occurs in various of nature's organisms, biologists in recent years have been able to duplicate this process in some beings which naturally reproduce sexually — frogs, salamanders, and fruit flies. Biologist Leon R. Kass describes the process:

> The procedure is conceptually simple. The nucleus of a mature but unfertilized egg is removed (by microsurgery or by irradiation) and replaced by a nucleus obtained from a specialized somatic cell of an adult organism (e.g., an intestinal cell or a skin cell). For reasons which are not yet understood, the egg with its transplanted nucleus develops as if it had been fertilized and, barring complications, may give rise to a normal adult organism.[34]

While no mammals have yet been replicated in this way, scientists continue their attempts. The theoretical knowledge for mammal (including human) cloning is available. The difficulties which remain are technical ones. Kass expects the birth of the first cloned mammal within a few years. At that time people will certainly rush to clone champion livestock to keep in perpetuity the producers of prime meat and milk. A few additional years may well see the technical obstacles to human cloning overcome.

Human cloning is not merely a matter of interest because it would be a startling scientific achievement, another Mount Everest climbed because it was there to climb. Its eugenic proponents offer a variety of reasons for its use.[35] Cloning, they argue, would offer a more reliable way than sperm banks for genetic improvement, for superior persons could be exactly duplicated. Body-cell banks could replace sperm banks, and genetic copies of dead individuals could be made from their frozen cells. Sets of genetically-identical persons could be produced for special tasks which require intense communication and certain physical characteristics: astronauts, soldiers, underwater explorers. Parents could choose the genotype for their prospective child: someone famous, a departed loved one, or even one of the parents themselves. And, of course, the sex of the child could be chosen. The generational gap could be overcome, at least between those persons who were genetically identical. And finally, organ transplants between clonal pairs would create no problems of tissue rejection. Such are the arguments.

To many people the matter of cloning conjures up the tyranny of Huxley's *Brave New World* and Orwell's *1984*. Clonees, they say, would not be allowed to marry or to reproduce in the natural manner nor could they choose vocations other than those for which they had been produced. Both Lederberg as a geneticist and Joseph Fletcher as an ethicist maintain, however, that it is quite the other way around. True, the dictatorship of the future would probably use genetic controls. But, says Lederberg, "it could not do so without having instituted slavery in the first place," and Fletcher adds, "Genetic controls do not lead to dictatorship; if there is any cause-and-effect relation it is the other way around." [36] However, the problem is oversimplified if we see a simple cause-and-effect relationship in *either* direction. Serious constraint of human freedoms in any sphere of life contributes to an ethos which tolerates constraints in other spheres.

In addition to the socio-political concerns, opponents of cloning raise several morally-significant scientific issues.[37] Natural sexual reproduction ensures the genetic adaptability of persons to changing environments, and it is not at all clear that cloned persons would be comparably adaptable. Further, if cloned persons suddenly returned to reproduction with members of the opposite sex, an accumulation of deleterious recessive genes and mutations might be dumped into the genetic pool. And, not the least of objections, what about the mishaps and mistakes created in the cloning process? If a large number of grossly abnormal creatures resulted from the frog experiments, might we not assume that something similar would happen in the process of human cloning?

Beyond these issues are those questions which arise out of reflections on human nature and sexuality. Would the rejection of sexual reproduction in cloning threaten the whole meaning of human parenthood and add one more threat to that crucial personalizing institution, the family? Would the rejection of sexual reproduction threaten a person's very *humanum*, inasmuch

as our bodies and sexuality are intrinsically part of our personhood? Would the cloned person's dignity and worth be threatened by having been deliberately denied a unique genotype?
And would there be a dehumanizing effect upon the scientist
himself, inasmuch as in the increase of his mastery over human
genesis he is subverting the sense of mystery and awe in the face
of human creation? These issues are raised by Kass and Ramsey.
But to Lederberg and Fletcher these questions seem rhetorical.
They are founded upon a set of religious premises upon which
not all Christians or humanists would agree. To the latter men
the real question is whether or not cloning contributes to the
fulfillment of human need. All else is relative to that. And to
that question we must return later.

Artificial Inovulation and In Vitro Fertilization

Many of the same questions which surround cloning reappear
with two other possibilities of the human genetic future. Artificial inovulation is the artificial insertion of an egg into a woman's uterus or Fallopian tubes. Technically it will be possible
within the next few years to remove a fertilized egg from one
woman's body and to transplant it into a foster mother who
could then carry the baby to term. Already this has been done in
other mammals, even using a temporary host mother from another species. Since 1962 fertilized ova from prize sheep have
been implanted into female rabbits, flown across the ocean, and
then implanted into other sheep for completion of the pregnancy — a marked saving on the transportation costs of livestock
breeding.

Varied uses for artificial inovulation have been speculated for
human beings. Some women want their own children but do not
want to go through pregnancy because of careers or personal
reasons. Others earnestly desire their own children and would
function well as mothers but for medical reasons (a heart problem, for example) are advised against pregnancy. Still other
women are sterile but so desire a child "of their own" that they
would be willing to receive an egg graft from an anonymous
donor.

Artificial inovulation could be combined with *in vitro* fertilization. *In vitro* means literally "in the glass" or in the laboratory test-tube. Harvard gynecologist John Rock proved the feasi-

bility of this in the 1940s, and during the following decade Columbia's Landrum Shettles carried Rock's experiments further, maintaining one embryo for six days. Then, as we have seen, by the early 1960s the Italian researcher Petrucci fertilized human eggs with human sperm in his laboratory and kept embryos alive for twenty-nine and fifty-nine days. The combination of test-tube fertilization with artificial inovulation could be used for the woman who is not sterile and yet cannot conceive because of malformed oviducts, the cause of many cases of infertility. Such a woman's unfertilized egg might be removed, fertilized with her husband's sperm *in vitro,* and then the embryo implanted in her womb.

Such embryo transplants are still in the future. Thus far all laboratory-fertilized embryos have simply remained in the laboratory until they died. But work is under way on artificial wombs and artificial placentas. As E. Fuller Torrey notes, *growing* the embryo in the laboratory appears to be a logical extension of what is already being done: "We don't hesitate to remove a fetus from the womb as early as 27 weeks in cases where medically indicated (especially Rh sensitization) and raise it in an incubator. And attempts are being made at Stanford University to keep human fetuses, expelled by a miscarriage, alive as early as 10 weeks old." [38] It is, however, quite debatable whether ecto-genesis (the entire process of "pregnancy" in the laboratory from the *in vitro* fertilization of the egg to the "birth" of the fetus from an artificial womb) would be a *logical* extension of present practice. That, of course, would depend upon what kind of logic one were using. It could be a *technological* extension of present practice, but it might also be a qualitatively different thing in *moral* logic. If, as it seems probable, workable artificial wombs and placentas are devised, then Huxley's Fertilizing and Decanting Rooms of the Central London Hatchery, envisioned in 1932, will be with us — if the choice is made to use these new devices for ectogenesis.

Let us look briefly at some of the moral arguments surrounding three major possibilities in the near future. The first is that of artificial inovulation using a host mother.[39] The perfectly healthy woman who does not want to interrupt her career with pregnancy's inconveniences, or the woman who wants children yet fears pregnancy and childbirth might choose this method. So also might the woman who is medically unable to experience pregnancy either because her health might be seriously endangered or because she lacks a uterus though is otherwise reproductively normal. In any case, the egg would be fertilized by the woman and her husband through normal intercourse and then transplanted to a voluntary host mother who would carry the fetus to term, bear the child, and hand it back to the original couple.

What are the risks involved? The medical risks are difficult to assess in the current state of the art, but they are certainly present. Any transplant handling of the fertilized egg runs the risks of chromosomal damage to the embryo. Even if these risks were, through scientific advance, made exceedingly slight, the human and personal risks could hardly be reduced by medical techniques. What of the host mother (whether a mercenary or unpaid volunteer) who becomes psychologically attached to that which is physically attached to her? What of the interpersonal feelings between the genetic parents and the host mother? What of the genetic mother who has good intentions at the start of the procedure but who months later finds herself psychologically unable to accept the child who has been carried and born by another? How would such a procedure alter the whole fabric of the parent-child relationship? What of the child's response to the discovery of his or her extraordinary origins? These difficult questions make the host-mother procedure gravely suspect as a morally humanizing option.

More viable morally is the egg graft. Here is the mirror image of artificial insemination by donor (AID), for now it is the woman who is sterile. She receives a ripe egg from an anonymous donor, the egg is implanted in one of her Fallopian tubes, and there it is fertilized by her husband through normal intercourse. For two reasons this process might be psychologically easier than AID. Conception in this case takes place through normal coitus. Also, in the egg graft the one who is not the child's genetic parent (the mother) is very much physically and psychologically involved through her pregnancy — unlike the husband in AID who has no physical involvement.

All of the moral considerations applicable to artificial insemination by donor apply to artificial inovulation by donor. If the former can be a morally responsible procedure in some instances, it would appear that the latter might receive even greater support since its psychological hazards are somewhat less. However, the medical issues are more complicated in such artificial inovulation. Egg donation is more difficult, obviously, than is sperm donation, and the implantation of the egg requires minor surgery. More importantly, the medical risk to the prospective child is far greater in the egg graft than in AID, for the handling of the delicate egg during the procedure brings the danger of chromosomal damage. If the damage were lethal and the embryo spontaneously aborted, the moral tragedy would be less than if the egg survived. The mishaps which might well occur in the further perfecting of this procedure are morally sobering. While our reasons for suspicion are fewer than with the host-mother possibility, in egg grafts the risks of genetic damage to the embryo remain and they are serious enough to warrant grave caution.

The third major option is the combination of *in vitro* fertilization with artificial inovulation. This process is a mirror image of artificial insemination by husband (AIH) if it were to be used as is now contemplated.[40] In this instance the woman produces perfectly good eggs, but she has malformed oviducts and the sperm cannot reach them. The proposed solution is to remove several eggs from the ovaries by minor surgery, fertilize them in the laboratory with the husband's sperm, grow the fertilized eggs for a day or two, and implant one of them in the woman's uterus for normal development there.

Our reasons (given in Chapter Three) supporting AIH in many siutations might appear to apply equally to the present procedure, but there are several important differences. One involves the nature of the conception process. In both instances the physician artificially intrudes. Yet, in AIH the actual conception takes place within the woman's body, while here both fertilization and the very early stages of embryonic development take place in the laboratory. Critics find this an unsupportable and qualitative moral difference. Leon Kass, for example, calls it "the most important *intrinsic* difference between artificial insemination and artificial fertilization." [41]

Lacking the strongly physical emphasis of certain natural law ethics, however, I find it difficult to concur in Kass' judgment. The motivations and adequacy of the would-be parents and the purposes for which the conception is taking place ought to weigh more heavily in our moral evaluations than should the place where the fertilization actually occurs. There may well be other things which make test-tube fertilization irresponsible, but it is not wrong intrinsically simply because it occurs in a test-tube.

Several other questions, however, might cast doubt on *in vitro* fertilization. One is the "disposal" of fertilized eggs which are not used. In order to maximize the chances for one successful implantation, the physician may have to fertilize eight or ten eggs. He may succeed with four or five of them and thus let several fertilized eggs die in the test tube. For those who believe that fully human life begins at the moment of conception, the process is, of course, morally repugnant at this point. If, however, one holds a developmental view (as I have earlier argued) one could say that these disposed eggs do have human value and hence there *is* moral ambiguity surrounding their deaths; nevertheless, their value, even to life's Creator, may be far outweighed by the value of personhood in the potential child of a hitherto childless couple.

Even more difficult is the persisting problem of genetic risk to the embryo implant. While scientists are divided on the amount of genetic risk, all are agreed that there is undoubtedly some. Kass and Ramsey both protest strongly against all *in vitro* fertilization for this reason. Kass objects "since the hazards are being imposed on another human being, the child-to-be, who obviously cannot consent to have such risks imposed upon him." [42] Similarly, Ramsey concludes that "unless the *possibility* of such damage can be definitively excluded, in vitro fertilization is an immoral experiment on possible future human beings." [43] For both, the experimentation necessary to achieve a risk-free procedure would undoubtedly produce genetic mishaps, a sufficient reason to say that this is morally forbidden.

Less definitive though still cautious in his judgment is Marc Lappé. He contends that the fear of gross monstrosities from the fertilization process is probably unfounded. Yet, when the fertilization is coupled with implantation, the risk data are less complete. There will be some loss of fertilized ova, but this also happens in normal procreation. True, "no one will be able to say when and if *in vitro* fertilization in man will become a risk-free procedure. But I have emphasized that traditionally no one has insisted that 'natural' reproduction be completely safe for the fetus before it is undertaken." [44] Nevertheless, Lappé concludes that moral stakes are extremely high. Risks should be exhaustively studied and genuine scientific consensus upon them should emerge before the first human implantation is attempted.

In addition to the genetic risk factor, those who categorically object to *in vitro* fertilization raise two other objections. For one thing, they resist the pro-natalist assumption that couples have a right to be fertile by *any* means. If the woman with blocked oviducts so desires to bear her own child, she should try corrective surgery. This, they say, would be more medically defensible because it would be treating the *disease* and not merely the *desires* of the patient. In addition to the fact that corrective oviduct surgery is now successful in only about 30 percent of the attempts, however, I find this position a curiously narrow conception of medicine's responsibilities. Caring for human health and wholeness ought to be the context within which curing specific ailments is viewed, and medicine's rightful concerns in such cases need not be limited to corrective surgery.

"The wedge argument," finally, is cited by the opponents of *in vitro* fertilization. "Once introduced for the purpose of treating intramarital infertility," says Kass, *"in vitro* fertilization could be used for any purpose." [45] According to Ramsey, once we justify this procedure for particular couples we have already accepted *in principle* the possibility of a whole succession of dehumanizing practices. "This intrinsic connection does not compel us to take those other steps also, but the argument for so doing has already impressed itself on our minds and persuaded us in the case at hand." [46]

The large-scale moral horrors which had seemingly innocuous beginnings in various areas of our common life ought to prevent us from dismissing the wedge argument too quickly. Taken by itself, however, it is not a persuasive argument against *in vitro* fertilization. The potential abuse of a thing ought not to preclude its justifiable use unless those abuses are deemed to follow inexorably from any use whatsoever. That therapeutic fertilization for the childless could lead to gross forms of genetic engineering is possible. It is far from inevitable. There are dangers, certainly, but as with a variety of technologies we must make numerous decisions along the way, carefully affirming what is responsible use and firmly excluding that which directly threatens our *humanum*.

While we ought not categorically rule out *in vitro* fertilization on the basis of the wedge argument, the genetic risks to the

potential child are still great enough to warrant a "No" to this
procedure in the present state of medical knowledge. Exhaustive
animal experimentation might one day lead to a responsible
consensus that the risks for human life in such operations are
no greater than the genetic risks entailed in ordinary procreation. *If* that day should come, laboratory fertilization might be
a humanly responsible help for the childless.

Some Further Ethical and Theological Reflections

Enough difficult ethical problems surround procedures in
negative eugenics, the diagnosis and treatment of specific genetic
defects in specific patients. But when we move from negative to
positive eugenics, the ethical problems boggle the mind and the
spirit. As Roger Shinn observes, up to this point in history the
most radical revolutions in both technology and society have
been deeply conservative in one sense — they have not touched
the genetic constitution of the human race. Now, however, the
possibility of changing that constitution is upon us.[47] The discovery of the DNA structure in 1953 by Drs. Francis Crick and
James Watson and the further illumination of its inner workings
by many others, notably Dr. Marshall Nirenberg, have set the
stage for our ability to remake humankind genetically. The
questions, of course, are what is possible and what is desirable?

Harvard historian Donald Fleming notes that the attitudes of
many bio-medical scientists are condescending toward religion,
and yet they share an attitude toward their own work and destiny
which is clearly religious in character. They believe that the
biological revolution will save humankind. According to Fleming,
three major elements constitute a full-scale revolution: "a distinctive attitude toward the world; a program for utterly trans-
forming it; and an unshakable, not to say fanatical, confidence
that this program can be enacted — a world view, a program, and
a faith." [48] By this definition there is an underlying revolutionary
temper in much contemporary bio-medical research. Joshua
Lederberg, Francis Crick, Edward Tatum, Robert Edwards —
some of the leading names in the field today — represent that
spirit. They are men of hope and vision. They are also men who
come perilously close to the view that in their particular hopes
and visions is the path of human salvation.

Other geneticists are more cautious about both the possibility and desirability of species-centered goals. British Nobel laureate Sir Peter Medewar maintains that "the end product of an evolutionary episode is not a new genetic formula enjoyed by a group of similar individuals, but a new spectrum of genotypes, a new pattern of genetic inequality, definable only in terms of the population as a whole." [49] Animal breeders know that breeding for all around improvement is not possible; certain characteristics are sacrificed in favor of others. Nevertheless, even Medewar admits that some significant genetic changes are possible — if society elects to pay the human price. But do we really know what constitutes a moral improvement in the human gene pool?

The same scientific situation thus elicits quite varying outlooks or dispositions toward the future on the part of different persons. Some respond with confidence and hope, others with more fear and anxiety. As James M. Gustafson rightly observes, interacting with our factual judgments are our theological and philosophical convictions about the world. Is a divine and providential process guiding the genetic future, or is all left to chance and human judgment? Is the human condition such that human judgments usually can be trusted? [50] My arguments thus far have assumed that there is indeed a divine intention for our human future, but God also gives his human creatures the freedom to create and to destroy the quality of life. I have assumed that there is both a grandeur and a misery about human nature: we are capable of quite selfless moral wisdom, and we are also prone to short-sighted and distorted, self-willed judgments. There is room, then, both for optimism and for pessimism about our genetic future.

A new scientific determinism pervades much of the genetic literature.[51] It is a technocratic logic which assumes that those things which *can* be done inevitably *will* be done. "Have we not," asked Dr. Hermann Muller in his last public statement, "eventually utilized, for better or for worse, all materials, processes and powers that we could gain some mastery over?" [52] However, coupled with this deterministic assumption frequently there is also a strange assumption of utter freedom: freedom for scientific manipulation of creaturely life. There is no limit, some seem to say, to what we can or should do to change the human condition. But we who attempt to perceive the world through Christian eyes should have difficulty seeing either a relentless determinism or a limitless freedom in human choice. We are not fated to do everything genetically which we now have or will have the power to do. Nor are we utterly free to manipulate our human future.

Genetic manipulation can be either responsible or irresponsible. Responsible human action, let us repeat, will take account of both the persisting ethical questions of individual rights and the wider social good. Some ethicists lean too hard on one side or on the other. Paul Ramsey is certain that even though some bio-medical innovations would be good for society they can never be right because they violate certain intrinsic human values. Joseph Fletcher is equally certain that genetic policies must always be judged by the social consequences they produce.

We need to hear both of these voices, but neither by itself is sufficient. Too great a certitude about inviolable human rights can result in an individualism which gazes fixedly upon the present with insufficient sensitivity to the changing needs of the human community. For example, if the genetic pessimists' predictions were to come true and humankind were clearly faced with a genetic apocalypse, then even Hermann Muller's proposals which admittedly breach on a vast scale the honored nexus between love-making and baby-making might become morally responsible. There is a relativity and a historicity about our notions of human rights that makes them less-than-absolute.[53] On the other hand, undue confidence in judging scientific policies simply by the amount of social good they can produce may well ride roughshod over individual rights and human values in the eagerness to achieve those social results.

In the present state of genetic knowledge our focus ought to be largely upon negative eugenics — eliminating specific defects in specific patients. Having said this, we cannot absolutely preclude the possibility that some day certain positive eugenic measures might be warranted both by the condition of the genetic pool and by increased scientific understanding. As in other forms of human experimentation, certainly in genetics we need concentrated attention to public policy.[54] Freedom for scientific research is an important value, but it is not absolute. The wider community — through intensified public discussion, interdisciplinary commissions, the political processes, and the considered opinions of religious groups — needs to clarify those principles which should guide the scientists. In the absence of clear public policy, scientists will continue to experiment with new genetic possibilities, with new ways of liberating human reproduction from its normal manner, with new ways to increase what the scientists themselves believe to be valuable human characteristics. But these are questions for all of us, not only for the researchers in the laboratories. Even if our social pluralism makes clear agreement on particular genetic issues unlikely, we might at least find some agreement upon what harmful results to individuals, to human marriage and parenthood, and to wider society ought to be avoided. We might find some consensus upon the broad questions of proportionality and distributive justice: how much in bio-medical resources ought to be allocated to such research in the face of numerous and elementary unmet medical needs which now exist? Beyond our own particular society, the entire international human community has a profound stake in these issues. One of the greatest imaginable threats to human well-being would come were genetic policy to become captive to myopic nationalistic interests and anxieties.

A hopeful Christian realism about human life can go far in counteracting the extremes of technological utopias and night-marish doomsdays which now creep into the genetic discussions. A hopeful Christian vision of what makes human life truly human will encourage those genetic efforts which are even now relieving much suffering and contributing to human wholeness. On the other hand, a wise Christian realism will challenge the biological engineers who are not content with humankind but are ambitiously intent upon improving the race. Without any ingratitude for the brilliance of their genetic achievements, some of us believe that salvation lies beyond any human revolution (even the scientific one) and that any human movement which claims ultimacy for its own vision breeds tragedy. Such is the posture of hopeful realism.

CHAPTER SIX

Humanizing the Dying Process

Cases

Mr. V. awoke in Room 5143 of the metropolitan hospital, remembering only his sharp chest pain at the family barbecue, the dizziness, and the sirens. After two weeks of struggling, the sixty-year-old factory worker died, alone in his hospital room. The only sounds had been the bleep-bleep of the heart-monitoring machine. A clear plastic tube had connected his windpipe to a respirator. Another machine had aided his badly-infected kidneys. A glucose tube was inserted in his left forearm. The nurse disconnected the machines and tubes, wrapped the body in a sheet, and with the help of an orderly lifted it onto a special stretcher with a false bottom. With the cover in place the rolling cart appeared to be empty, and none of the patients seeing it in the corridors would suspect that the orderly was pushing a dead man to the basement vault. The nurse returned to her desk to fill out necessary papers and notify the physician who would contact the relatives.[1]

A man in his thirties was found at the door of the emergency room of a New York Hospital, left there by companions who had disappeared. He was not breathing, and artificial respiration was begun immediately. Laboratory diagnosis later confirmed the staff's suspicion — an overdose of heroin. Neurological tests the next day, while the patient was being maintained on the respi-

rator, showed permanent damage and no brain activity. The
staff was divided into three camps. One group said he should be
declared dead and the lung pump stopped. Another group be-
lieved the patient should be declared living, though hopeless,
and should be allowed to "die all the way." Others argued that
if his heart was still beating, even though on the respirator, he
was still alive, and he ought to be maintained as long as possible.[2]

A massive cerebral hemorrhage struck Mr. A's father four years
ago. He has been in the hospital continuously since then, unable
to eat or speak and showing no neurological signs of being able
to communicate. He is incontinent, is fed completely intra-
venously, and is attended by three shifts of private nurses around
the clock. The son is plagued by guilt — guilt at the thought of
requesting that the doctors do something that will end his father's
"subhuman" existence and, at the same time, guilt over the
staggering expenses, the consumption of medical resources, and
the family strain.[3]

Contexts of the Death-and-Dying Debates

The concern for dying a good death has always been related
with the concern for living a good life. Montaigne observed that
to die well requires greater moral stamina than to live well. Karl
Jaspers, putting it a bit differently, has described philosophizing
as learning how to die, which is one and the same thing as learning how to live. A convergence of powerful social experiences
in our time has raised questions about the quality of life to a
new pitch. A tragic war, the rise of human liberation movements,
the emergence of counter culture groups, the press of ecological
crises — all of these have also, at least by implication, heightened
our consciousness about the quality of death.

The context for discussion of death obviously has been changed
significantly by medical technology. Earlier generations did not
face the same questions about prolonging the life of the dying
nor did simpler medical techniques pose questions about the
very definition of death itself.

Yet, the discussion is complicated by what Geoffrey Gorer has
called "the pornography of death." Our grandparents held things
sexual to be unmentionable, but they spoke openly about death.
We tend to reverse that order. Our playwrights have replaced

deathbed scenes with bedroom scenes. But what is concealed
becomes the object of fantasy and obsession. Hence our fascina-
tion (particularly with violent death) paradoxically exists side-
by-side with our prudery about death.[4]

In spite of our reluctance to face death openly as a normal
part of God's creation, certain medical developments now force
the issue. Whereas once we asked if we morally could do anything to hasten the death of those in hopeless misery, now we are
also asking if we can morally omit doing a number of things we
now can do which prolong the dying process.[5] Physicians and
nurses, like the rest of us, lack a clear mind on the matter. Their
professional consciences have been significantly shaped around
two principles which now increasingly conflict: the prolonging
of life and the relief of suffering.

The Hippocratic Oath does not solve the problem. Its pertinent sentences read, "I will use treatment to help the sick according to my ability and judgment, but never with a view to
injury and wrong-doing. Neither will I administer a poison to
anybody when asked to do so, nor will I suggest such a course." [6]
The Oath does not exalt the continuing of biological existence
as such. Rather it emphasizes the patient's well-being. But whether the use of extraordinary means to prolong life is for a certain
patient's well-being or whether it is "injury and wrong-doing"
is the unresolved question. Moreover, many are now raising the
question afresh as to whether modern medicine has so altered
the context that Hippocrates' dictum against poison needs rethinking.

How Shall We Define Death?

The question of death's definition has arisen in our time
because of what medical technique now makes possible. Scientifically we know that certain organs can be transplanted from a
dead person to a recipient. We also know that the cadaver donor
must not be "so dead" that deterioration has made the kidney or
heart useless for the transplant. We know *scientifically* when
removal of the organs is still viable. But when is the removal
morally viable? We can determine *scientifically* when the brain's
cortical functions have become permanently damaged so that
consciousness is no longer possible. It goes beyond a strictly
scientific judgment, however, to say that such an irreversible

coma is death. That is a *moral* judgment based upon theological and philosophical considerations. And it has, to be sure, immense practical implications: are we dealing, in this particular instance, with a living patient or are we dealing with an unburied corpse whose bodily processes are being artificially maintained?

Before pressing the moral dimensions, we need to rehearse briefly the scientific picture. Not many years ago, physicians were united in a medical definition of death: when spontaneous respiration and heartbeat ceased the person was dead. Nowadays, death as a *process* has become common medical currency.[7] The process has several dimensions. When the body's vital functions of respiration and heartbeat cease there is *clinical death*. In some cases resuscitation can reverse clinical death. Sometimes the patient is restored to an active, meaningful life. In other cases of clinical reversal, however, considerable brain damage has already occurred; spontaneous respiration and circulation have been restored but the capacity for conscious personal existence is gone. Following cardiac and respiratory failure, *brain death* soon begins to occur. The higher brain functions (controlling consciousness) die first, followed by the lower brain functions (controlling the nervous system and heart-lung functioning). In some situations brain death can be partially arrested after permanent damage to the higher functions has occurred. When the brain completely dies, however, *biological death* occurs — the permanent extinction of bodily life as the result of the loss of cardiac-respiratory functions. Yet, since the body does not die all at once, physicians speak of *cellular death*. Having different cellular compositions, some parts of the body die more rapidly than others. Fingernails and hair, for example, will grow for a time after the body is biologically dead.

About this process of life's cessation there is little scientific disagreement. However, medical people tend to divide into three schools of thought concerning the criteria for determining when death has occurred.[8] The first and most radical position uses only brain tests as its criterion. The electroencephalogram (EEG) is a graph made by an instrument which records the electric impulses or waves in the brain. If the EEG is flat (the graph shows no evidence of brain waves) this is taken as sufficient indication that the patient is dead.

The second school of thought uses the EEG also, but in combination with several other tests. Under the chairmanship of Dr.

Henry K. Beecher, the Harvard Medical School's Ad Hoc Committee defined the irreversible coma as the permanent cessation of both higher and lower levels of brain functioning and hence the irreversible loss of cardiorespiratory functioning. The characteristics of the permanently nonfunctioning brain, said the committee, are these: unreceptivity and unresponsiveness; no movements or breathing; no reflexes; and a flat EEG. If the same tests are repeated after twenty-four hours, the individual is to be declared dead. If the patient is on a respirator, death is to be declared and *then* the respirator turned off.[9] Confirmation of the tests after at least twenty-four hours by at least two physicians prior to turning the respirator off guards against the suspicion that the patient died as a *result* of the machine's having been removed or that the physician was hastening the patient's death because someone was waiting for transplant organs. The Beecher Committee's widely-known report has made irreversible coma or total brain death the sign of death, and it has recommended careful procedures for establishing its certainty.

The third position is the most traditional. Like the Beecher Committee, adherents of this school wish to use more than one test for determining death. Death itself, however, is not located primarily in the loss of brain function but in the loss of the integrated functioning of all of the body's parts and systems.

These attempts to establish scientific criteria are significant. Yet being able to determine *when death has occurred* is not the same as *defining death*.[10] We must have some notion of death in our minds (a religious, philosophical judgment) before we know what it is we are looking for in the medical tests. Or, perhaps more accurately, we must have a notion of what life means, and we can then define death by its absence. Only upon this basis can we establish medical criteria for telling us when death has occurred.

We are faced once again with the definitions of human and personal life (see Chapters One and Two). The varying positions we examined earlier in regard to abortion apply here. Those of the genetic school who have argued that human life begins upon the fixing of the genetic code in conception will argue that near life's ending human life is still present even in the permanent absence of higher brain functions. Even though the individual is permanently unconscious, has no awareness, self-control, or capacity for interpersonal relationship, that pa-

has human life. At the other extreme, those of the
ısequences school feel it unwise to call this life "human."
ıl facts are insufficient to define that which essentially
ıs   ral quality; our definition must come from the kind of
social policy we desire.

I have argued for a version of the developmental school. It
does make sense to affirm that any life with a unique genetic
code is, indeed, human life deserving of our profound respect.
But what is at stake is not only human life as such but that
special quality of human life we call "personal," the capacity for
consciousness, relatedness, self-transcendence. Without giving
highest priority to the personal quality we easily slip into a
biological idolatry.

A recent exchange between two scientists, Robert S. Morison
and Leon R. Kass, illustrates the importance of these distinctions.[11] Morison argues that understanding death as a sharply
defined and specific event introduces artificial discontinuities into
what is essentially a continuous process. Just as the longer a pregnancy proceeds the more value the fetus acquires, so also at the
other end of life: "The life of the dying patient becomes steadily
less complicated and rich, and, as a result, less worth living or
preserving. The pain and suffering involved in maintaining what
is left are inexorably mounting, while the benefits enjoyed by
the patient himself, or that he can in any way confer on those
around him, are just as inexorably declining." [12] We must, indeed, respect human life, argues Morison, but recognize that it
is not of one absolute value. The costs in human relationships to
those around the dying one and to society at large must also be
assessed in the question of unduly prolonging life.

Leon Kass, however, responds that death is a concrete event
and not just a process. "What dies is the organism as a whole. It
is this death, the death of the individual human being, that is
important ... not the 'death' of organs or cells, which are mere
parts." [13] We cannot identify the whole with one of its parts
(presumably even the brain). The trouble with Morison's position, argues Kass, is that "he does not distinguish the question
of when a man is dead from the question of when his life is not
worth prolonging." [14] The result is that the definition of death
becomes a socio-moral question rather than a scientific one.
When this is done we begin to weigh the value of the patient's
life against the costs to those around him, a dangerous procedure.

There is truth in each of these positions. Morison is right that the definition of death is not, strictly speaking, scientific. It is a moral judgment made upon the basis of life's relational value and capacity. Kass, however, correctly insists upon due regard for the rights, protection, and welfare of each individual patient. These affirmations can be fruitfully combined if we make two sets of distinctions. First, we can affirm that death is indeed a process and at the same time affirm that "the moment of death" is still a useful moral symbol. On this point Paul Ramsey perceives the real question: "when in the continuum of the dying process there is a life still among us who lays claim to the immunities, respect, and protection which in ethics and/or by law are accorded by men to a fellow man." [15] The second important distinction (which Ramsey does not clearly make) is the risky yet necessary one between human life and personal human life. Both lay claims upon us, but the claims are not the same.

The definition of death is ultimately religious and moral. The establishment and application of the criteria for knowing when death has occurred is a medical task. All of us have a voice in the former judgment; only medical professionals are competent in the latter.

In defining death we need to risk the distinction between personal human existence and that kind of human existence which is "post-personal," which has irretrievably lost its capacity for personhood. Granted, in specific cases the line is not always clear, but the distinction is still important. Without it we confuse personhood with a collection of physiological life signs. When life has lost its full humanity, its personhood, and yet is still among us in its life signs, it deserves our respect and our care. It deserves warmth, cleanliness, and comfort. It also deserves not to be confused with personal life, for in that confusion it may become artificially metabolized incurring a whole range of human costs.

In short, we need something more than a genetic norm to define both life and death. Daniel Callahan is correct:

> Genetically, a body still circulating blood is in some sense a "human life," if genetic membership in the human species is the norm. Thus if the moral aim is to preserve whatever genetically counts as "individual human life," then an artificially sustained body meets the standard. But if the moral concern is with personhood — thus presupposing an electri-

cally active brain — then, in the absence of brain activity, no "person" is present.[16]

Somewhere along the line we have to be willing to say that we are here no longer dealing with a human *person*. Death is more than a biological event; it is a personal process.

The Options: I. *"Striving Officiously to Keep Alive"*

The patient is clearly dying. There are three broad options open to him (if he is able to make a choice), to his family, and to the members of the health care team. First, all possible means including extraordinary or heroic measures can be used to keep the patient alive. Second, heroic therapy can be rejected or withdrawn and only ordinary medical care given. Third, some positive step can be taken to kill the patient immediately or to hasten the downward trajectory of his life. Let us look at each of these in turn.

A seventy-three-year-old man "who, having survived three prostate operations, a pulmonary embolus, a fall out of a wheelchair and several attacks of diverticulitis, chose to disregard his internist's recommendation that he undergo surgical exploration for removal of an intestinal polyp. His attitude was: 'If the polyp is benign, it's doing me no harm; if it is malignant, it probably has spread. I prefer to take my chances rather than to go through strenuous surgery again.' " [17] Commenting upon this case, Dr. Morris A. Wessel observes that the patient's fear was accurate and he did die of widespread cancer within a year. "What amazed me, however," Wessel adds, "was that the patient's physician, a respected and beloved internist, became increasingly angry at the patient and the family for refusing to follow his recommendation for exploratory surgery. His intense anger limited his capacity to offer comfort to the patient and his family, and limited their capacity to accept what he did offer." [18]

This case represents a fairly typical attitude among medical professionals: the reigning duty is to cure and keep alive. One professor of hospital administration says, "When I worked as a nurse, our goal was to keep the patient alive by any means until the next shift came on duty. Never have the patient die on your shift." [19]

It ought not surprise us that medical professionals, particularly physicians, tend toward this orientation. Their professional consciences have been given shape significantly around the principle of preserving life, and in their training the focus on that life is heavily physical and biological. Further, the doctor's attitudes are conditioned by his concentration upon the individual patient. The individual is his prime responsibility and, apart from a minority of rural family doctors, most physicians today have little time or opportunity for understanding the patient in his network of family and community relations. In addition, the physician is acutely aware of the importance of the trust relationship which he must never undermine. He must never let anyone fear that the doctor who is supposed to be the patient's healer might one day become the patient's executioner. Professional attitudes and relationships thus bias large numbers of physicians toward expending maximum technological effort upon each individual dying patient.

Two groups of terms need clarification.[20] *Extraordinary, heroic, maximum,* and *unusual* are applied to some medical procedures. *Ordinary, customary,* and *usual* are applied to others. These are relative terms. They are relative both to the state of medical technology and its availability and to the non-medical factors in a particular situation. Roman Catholic moral theologians generally have spoken of ordinary means as those medicines and treatments which offer reasonable hope of benefit to the patient and which do not involve excessive pain or expense. Extraordinary means, on the other hand, are those which do not promise reasonable benefit and cannot be administered without excessive cost, pain, or other considerable inconvenience. Physicians themselves tend to think somewhat more pragmatically: "ordinary means are established medical and surgical procedures appropriate to a given illness within the limits of availability; extraordinary means are those procedures (including medicines) which are incompletely established, frankly experimental, or bizarre." [21]

Against the opinions of those physicians who would always use maximum efforts to extend the patient's life are those of some colleagues and of most Christian moralists. Indeed, Pope Pius XII said in 1957, "Normally one is held only to use ordinary means according to the circumstances of persons, places, times, and cultures, that is to say, means that do not involve any great burden for one's self or another." [22]

A Bethesda doctor in charge of a cancer ward for seven years reports that never once has a patient asked him to be allowed to die.[23] (Perhaps he was asked in ways he could neither understand nor hear.) The physician gives three reasons for keeping each patient alive as long as possible, reasons which are representative of this position and deserve responses:

(1) When physicians withhold maximum efforts, patients lose hope and die. It becomes a self-fulfilling prophecy. (Surely if there are grounds for hope the doctor ought to convey that hope in his actions as well as words. But the decision must be made as to whether maximum efforts are prolonging meaningful personal life or whether they are only prolonging the dying process.)

(2) Since the patient is usually semi-comatose, his pain can be controlled and thus it is not a matter of prolonging his suffering. (Again, however, is meaningful life being extended? And, considering the terminal nature of the illness, what are the emotional and financial costs to the family? What are the costs in medical resources that might have been used by those who do have hope?)

(3) If doctors are to make decisions about expending extraordinary efforts on some but not on others, mistakes will sometimes be made and efforts withheld from some who could have been saved. (But in practice these decisions are not made when the question is whether the patient will live or die; rather, they are made when beyond reasonable doubt the patient is dying. The real question has to do with the nature of the death he will die and the length his dying will be artificially extended.)

So much hinges upon the frame of reference with which we are deciding. If we see death as the supreme enemy and a patient's death as a medical failure, then we will also see extraordinary measures as mandatory. But if death in a given instance can be a friend, if the physician's success is not narrowly calculated in terms of saving physical life, and if the care for the patient as a person who is linked in bonds to his family, to his society, and to his Creator is even more important than the cure of a physical condition — if these are the reigning perspectives, then the use of heroic medical measures is always elective. Only a crude vitalism, the prizing of physical life at any cost, would argue otherwise. Arthur Hugh Clough's parody on the Ten Commandments makes a serious point:

Thou shalt not kill, yet need not strive officiously to keep alive.

The Options: II. Cooperating with the Patient's Dying

After thirty-five years of specializing in the care of cancer victims, Dr. Edward H. Rynearson comments on the dying patient who is beyond any therapeutic hope, numbed by pain and drugs: "There are too many instances, in my opinion, in which patients in such a situation are kept alive indefinitely by means of tubes inserted into their stomachs, or into their veins, or into their bladders, or into their rectums — and the whole sad scene thus created is encompassed within a cocoon of oxygen which is the next thing to a shroud." [24]

The classic novel of an earlier day depicted the scene where the dying person met death giving his farewell address to the family and friends gathered in his bedroom. The more typical scene today is that described by Rynearson above. And the irony is that in prolonging the dying process the new array of medicines and devices frequently hastens *personal* death: self-consciousness, self-control, and the capacity to relate to others may be cut short by drugs and machines in the effort to prolong the body's existence. [25]

Thus many religious spokesmen, some physicians publicly, and many physicians privately now advocate withholding extraordinary measures of medical support and of terminating such measures which have been started in cases of irreversible dying marked by great pain or by permanent unconsciousness. Such decisions frequently are called "indirect euthanasia" or "passive euthanasia." Somewhat more accurate is "cooperating with the patient's dying."

From the patient's side these decisions can be either voluntary or involuntary. In a voluntary situation the patient, while still competent and rational, gives instructions to cease medical opposition to his death. Or the patient even prior to his terminal illness may have drawn up a "Living Will" — a formal document addressed to one's family, physician, clergyman, and lawyer stating the general conditions under which the person wishes no artificial or heroic medical measures to be applied. Still more common, however, is the involuntary situation. There is no written statement and the patient's wishes are unknown, but the choice to stop heroic medical measures is made on his behalf by others.

A personal covenant with the dying one means that our first

responsibility is not to save a physical life and then only later to worry about the whole person. Our first responsibility is to take into consideration the person's wholeness — involving emotions and significant relationships — at each step of the way. Our first responsibility is to care. This is even more basic than curing, and acts of care will center principally upon the person rather than principally upon the disease.

Basic human and Christian faithfulness dictate that ordinary medical care be mandatory, not elective. Again, however, what is ordinary cannot be prescribed in advance. Warmth, cleanliness, fluids, and the easing of bodily positions are all basic. Beyond these, the particular context must inform the decision. For example, while antibiotics to stave off pneumonia are normally routine and ordinary, cooperation with the person's dying in a certain situation may make them extraordinary. Indeed, at times to withhold antibiotics may be a mark of profound respect for the quality of human life. An Anglican dean, Bryan Whitlow, puts the matter in proper perspective: "The Christian does not respect life any less for recognizing the boon of death. Because life is what it is, there frequently comes a moment when it is good to die (and therefore good to allow another to go unvexed to death). Where Christian insight is deepest, death itself, when it comes, has an element of voluntary surrender." [26]

But several important issues remain. Who should decide? Preeminently the patient. If prior to unconsciousness he can make a rational decision undistorted by heavy sedation or severe pain then he, of course, has the right to decide. Hopefully, he will include those to whom he is most closely bound in human covenants in his decisional process. But when the patient has lost capacity for decisions, who then? Some physicians claim this right for themselves alone, but they are mistaken. It also belongs to others on the health care team, including clergy and chaplains. Most importantly, however, it belongs to the family. To be sure, some families may be so overwhelmed by guilt feelings that they push for extending the patient's life at any cost. Some others may be utterly dominated by pecuniary reasons. These minorities remind us that the family's right to decide also has its moral limits. In short, when we must decide about life and death on behalf of another, it clearly ought to emerge as a communal decision made in a process together by those bound to the patient in special ties and responsibilities. Dying is a process not only for the patient but also for those who most intimately must face the loss.

Is there any moral difference between stopping a medical treatment once it has been started and not starting it at all? While many physicians are more reluctant to stop something than not to begin it, it is difficult to see any qualitative moral difference. In both instances the intention is the same: to cease from giving that which would prolong the patient's dying. And in both instances that which will actively cause the patient's death is the same: his disease. Understandably, there may be different subjective and psychological feelings in withholding as opposed to withdrawing, but any meaningful moral distinction is hard to defend.

Related is the difficult question, is this a form of euthanasia? If euthanasia is the direct administration of a death-dealing substance to shorten the life of a dying patient, is there any significant moral difference between the active and the passive, the direct and the indirect, killing the patient and willingly allowing him to die?

Joseph Fletcher argues that both indirect and direct euthanasia are the same in principle:

> Either way the intention is the same, the same end is willed and sought. And the means used do not justify the end in one case if not the other, nor are the means used anything that *can* be justified or "made sense of" except in relation to the gracious purpose in view. Kant said, as part of his practical reason, that if we will the end we will the means.[27]
>
> A decision *not* to keep a patient alive is as morally deliberate as a decision to *end* a life.... Disagreements concern only the "operational" or practical question — who does what under which circumstances?[28]

Traditional Roman Catholic voices adamantly maintain a clear moral distinction between "the direct killing of innocent life" and the ceasing or withholding of treatment (which they insist is *not* a form of euthanasia). A number of noted Protestant thinkers concur. Karl Barth and Dietrich Bonhoeffer, for example, contend that any direct action to kill the patient is a usurpation of God's right to define the limits of life and, as such, is morally comparable to murder.

Paul Ramsey counters Fletcher's argument. The only real

form of indirect euthanasia, he insists, is the use of pain-relieving drugs which may also have the foreseen result of shortening the patient's life. This is morally permissable under the principle of double effect (see Chapter Two). The doctor's intention is to ease the patient's pain, not to kill him. That the drugs may hasten his death (and of this we are never quite certain) is an unintended even though foreseen possibility. Further, Ramsey argues, ceasing or withholding treatment is a significantly different kind of moral choice than directly killing:

> In omission no human agent causes the patient's death, directly or indirectly. He dies his own death from causes that it is no longer merciful or reasonable to fight by means of possible medical interventions. Indeed . . . we cease doing what was once called for and begin to do precisely what is called for now. We attend and company with him in this, his very own dying, rendering it as comfortable and dignified as possible.[29]

Is there then a significant moral distinction between omission of treatment and directly causing the patient's death? There is, in my judgment, a difference more significant than Fletcher sees and less clear than Ramsey and others believe. Fletcher is right that the deliberate omission of treatment *is* euthanasia of an indirect or passive sort. For both direct and indirect euthanasia the doctor's intention is the same (he wants the patient for his own good to die) , and the consequences of the action or inaction are the same (the patient dies) . Others are right in insisting that the means which are used are of considerable moral significance— whether the patient dies by omission or by our commission. But the significance of the different means is neither clear-cut nor absolute.

To argue that by ceasing or withholding life-sustaining treatment we are thereby leaving the patient's outcome in the hands of God is dubious theological reasoning. In any event we cannot avoid "playing God" if by that we mean making life-and-death decisions and taking responsibility for them. The decision to refrain from treatment is a decision for the patient's earlier death; even though the disease kills him, by our decisions that disease could have been kept at bay longer. To argue that *God* sets the time of the patient's terminus when we omit treatment but that *we* set that time if we actively administer death presupposes an untenable understanding of how God works in human life. It presupposes a deity who works through physical causation rather than one who works through persuasion and influence. It assumes a mechanistic rather than a personalistic model in understanding God's activity, and if we opt for the former we would be consistent by refusing to intervene medically in *any* disease at *any* point. Rather, in both acts of omission and commission we ought to attempt to enact our care for the patient in personal response to our perception of God's caring for him.

Nevertheless, there are reasons for *preferring* indirect methods to direct euthanasia, without excluding the latter on principle. The first reason is one of practical morality. The trust between physicians and their patients is perhaps better protected if the patient knows that his doctor would choose direct euthanasia only as the last resort in a tragic situation. In short, we want our doctors to be strongly but not absolutely biased in favor of sustaining life. We want them strongly but not absolutely biased against the direct killing of human life.

Furthermore, the preference for indirect over direct euthanasia whenever the situation warrants the choice simply reminds us that there are limits to our human judgments. Regardless of the sameness in both intentions and consequences, we do feel differently about allowing the sufferer to die than about killing him. The inchoate awesomeness which we feel more keenly in the direct act of taking life rightly reminds us of the pro-life bias to which we are Christianly and humanly committed. Yet, even more it is in a pro-*personal*-life bias. Hence, in spite of our reluctance to resort to direct euthanasia except as the last and person-affirming resort, we must hold it open as an option. There is, in the final analysis, an important difference between prolonging meaningful human life and prolonging the death process.

The Options: III. "Drinking the Hemlock"

While Socrates drank the hemlock because he was condemned by the civil authorities, history is replete with examples of and debates about other forms of "hemlock" for another kind of condemnation: incurable suffering.[30] Euthanasia, literally a "good death," is frequently advocated for two types of situations. One is voluntary. Here the terminally-ill patient consciously makes the choice for relief from a slower and intolerably pain-filled death. The other is involuntary. Here, for example, is the accident victim, permanently unconscious and vegetable-like because of a shattered cerebral cortex, and his family and the health care team face a decision.

I have already suggested that in some situations direct euthanasia may be a morally responsible last resort. The issue, however, is momentous and complex, and this brief treatment risks gross oversimplification. Yet at least we can raise the major objections and indicate the directions of possible response.[31]

It is said that euthanasia is a direct attack upon the Christian and humanist affirmation of the sanctity of human life. Euthanasia not only wrongly deprives the individual of life, but also its public sanction would have grave social consequences in a multitude of ways. We have dealt with these same issues at somewhat greater length in the abortion question, and here a similar response is warranted. While euthanasia, like abortion, may in certain situations be a responsible decision, it would always be undertaken with a heavy heart. Our awareness of the tragic ambiguities in such decisions testifies to life's preciousness. Indeed, the psychic pain for family and friends would usually be far greater in deciding to terminate the post-personal life of a comatose one than in intervening in the pre-personal life of a fetus. Unlike the abortion, the act of euthanasia involves established relationships and webs of personal ties and memories. Yet, it is personal life which God and we value above biological existence, and the insistence upon the continuance of life which tortures and degrades the personal can be a far greater threat to society and to human values than is its deliberate ending.

It is said that if euthanasia is voluntary it is suicide and if involuntary it is murder. But when suicide is wrong, it is wrong because the person has taken his life solely on his own judgment, perhaps in a mood of despair and hostility, and avoiding and evading human responsibilities which yet lie before him. In suicide, death for medical reasons is not immanent. Surely, both in motives and in situation suicide is morally distinguishable from voluntary euthanasia. What of murder? Murder is wrong not simply because it is the premeditated killing of human life but also because it is the malicious and unjustified killing of human life. Involuntary euthanasia is premeditated killing. But its motives, its purposes, and its consequences are all aimed at mercy and not at malice.

It is said that suffering may be ennobling and a means of

God's grace. It is true, it may be and often is. But redemptive suffering is *meaningful* pain, not the mindless and dehumanizing pain of certain cancer patients whose choice is either that or drugged unconsciousness. If it is difficult to see the redemptive dimension in such a case, it is also difficult to see it in most instances of the smashed cortex victim whose body lingers on for weeks, months, or even years. Even though many persons make a profound and voluntary religious affirmation through suffering, this cannot justify our forcing others to suffer against their will.

It is said that euthanasia might be chosen impulsively by the conscious patient or for unworthy motives by the family of an unconscious one. Both, indeed, are possible, but careful procedures can mitigate against abuses.[32] Procedures can require that there be a time lag between decision and enactment sufficient for the patient to reconsider and change his mind. Further, the family decision ought to be made within the community of vital concern — in consultation with the doctors, attending nurses, and clergy. Beyond these safeguards (as Joseph Fletcher has rightly minded us) "what reply is needed other than *abusus non tollit usum*, the abuse of a thing does not rule out its use." [33]

It is said that we ought not raise euthanasia as a matter for public debate. We should simply leave such matters to the doctors. But with what right do we place this burden of decision upon the doctor or by what right could he alone make it?

It is said that euthanasia would foreclose the unexpected recovery or the use of the suddenly-appearing new cure. Indeed it would — if recovery were possible or if the cure were to appear. We cannot say with certainty that mistakes would not be made. But there is reasonable certainty in the alternative: the certainty that many more persons are being condemned to ignoble and intolerable pain, that many families are being fractured by the prolonged vegetation of the irretrievably comatose one, that immense medical resources are being denied those who do have hope. Decisions must be made carefully, case by case.

It is said that euthanasia is a direct affront to God's lordship over human life. Once again, however, this argument betrays a puppetmaster notion of the manner of God's action as well as an unholy identification of God's will with the prolonging of bodily existence regardless of its personal capacity. In Christian faith we live in the tension between reverent gratitude for the goodness of life, on the one hand, and, on the other, the conviction that death is not the final enemy. If we can contemplate the precarious possibility that in *some* cases killing may be an act of merciful love and an expression of God's humanizing intentions for life, then we are resting neither in a life worship which is blind to life's quality nor in a death fear which is blind to transcendent hope.

Attention to general rules is important in Christian ethics. "Do not kill innocent human life" is an immensely important rule. But, if and when those medical situations arise in which the mere omission of treatment will not suffice, and *if* there is no other human way to benefit the dying one, then "it is better to act so as to kill than to omit to act and therefore torture." [34] Christian action is informed by abstract truths, but in the final analysis it must be bound to the concrete needs of the neighbor. In a chapel talk at Union Theological Seminary some years ago, Reinhold Niebuhr spoke in reference to the Dr. Herman Sanders euthanasia trial. Niebuhr said that laws against mercy killing might be a good thing in order to emphasize the sanctity of human life and to accent the crucial importance of the issues surrounding its protection. But, he added, it may be even better to have physicians who know when the law has ceased to be a moral thing, who know when the law has become an instrument of evil which demands unnecessary and prolonged suffering. [35]

Death, the Law, and Public Policy

The Sanders trial of 1950 still occupies pages of comment in the literature on medical ethics for the basic legal and public policy questions surrounding the prolonging of the dying patient have not been resolved. Dr. Sanders was tried for injecting air into the veins of his cancer-stricken patient, a deed to which he readily confessed. The nurse in attendance testified that the patient was still gasping when the physician injected the air, yet the jury of laypeople acquitted him on the grounds of his motive of mercy. (The medical society, however, refused to recognize Sanders' license to practice for several years.) The legal and policy questions surrounding death have become considerably more complicated since the Sanders trial, and the whole subject promises to become still more involved with the predictable quantum leap in medical technology in the last quarter of this century.

In American law there is no unclarity about direct euthanasia. It is first-degree murder even though the actor's intention is merciful. But, as legal scholar George P. Fletcher notes, a gap exists between theory and practice. Though the law itself remains severe and uncompromising, the people who administer the law may be otherwise. "There is no case in the Anglo-American tradition in which a doctor has been convicted of murder or manslaughter for having killed to end the suffering of his patient." [36]

Even so, a moral urgency exists for legislation which will sanction and carefully regulate euthanasia. It is not a choice which great multitudes will or even should make, but it is an option which ought to be available for those whose situations might make the act an affirmation of humanity in dying.

Numerically, the far greater numbers of problems arise with the ceasing or withholding of life-prolonging treatment. Here the law is in considerable confusion. For one thing, doctors presently are in position to shape their own law in dealing with these situations.[37] As yet there have been no convictions in American law for a physician's failure to provide treatment which might have prolonged life. Legally it is clear that there is always potential liability here, but the law thus far has always been interpreted so that everything hinges upon the special relationship existing between a particular doctor and a particular patient. In addition, while acts of commission (e.g., injecting air into the veins) are clear-cut, acts of omission are more flexibly interpreted. Even though turning off a respirator requires a physical act, it is generally treated as an act of omission, and not all omissions in medical practice are illegal. The net result in present law is this:

> The doctor's duty to prolong life is a function of his relationship with his patient, and, in the typical case, that relationship devolves into the patient's expectations of the treatment he will receive. Those expectations, in turn, are a function of the practices prevailing in the community at the time. And on what do those practices depend?... It all depends on *what doctors customarily do*.[38]

Usually, court-interpreted law is no more precise than that.

Some are willing to live with this imprecise state of affairs as the best workable solution. But others disagree. In the early seventies the state of Kansas took the first step in the Anglo-

American legal world to enact a definition of death into statute
law. Significantly, it makes either "the absence of spontaneous
respiratory and cardiac function" or "the absence of spontaneous
brain function" the medical-legal indication of death.[39] Ian
McColl Kennedy, a British legal scholar, holds that such laws
are undesirable. By legitimating brain death such a law biases
medical practice in the direction of transplant surgery at the
risk of proper care for the dying individual who is a prospective
organ donor. Furthermore, such a law defines the limits of the
physician's duty to the patient — an overly-rigid solution in the
face of constantly changing medical technology. These matters,
argues Kennedy, should be "developed by the courts with the
cooperation of the medical profession." [40]

In defense of the Kansas statute, Don Harper Mills, an American lawyer-physician, praises the recognition of brain death as
clarifying the murky legal situation.[41] This definition in turn
clarifies the legal uncertainty which presently plagues doctors
when they must decide whether to avoid resuscitation attempts
or discontinue artificial maintenance of a patient. To leave such
matters to the courts in this country, maintains Mills, is to leave
things in confusion since each court jurisdiction makes its own
decisions. Not only would uniform statute law immensely clarify
the present situation, it also would give recognition to the conviction that in such crucial matters as the definition of death
the *public* interest is at stake, not simply that of the medical
profession.

In addition to affecting the doctor's responsibilities, legal
unclarity also surrounds the patient's rights. Does a patient have
a legal right to choose an earlier death by refusing heroic medical
treatment? At present no American court has ever successfully
ordered a legally competent adult without dependent children to
undergo medical treatment even when refusal would almost certainly lead to death.[42] The sticky problems come in interpreting
this right of refusal.[43] Some cases have centered upon the question of consent: was this individual legally competent when
requesting no further extraordinary medical treatment? Many
other cases, however, have turned upon the question of who has
the final right to decide. Can the family legally request the cessation of heroic treatment for a permanently comatose patient?
Can a doctor force a legally-competent patient to continue receiving heroic treatment? If both doctor and patient agree upon

discontinuing extraordinary medical measures, can family members legally insist upon them anyway? The legal waters are muddy at these points.

Some continue to argue that we ought not have a public policy at all on the matter of the patient's right to die. In actual practice we do have a functioning policy — that the individual doctor (sometimes after consultation with others) ought to decide what is in the best interests of this particular patient. But this is a poor policy. It is unfair to the doctor. Physicians frequently carry excessively heavy moral burdens in this regard, and they do so conscientiously. Some families willingly thrust the burden onto the doctor, but even if he is willing to shoulder it he should not have to be its primary bearer. It is a poor policy because it is unfair to the patient. All too often there are serious differences between what the doctor thinks are in the patient's interests and what the patient himself believes. Robert M. Veatch points out two reasons for this.[44] One is that physicians as a group tend to have an unusually high anxiety about death. "This may be in part because individuals with a high fear of death choose to enter a 'death conquering' profession and in part because of socialization after one enters the profession." [45] Another reason is that some doctors appear to affirm what they take to be a special professional norm: life must be prolonged at whatever cost. As a net result, the doctor with the best of intentions frequently violates the patient's freedom to decide about the manner of his own death. The adult patient is treated as a child.

One step toward a more shared decision-making process is "the thanatology committee" which some hospitals have established. Here non-physician members of the health care team are drawn into the consultation process with the doctors, patients, and families. Some such committees have proved extremely useful and have enjoyed good physician support. In other instances, however, they have been dominated by physicians themselves, a process which simply reinforces the misconception that doctors as a group have special rights and duties in making these decisions about the manner of one's dying.[46]

Beyond committee attempts at broadening the decision-making process, we need carefully framed and universally accepted legal policy in our society. By the early 1970s laws for this purpose had been unsuccessfully proposed in at least two states. Hopefully, more laws will be attempted and will succeed. They should clarify the rights of the patient to refuse treatment and insist that those rights be made known to him. When he is beyond the power to decide, the law should stipulate the line of authority for these decisions in the patient's family (or, in absence of a family, in a court-appointed representative to protect the patient's interests). Our present unstated but operational policy of leaving the final verdict in the hands of physicians is neither fair to them nor to their patients.[47]

Even now there are urgent needs for clear legal policies concerning the determination of death and the rights of refusing heroic treatment. Given the developments of modern medicine, however, additional longer-range policy issues will soon be thrust upon us.[48] Life-extending therapies will force us to make more conscious decisions about the allocation of resources between persons who are older and those who are younger. The allocation of medical resources between the rich and the poor, presently a glaring problem, will become even more evident as we realize how true it is that the affluent live longer while the poor die sooner. When we have medicological powers to sustain life for much longer periods of time, additional complex decisions about personal rights to choose the time and manner of dying will demand resolution. While public policy cannot anticipate the medical technology of the future, it is also true that the future morality of death and dying will be even more chaotic unless we face more squarely the policy issues which are now inherent in our present medical powers.

Caring for the Dying

Caring about another person means that he does matter. It involves a profound respect for the individuality and otherness of this human companion. Caring means that we will try to relate to the other in ways that will help him to actualize himself. Caring about the dying person means all of this — even self-actualization, for surely the dying of a good death can be part of life's meaning and not simply its terminus.

Caring means being truthful with the dying person. Voluminous discussions of truth-telling in the literature of medical ethics point out the related problems. Can we be sure the patient really wants to know the seriousness of his condition? Will knowledge of its gravity condemn him to a needlessly despondent dying?

Can the doctor, though pessimistic about the prognosis, really be certain of his medical judgment? And if he is mistaken, will the physician have damaged the patient's will to live?

Undoubtedly there are those times of genuine medical uncertainty when withholding the prognostic guesses may be warranted. More frequently, however, the medical picture is reasonably clear. In those cases, our attempts to withhold or distort information are more often based upon our own self-protecting and death-avoiding instincts than upon a realistic assessment of the patient's ability and need to cope with the facts. Research points up disparities between those who attend the patients and the patients themselves. "According to one study, for instance, only *twelve percent of physicians* claimed that they 'usually' follow the policy of telling cancer patients of their diagnosis, while another study revealed that *98.5 percent of patients* being examined in the 'Cancer Detection Center' of a hospital claimed they wanted to be told." [49] Secrecy, distortion, and paternalism will inevitably twist and distort the relationships between the patient and the physician and family. Deliberate withholding of information about his condition may well be a theft of what is rightly his.[50] If the patient is to realize his fullest possible humanity even in his dying, he must be able to know *that* he is dying and be able to respond to that fact. Only then can he prepare for his death, share the last feelings he wants and needs to share, and join responsibly to the extent of his ability in plans for the changes his death will mean for the living.

Even more fundamentally, however, caring means *being* truthful with the patient, and this is far more complex than merely "telling the facts." Speaking the truth is only part of being the truth to the other, being in that kind of relationship which affirms and nourishes his divinely-intended humanity. In this deeper sense, truth is served neither by tissues of fabrication *nor* by bludgeoning the patient with cold objective facts. Responsible speaking of the truth to the dying one takes place in a relationship of deep caring, of helping the other to know he is not forsaken or abandoned. It takes place in a relationship which helps the other realize his personhood even in (and perhaps especially in) his dying. As James T. Laney aptly says, "Truth is responsibly uttered when it assists one to come to terms with death and yet at the same time 'win' his life." [51]

Caring involves a covenant of faithfulness with the dying

person, "companying with him" in the process.[52] The Apostle
Paul describes the "sting of death" as sin. Sin always involves
alienation, and the sting which dying persons so frequently seem
to experience is being left to suffer in loneliness, being deserted
in their dying, being unaccompanied on their journey.

Sometimes they experience the desertion physically. A physician comments:

> Thus we have the spectacle of the dying patient who is receiving more than his share of medical technological help and less
> than his share of human attention. In earlier periods when
> doctors could do less medically for their patients, they felt
> obliged to be present to be of comfort during death; now,
> when medicine has more to offer, doctors appease their super-
> egos by writing orders for a variety of life-prolonging measures
> and leave the patient to die without personal attention.[53]

Oliver Wendell Holmes reportedly said to a doctor, "Don't just
do something, stand there!" Medical personnel need to remember
his advice. Frequently, even in medical literature, the dying person is termed "a failure." If he is that, he will be abandoned
(albeit left surrounded by respirators, pumps, intravenous tubes,
and drainage apparatus) in favor of those patients with whom
the physician can "succeed." Indeed, studies indicate that nurses
tend to respond more slowly to the call lights of the terminally
ill.

Physical desertion of the dying one usually is intertwined with
the manner in which we have institutionalized the dying process.
Over two-thirds of our society's deaths now occur in hospitals
and nursing homes, when in physicians' judgments many of these
patients could be at home among family, friends, and familiar
surroundings. Perhaps "Get Dying Back into the Home" would
make an acceptable bumper sticker, but the systemic change
would be difficult. Paul Ramsey is undoubtedly right in saying
that if such change were brought about the clergy would have
on their hands numerous distraught relatives, "but for once they
would be shattered by confrontation with reality, by the claims of
the dying not to be deserted, not to be pushed from the circle
that specially owes them love and care, not to be denied human
presence with them." [54]

For those patients for whom institutionalization is necessary in
their dying, surely more places like the remarkable St. Chris-

topher's Hospice, London, could be developed.[55] This is a hospital for the dying. The patient who goes there knows exactly that. But it is a place where death is faced realistically within a remarkable context of human warmth from both families and staff. Here are to be found plenty of human touching, wine and ale, and a deep conviction of God's care which continues to be "made flesh." At St. Christopher's there is a remarkable lack of medical apparatus; even nasal tubes and intravenous feeding are rejected. All feeding is done by human hands, and even if the patient does not get enough physical nourishment he gets what is more important — the personal nourishment of one who cares enough to sit on his bed several hours each day.

Sometimes the desertion of the dying one is not so much physical and institutional as it is psychological and spiritual. Those who company with the patient are unwilling to engage in double-talk, yet not knowing how to speak the truth in anything but harsh bluntness they retreat into silence or join the great cultural denial of death with condescending cheeriness.[56] Thus the patient is psychologically and spiritually unaccompanied in what Dr. Elisabeth Kübler-Ross has described as the stages of the dying process: denial and isolation, anger, bargaining, depression, and acceptance.[57] Death is not only a physical process; unless it comes suddenly it is also an emotional-spiritual process in which the covenant of caring plays a profound role.

In the final analysis, our attitudes about death and dying profoundly affect our attitudes about life and living. Christians are called to celebrate and treasure personal life without at the same time slipping into a biological idolatry which fearfully demands life's continuance at any price. By coming to grips with the inevitability of our own deaths we might be able to resist "cadaverizing life." We might rather be able to consecrate life and hence be authentically available to the needs of the dying one.[58] Some forms of death are, indeed, brutal and dehumanizing. But death itself is not the final enemy for those who somehow are convinced that whether we live or whether we die we are the Lord's.

CHAPTER SEVEN

Organ Transplants:
Their Human
Dimensions

Cases

A 43-year-old high school teacher was so afflicted by heart disease that he had to give up teaching. At the time he entered the hospital, he was so weak he could not feed himself and needed the constant care of nurses. After receiving a heart transplant from a human donor he was able to return to his work. He has recently painted his house, he rides a bicycle regularly, and he and his wife are planning to adopt a baby girl.[1]

Jerry Strunk, confined to a state mental hospital in Kentucky, was judged by physicians to be the best potential kidney donor for his brother. Although an adult, Strunk was mentally incompetent to give a valid consent for the donation. While the mother of the two young men favored the operation and requested that the court authorize it, Jerry's state-appointed guardian objected. A lower court decision, later upheld by the Kentucky Court of Appeals, approved the transplant saying that Jerry's well-being "would be jeopardized more severely by the loss of his brother than the removal of the kidney." [2]

Two years after the removal of one cancerous breast, Mrs. Blake developed serious kidney disease. One kidney was removed for malignancy. A year later the other kidney became dysfunctional and was removed, but no cancer was found. Kept on dialysis, the patient and her family raised the question of a transplant. While her brother was willing, indeed anxious, to donate a kidney to Mrs. Blake, the medical staff were not eager to accept his offer. They knew that post-transplant patients receiving those drugs (immunosuppressives) which combat the body's attempt to reject the new organ are statistically more likely to develop malignancies than is the normal person. And Mrs. Blake's malignancy history was not good. On the other hand, a cadaver kidney would not offer her as great a chance for success as one from her brother.[3]

The Development of Organ Transplants

The history of organ transplants is both brief and long, depending upon one's frame of reference.[4] Interest in transplant possibilities and rudimentary experiments are ancient. Greek mythology pictures Medea arranging a transplant of blood between Jason and his father, and records suggest that skin was grafted from one part of a person's body to another as early as 600 B.C. in India. Successful human tissue transplantation from one person to another, however, awaited the seventeenth century. The first transplant textbook is probably an eighty-page pamphlet on blood transfusion published in Bologna, Italy, in 1668. Indeed, blood transfusion "represents the greatest and most successful transplantation of tissue." [5] Heterografts (transplantation of the tissue of one species into an individual of another species) were performed prior to World War I in Europe, with kidney donors for human beings sought from among rabbits, goats, pigs, and primates. Homografts (transplantation between individuals of the same species) began in human beings in the 1920s with skin transplants between identical twins.

The intense interest and public discussion of the complex moral questions surrounding such procedures, however, awaited the 1950s with the onset of kidney transplants. In 1951 Dr. David Hume of Boston did the first modern kidney transplant, followed by a number of similar experiments all using cadaver organs. The longest survivor lived six months. A major medical and moral decision came in 1954 when Hume's Boston colleagues Dr. Joseph Murray and Dr. John Merrill performed the first living-donor renal transplant. In this case Richard Herrick received a kidney from his twin brother, later married, became a father, and died eight years after the operation from a heart attack apparently related to his original kidney disease.

With rare exceptions, kidney transplants throughout the 1950s had poor results, largely because of the strong tendency of the recipient's body to reject the foreign organ. By March 1961, however, the first powerful immunosuppressive drug, azathioprine, was ready for use on a transplant patient. Its discovery led to a dramatic improvement in transplant results and consequently a sharp rise in the number of renal transplants attempted.

The growth of immunosuppressive therapy paved the way for the first human heart transplant by South Africa's Dr. Christiaan Barnard on December 3, 1967. (Four years earlier a Mississippi surgeon, Dr. James Hardy, had unsuccessfully attempted a heterograft using a chimpanzee's heart in a sixty-eight-year-old man. The widespread feelings that Hardy had transgressed moral limits in that case was a large factor in discouraging further cardiac transplants attempts for several years.) Barnard's patient Louis Washkansky lived only about two weeks with Denise Darvall's heart, but that was long enough to prove the feasibility of the procedure and to arouse intense world-wide interest and debate. Within weeks several other heart transplants were performed, and the following year saw almost a hundred. The number of attempts rather quickly subsided, however. Even though by the early 1970s a number of heart recipients had lived several years, the much larger number who had succumbed to rejection problems had somewhat sobered the earlier enthusiasm.

Successful organ transplants depend in no small measure upon successful immunosuppressive therapy following the surgery. Most severe rejection crises occur within four months, and delicate medical decisions must strike the balance between enough of the drugs to prevent organ rejection but not so much that the patient cannot ward off other infections. To complicate matters, some of the drugs have other unpredicted side effects; postoperative psychoses, for example, have been linked to certain immunosuppressants used in cardiac transplants. However, new drugs are now appearing plus techniques which may change the cell surfaces in the donated organs so that they will not trigger rejection mechanisms. Up to this moment the high risk of rejection has posed some of the difficult moral problems with transplants. If (as experts predict) the rejection barrier is broken, some of the moral issues will shift; but then we shall face moral problems at least as difficult — stemming from the virtual certainty of success.

The "Just" Organ Transplant

As we turn to the moral dimensions of organ transplants, I propose that we draw upon an important framework in the history of Christian and Western ethics: that of the "just war." [6] While this analogy may seem odd, there are, I believe, persuasive reasons for it. If the wisdom of past centuries in our moral tradition can shed any light upon apparently new dilemmas in the present, surely it is well to draw upon those sources. And the just war tradition is "that most uninterrupted, longest-continuing study of *moral decision-making* known in the Western world." [7]

Further, in both instances we are dealing with the controlled uses of regrettable violence. In spite of its therapeutic intent surgery is always violent, and transplant surgery usually involves major violence to the body. The just war theory has tried to deal with the ambiguity which violence always involves: the need for action and the need for restraint upon that action. It steers a course between the pacifist position (no violent warfare is ever morally admissible) and the holy crusade (since God is on our side and we are battling the devil, anything goes). The ethics of organ transplants similarly must be forged in that ambiguous middle ground between, on the one side, the position that while organ transplants may be technically feasible they are never morally justifiable, and, on the other side, the contention that whenever transplants are technically feasible they can be performed without any moral qualms. Put another way, in organ transplants as in war we are concerned about "the morality of means" as well as "the morality of ends." Not only *what* we are attempting to achieve needs moral scrutiny, but *how* we intend to do it as well.

The just war theory, like virtually every other moral theory, has been twisted and misused. For that reason some people have written it off as useless at best or as inherently inimical at worst. Yet, if the Indochina tragedy has taught our society anything, it should have taught us that precisely the issues raised by the just war theory must be faced openly in any contemplated violence.

Organ Transplants: Their Human Dimensions

Every use of violence is interlaced with the tragic. St. Augustine, who gave this theory early formulation sixteen centuries ago, was keenly aware of this:

> Let every one, then, who thinks with pain on all these great evils, so horrible, so ruthless, acknowledge that this is misery. And if any one either endures or thinks of them without mental pain, this is a more miserable plight still, for he thinks himself happy because he has lost all human feeling.[8]

Though Augustine's words clearly apply to warfare, they seem a gross overstatement if applied to organ transplants! Yet the words might strangely apply here, too, for anyone who contemplates these procedures without feeling the pain of moral ambiguity has lost feeling for the *human* dimensions of organ transplants.

The Last Resort

Thus, if the parallelism is appropriate, each of the key questions raised by the theory of the just war ought also to be raised about organ transplants. The first is this: is it the last resort? If war is ever to have moral justification, it cannot be used before all other reasonable means have been tried and failed.

In 1968 the Judicial Council of the American Medical Association proposed a set of guidelines for physicians in organ transplantation. While that statement unfortunately omits several issues which the just war framework does raise, the A.M.A. norms are appropriately clear on several others, including the last resort. "Transplantation of body organs should be undertaken only after careful evaluation of the availability and effectiveness of other possible therapy." [9] Organ transplants are hardly something to rush into. They are radical therapy, and few physicians would recommend (nor should they recommend) a transplant procedure if anything less violent held reasonable promise of benefitting the patient.

The Just Intent

If military force is ever justifiable, it is for defensive and never aggressive purposes. This second rule has its parallel in the physician's intention toward the patient. His intention must be defensive — to defend this particular patient's welfare. His *pri-*

mary intent is not to advance the state of medical knowledge about transplants (in which case the patient would be used, probably without his awareness, primarily as a means to an unknown future good).

Obviously, there is a problem here. Experimental and therapeutic procedures often do not fall into two neat categories. Medical realities point to much more of a continuum. Corneal transplants and blood transfusions long have been established as reliable therapy. Renal transplants are now considered much more therapeutic and considerably less experimental than they were just a few years ago. Heart transplants, while they can provide great therapeutic benefit where they succeed, are still very experimental as are most of the less dramatic transplant procedures such as lungs, nerves, stomachs, intestines, ovaries, livers, and endocrine glands.

Nevertheless, guinea pigs and chimpanzees will never completely suffice as subjects for perfecting human surgery. Somewhere along the line there must be human guinea pigs for whom the transplant attempt is frankly experimental and for whom therapeutic benefit is little assured. Such procedures may well be responsible if there is no other hope. But the covenant of partnership also means that the patient has utter assurance that he will not be used without his free and informed consent primarily as a means to medical progress. There is, after all, a warning in the grim humor of the sign erected along a busy highway shortly after the first heart transplant: "Drive Carefully — Christiaan Barnard Is Watching You." [10] The A.M.A. Guidelines rightly recognize the importance of the just intent: "The physician's interest in advancing scientific knowledge must always be secondary to his primary concern for the patient." [11]

The Just Declaration

If the use of military force is ever morally justified, there must also be an open declaration of the nation's intent made by the civil authorities who bear such responsibility. Sneak attacks are immoral. This rule, following naturally from the previous one, raises the parallel question for organ transplants: is there free and informed consent given by the persons involved?

In Chapter Four we examined the issues of consent in reference to experimentation on human subjects. The same considerations regarding free and informed consent apply to organ transplant situations, even where the procedure is considered beyond the experimental stage. In addition, however, organ transplants raise some particular issues which we can see in relation to the several types of "consenters" who may be involved.

The living donor (in the case of paired organs) poses several subtle consent problems. Transplant surgeons would far prefer to do without living donors; no one relishes the thought of removing a healthy organ from a person's body. But cadaver kidneys are in short supply, and the success rate with the living related donor is still significantly higher.

Free and informed consent means that the potential donor be made aware of both physical and psychological risks. The physical risks begin with the donation surgery itself, and while statistically the hazard is very low it cannot be overlooked. After return to normal life the donor's physical risks simply come from the fact that now he has one kidney instead of two. While one is sufficient to clear the blood's waste products, if accident or disease strikes that kidney then the donor himself becomes a transplant candidate.

Psychological hazards are more elusive. Living donors usually come from the patient's own family both because of tissue matching and because of the responsibility felt for one's blood relative. (Indeed, some transplant centers will not use unrelated living donors at all.) But how free is free consent given by a relative? Unfortunately, families occasionally do put heavy pressure upon one of their members to "volunteer," and the one thus drafted can feel immense guilt if he refuses such induction.

How informed is informed consent? It is impossible to answer with precision. The law assumes that competent adults may donate paired organs but that since minors are incapable of giving valid consent written permission of parents or guardians is required. Yet the moral problem is not resolved by the legal answer. What of the seven-year-old New Haven girl who gave a kidney to save her twin sister? At that age, even though she felt her choice was free, could it have been sufficiently informed to be meaningfully free? The court gave an advisory opinion in the affirmative.[12] In several other cases, advisory opinions of the courts have indicated that (in addition to parental consent, grave medical necessity, and voluntary consent by the healthy sibling) there must be "psychiatric testimony that the operation was necessary for the continued good health and future well-being of the *donor*."[13] The situation of minor twins is both psychologically and morally complex. Psychologically, there is always the danger that parents might not treat each twin as an individual personality; the temptation to think of the two as one is subtle.

Even though it may be legally permissible, *ought* anyone give permission for a minor, particularly those on the younger edge of the age of understanding, to be an organ donor? After all, the donor child can hardly be aware of the full implications of the risk factors. Moral generalizations here are difficult at best. At the very least we ought to be unusually cautious about giving permission on behalf of others and about making judgments about their future psychological and spiritual well-being.

In dealing with donors of any age, physicians will wisely pay as much attention to the psychological factors as to the physical. Dr. Henry K. Beecher reports a typical practice: "The donor is told that if he does not want to give a kidney no one will know, for the physician will state that the donor is unsuitable. In these circumstances about three of five donors are found to be genuine volunteers."[14] Beecher's estimate, we should note, also suggests that about *40 percent* of those persons contemplating donation are *not* genuine volunteers — a rather significant portion. Hence, the uncertainty among doctors concerning the use of family donors is quite understandable.[15] Some deliberately discourage them, fearing involuntary consent and family blackmail. Others are more persuaded by the more promising results for the recipient. In any event *primum non nocere*, "first of all, do no harm," is a deeply-ingrained medical norm with which physicians wrestle in dealing with volunteers, for the major surgery required of the organ donor affords him no physical benefit whatever, only physical loss.

Thus far I have emphasized the obligations of others to respect the rights and needs of the potential donor. But how do we perceive the obligations of the potential donor himself? Different emphases come from different religious streams on this issue.[16] While the Roman Catholic Church has not declared an official position on organ donation, its statements and discussions have centered around "the principle of totality," and this has given a decidedly cautious cast to organ donation. The principle maintains that the part exists for the sake of the whole. Conservatively interpreted this would mean that self-mutilation is justifiable if it is for the sake of *one's own* total well-being, but only for that reason. Pope Pius XI put it this way in 1930: individuals "are not free to destroy or mutilate their members, or in any other way render themselves unfit for their natural functions, except when no other provision can be made for the good of the whole body." [17] At that time Pius XI was primarily concerned about eugenic sterilization, and in reiterating the principle of totality Pius XII used it to condemn the Nazi abuses in human experimentation. Nevertheless, a conservative interpretation of the principle will not allow self-mutilation (including organ donation) for the sake of one's neighbor.

Many contemporary Catholic moralists, however, argue that in two ways the church can approve of organ donation. One is to expand the principle of totality beyond a sheer physical interpretation to include the person's spiritual totality. Father Martin Nolan points out that Pius XII himself opened the door for this interpretation in saying, "To the subordination however of the particular organs to the organism and its own finality, one must add the subordination of the organism to the spiritual finality of the person himself." [18] Nolan comments that while the church's teaching does not allow one to risk serious maiming or death, yet, "If the total good of the whole person, achieved in self-gift, is considered, vast new possibilities arise. Experimentation for the good of another becomes a moral possibility, perhaps at times a demand." [19] Father John J. Lynch, on the other hand, suggests that the church can approve of organ donation because even more decisive than the principle of totality (however that be interpreted) is "the law of fraternal love — whereby one may do for another whatever one may legitimately do for self." [20]

Protestant ethics has had less difficulty with organ donation. In fact, its bias has been in the direction of encouraging living donor gifts. Whereas in Catholic theology love is usually seen as a state of harmony (hence totality becomes one's personal harmony), in Protestant thought love is primarily seen as *agape*. Love of one's neighbor is to take its shape from God's free and gracious gift of himself to the world. And what can be a more gracious gift to the neighbor than one's kidney?

Paul Ramsey rightly sees the necessary tension between the two points of view. If Protestant ethics need not resort to any "sticky (psychological or spiritual) benefits theory" to affirm the possibility of organ donation, Roman Catholic thought (along with traditional Jewish ethics) reminds us of our appropriate concern for embodied existence and for the integrity of the flesh.[21] Put another way, without remembering the human right to bodily integrity and physical harmony, not only are we in danger of an unbiblical body-mind dualism but we also risk encouraging masochistic inclinations. On the other hand, without remembering the Christian claim to give ourselves in love to the one who is in need, the principles of totality and bodily integrity easily become mere masks for egocentric self-preservation.

Medically, it is clear that the removal of an organ from a living donor is of no physical benefit to that person whatever. It is only a loss. Psychologically, it is clear that situations vary immensely. The donor in one instance may receive vast satisfaction.

However, when the organ recipient has died shortly after the transplant some donors have been faced with serious psychic problems; some have brooded about causing the other's death while others have mourned the futility of their own organ loss. Morally, the central issues hinge around the degree of physical risk involved for the donor (in kidney donations statistically quite slight), the motivations for giving the organ, the health of the relationships within the family, and the reality of the donor's free and informed consent. With favorable indications on these matters, the organ donation can indeed be a gift of life, a responsible and morally-beautiful act. With unfavorable indications, it can be quite otherwise.

If the just declaration rule raises important issues about the living donor's consent, what about *the cadaver donor?* Pictures of the present availability of cadaver organs are sobering. One estimate holds that of the 100,000 or more patients dying of kidney disease in this country each year at least 8,000 could be saved by transplants; now, however, because of the lack of available organs and facilities 7,000 of the 8,000 will die.[22] Another estimates that 15,000 kidneys could be made available annually from persons dying of brain damage, but in fact the great majority of them are committed to the ground or to the flame.[23] Still another calculates that if all patients who died in hospitals as a result of brain damage were to become cadaver organ donors, there would be absolutely no shortage of either kidneys or livers, even though when heart and lung transplants become routine these organs would still be in short supply.[24]

A 1968 Gallup poll indicated that seventy percent of the American adults claim to be willing to donate an organ upon their deaths. There was little difference among members of the major religious groups in this regard, though persons of higher education tended to look upon donation more favorably.[25] Unfortunately, only a very small proportion of that seventy percent carry out their intentions by making pre-death arrangements for donations! The Uniform Anatomical Gift Act, now valid in all fifty states, provides the legal framework for this process. Private foundations (notably The Kidney Foundation) and numerous medical schools provide the machinery.

The Gift Act affirms the right of anyone who is at least eighteen years of age and mentally competent to will as a gift his body or any parts of it upon death for transplantation or research. In addition the Act provides that the next of kin cannot overrule the person's wishes (though family members may give permission for cadaver use if the person had made no formal decision before his death).

There are some important moral judgments behind the Uniform Anatomical Gift Act.[26] For one thing, the organ transaction is strictly a gift. Neither buying nor selling is involved. In this sense at least, life cannot be bought, it can only be given and received. Further, the act is uniform. It establishes a common basis for action among all of the states, an increasingly important factor in a day when organ needs and availability are being computerized and donor organs are flown to distant recipients.

Most obviously, perhaps, the Gift Act leaves the decision about organ donation in the hands of the individual (or, if he has made no decision, in the hands of the family). Neither the medical profession nor the state are given the rights of decision. Differing from this approach, a number of proposals have been made on the assumption that the more rational and efficient way to meet the need for organs is to give the medical profession permission for "routine harvesting" of usable organs in the event of any death except in those cases where the patient or the family had specifically forbidden organ removal. Israel, France, and Sweden have experimented with such laws. The state of Virginia goes part way by giving permission for organ removal without prior consent if there is not enough time to notify the family and if no one knows of any stated family objections.[27]

Greater moral wisdom lies, I believe, in the position taken by the Uniform Anatomical Gift Act. It is true that the emphasis upon voluntary giving rather than upon routine taking of organs may well insure a perpetual shortage of cadaver organs. And this is morally serious. On the other hand, the rule of organized, voluntary giving seems to recognize the danger in our developing a "spare parts" mentality about our bodies. It recognizes the problems that would be faced in their hours of grief by families who feel deeply about the body remaining intact and yet who would have to resist routine hospital procedures. It recognizes that however great the need for transplant organs, we need to be at least as concerned about how those organs are obtained. And it recognizes that in matters as personal as this, society will be better if it can rely upon voluntary giving rather than upon routine taking.[28]

Nevertheless, if this voluntary policy is to remain morally defensible in the face of the great need for cadaver organs, it must be strongly interpreted and encouraged. For one thing, the relatively young person is the most likely cadaver donor candidate, and the death of this age person frequently is a sudden tragedy for the family. If the person has not made a prior decision about donation, the family may find it difficult in such a highly emotional time.[29] To be sure, there are exceptions. Some transplant surgeons testify that in some tragic deaths — motorcycle accidents, shootings, etc. — the family will plead that the body's organs be used so that at least *some* good might come out of this.

Prior consent for donation needs persuasive advocacy also because there is much misguided resistance to the idea. Unfortunately, some of this comes from funeral directors who object that organ removal makes neat embalming difficult. And if the whole body has been willed for research the threat to this service industry is great indeed. Joseph Fletcher quotes one of the "bier barons" as saying, "With no body, there is no funeral. If there are no funerals, there are no funeral directors." [30]

Further resistance comes from certain Christians who for reasons of plain superstition or unwarranted physicalist interpretations of the resurrection of the body abhor the notion of a donor card. Surely, the church should defend the rights of those who have such convictions. It is also the church's ministry to make clear the opportunity for self-giving love at the time of our dying. When the Apostle appealed to the Roman Christians to present their bodies as a living sacrifice (Romans 12:1), he may not have been thinking of organ transplants; he certainly *did* have in mind that fundamental obligation to recapitulate God's agapaic love on behalf of the neighbor in need. Paul did know that we do not own our bodies; we are stewards who hold them in trust.

In addition to that of the organ donor, *the recipient's* free and informed consent is also crucial. Unfortunately, at times the patient's agreement is bypassed, as if narrowly medical judgments were the determining factor. Consider the difference is two statements by transplant surgeons. Dr. Keith Reemtsma says, "The risks and results of such procedures . . . should be explained. *The patient should be given the opportunity freely to decline treatment* which carries significant risks and uncertain outcome." [31] On the other hand, listen to Dr. Francis D. Moore: "If he is in full possession of his faculties, he should be given a clear picture of the hazards involved and allowed to join in the discussion. *Yet under no circumstances should the final decision be left in the hands of the patient;* he has not the education, the background nor dispassionate view necessary to make a decision in his own best self-interest." [32]

Here again we are faced with the problem of extraordinary medical treatment (see Chapter Six). As many physicians and ethicists have recognized, to say that there is no other hope does not mean that there is no other choice.[33] The refusal of a life-saving transplant may well be far different from suicide. It may be the responsible decision of a patient who has weighed the probabilities of surgical success and the quality of life which might follow. It may be the considered judgment of one who has assessed the financial and emotional costs to his family and the costs of medical resources to his society. We must reply to Dr. Moore. Certainly most patients will not understand the medical details. However, the assumption that the patient cannot and should not finally decide about his own human future as it is intertwined with the lives of others can only come from a grossly distorted perception of the doctor's professional role in this matter.

"I was a victim of chronic membranous nephritis, which culminated in end-stage renal failure, dialysis in hospitals, dialysis at home and five renal transplantations," writes Chad H. Calland, himself a physician.[34] Dr. Calland's personal experience led him to conclude that the fears and anxieties of kidney dialysis and transplant patients are well founded and not paranoid. The problem is that the nephrologist (dialysis specialist) "has devoted his attention to his patient's biochemical findings rather than to his patients," and "the transplant surgeon has minimized the morbidity and mortality of graft rejection and of immunosuppressive therapy." [35] Thus the emphasis is heavily upon curing the patient's kidney ailments rather than caring for the patient as a person. However well-intentioned this may be, it inevitably hinders a patient's free and informed decision about a transplant.

Yet, the dilemma from the doctor's viewpoint is a real one. Gerald Leach recognizes this: "The more transplant surgeons are attacked for being over-heroic, the more defensive they will feel, the more they will be limited to operating only on very sick patients and so the fewer patients will be saved." [36] The surgeon does not deliberately wait until the appendix has burst and peritonitis sets in before he operates, because it is clear to everyone that an appendectomy is reasonable therapy, not over-heroic. But organ transplants are not in the same category yet, and the surgeon is keenly aware that they will not soon become less-experimental unless more permissions are given. We are left once again with the tension between the rights of this particular patient and the wider possible benefits for patients yet to come. Both concerns are important, but the patient's right to make that final decision should remain clear and unassailed.

What about the unconscious patient? Some agree that even though the patient will die without treatment a transplant ought not be performed without his conscious consent. This, however, makes of the patient's right to consent a rigid and inflexible moral absolute which hardly serves the cause of responsible decision-making. Surely, the family has the right to decide if the patient is unconscious, and in the absence of the family the medical team must decide. While the making of life-and-death decisions on behalf of another ought never be a standard or welcome procedure, sometimes it is unavoidable.

Just Conduct: Non-combatant Immunity

The next major criterion in just war theory deals with its conduct. Three related questions are at stake. Is the immunity of non-combatants protected? Are right attitudes present? And is the rule of proportionality followed? All three remind us of important moral questions about organ transplants.

Non-combatant immunity as a moral rule of warfare says that, if the use of violence is ever to be morally justified, every possible measure must be taken to protect the innocent from becoming unwitting victims. In the case of organ transplants, the most obvious "innocent" one is the dying patient whose organ will be transplanted into another. He must be protected from being victimized by someone else's need.

In Chapter Six we examined the current debates over the redefinition of death. The desire to update death, of course, has been prompted in significant measure by the feasibility of organ transplants. The donor must be dead but not "so dead" that his organs have deteriorated beyond usefulness.

The danger comes from two directions. The prospective donor can receive either too little or too much treatment. In medical ethics discussions to date the former possibility has received greater attention. Early heart transplants at the Groote Schuur Hospital in Capetown were criticized by both surgeons and jurists on grounds that "the potential heart donors were declared dead somewhat hastily." [37] Since then the medical profession has wisely insisted that the dying patient receive all the care due to him as a person and that he not be treated simply as a donor prospect. Unless he has consciously and freely stipulated otherwise, no relaxation in care is justified by the fact that he is willing to donate his organs upon death. The A.M.A. guidelines and current procedures in major transplant centers are both clear on this point. Accepted practice insists that the death of the donor must be determined by physicians other than the transplant team. This is both compassionate and wise. If Christian compassion insists upon giving all care due to the dying patient, Christian wisdom also knows that our own driving concerns can distort our judgments.

The stickier of the two problems is that of *too much* treatment for the dying donor. Drs. Roberta and Richard Simmons give these examples:

> ... should the neurologists and transplant team be allowed to consult each other before the donor's death concerning the treatment that will benefit the organ to be donated? If the

fluid balance of the patient is neglected, as occurs sometimes with hopeless patients, the patient will die with a useless kidney. Should the transplant team be allowed to question this type of inadequate therapy? Usually what is good for the kidney will be good for the patient.[38]

Here then is the problem. Had this particular patient not been a likely donor extraordinary treatment perhaps would not have been undertaken. Knowing that he *is* a potential donor, however, the physician may try to preserve the organ, and in that process he will extend the dying process of the patient. What is good for the kidney is bad for the patient *as a person,* and vice versa. Moreover, someone is waiting who desperately needs that kidney.

Moral generalizations about these situations are not easily made. Recognizing this ambiguity, some hospitals have set the following policy: if in order to save his transplantable organs a comatose patient is sustained beyond the normal time period, financial charges stop when the patient is declared dead even though the body may be kept under treatment on the ward for an extra day or even two or three. Financially, there is some justice in this policy. How fair it may be to the emotions of the family is another question. If in their eagerness to see the organs used the family is willing to bear this additional personal strain, the practice perhaps is justifiable. Yet caution in each particular situation is warranted, lest the dying one lose all rights to die unhindered by artificial supports.

Just Conduct: Right Attitudes

The classic doctrine of the just war holds that "those who resort to violence as an act of justice should avoid vindictive anger and malicious revenge." [39] While vindictiveness and malice certainly are not the typical problems encountered in organ transplant situations, there are other attitudinal dangers that need to be avoided.

The A.M.A.'s guidelines speak to this concern in regard to physicians in two ways. First, doctors should not encourage expectations in the potential organ recipient beyond those which are reasonably justified by the circumstances. Second, realizing the newsworthy nature of transplant developments, physicians should be objective, factual, and discreet in their reports to the communications media, and whenever possible reports to the press should be delayed until scientific reports can first be made to the medical profession itself for review and evaluation.[40]

In short, physicians' attitudes should be cautious and objective about the potential results of organ transplants. It may be difficult for the organ recipient to sort out the message coming from his surgeon and the message he has absorbed through the news media. The media handling of some transplant developments undoubtedly has contributed to unrealistic expectations in patients and a general social clamor for more fantastic medical breakthroughs. Harmon Smith characterizes the scene at the time of the first heart transplant: "That unrestrained enthusiasm bordering on irresponsibility created something like a carnival atmosphere at the Groote Schuur Hospital is attested in part by the fact that at least one camera crew surreptitiously gained access to Barnard's operating theater." [41] While doctors cannot control what the press does with their statements, they can significantly influence the manner of coverage by their procedural care and their objectivity. One transplant surgeon recently told me that he always accents the negative when discussing a possible transplant with a patient; from past experience he now routinely assumes that each new patient will come with unrealistic expectations. And such expectations take their toll in human costs.

Attitudes will color the moral quality of the transplant procedure in other ways as well. Consider, for example, the situation described by Leroy Augenstein. A man who had received a kidney from an accident victim was diagnosed as needing a second transplant. He and his wife promptly moved into an apartment across the street from the hospital so that he would be available for surgery on short notice when another kidney donor appeared. After waiting for some time, however, the couple realized that something was happening to them: whenever they heard a siren they found themselves wishing that this would be an accident victim who would die in the hospital under ideal conditions for a kidney donation. "As a consequence, two very fine people began to view themselves as ghouls: they knew what was happening, and why, but were unable to stop it." [42]

The matter of right attitudes involves not only physician and organ recipient but also all others whose bearing affects the moral quality of the transplant procedure — families and friends, donors and medical support staff, press and public. In varying ways these attitudes will affect the ability of the ill person to make a free and informed decision; they will bear upon his right to privacy during and following a transplant. Such attitudes will affect the motivations and outlook of the potential donor. They will also shape the stance of the medical professional toward patient, press, and public.

Just Conduct: Proportionality

The norm of proportionality in warfare holds that the constructive results achieved by force must be at least commensurate with the evil (the violence) used to obtain those results. In other words, one simply does not destroy a village in order to save it.

In organ transplants, too, counting the cost is always an important part of the moral judgment. Is the cost to the living kidney donor likely to be outweighed by the benefit to the recipient of that kidney? What of the costs of the recipient and the patient's family? Will the quality of life that is the probable outcome of this operation be worth whatever physical, emotional, and financial prices that must be paid?

Beyond the particular transplant situation, the rule of proportionality raises an important question about the wider medical context, a question too frequently overlooked. Considering the broad range of medical needs, is the investment of skills and dollars in organ transplants proportional to the good that is achieved? More graphically, how should we spend $50,000? On one young man needing a heart transplant? On two or three children in need of kidney transplants? On a hundred children suffering from malnutrition? On five thousand persons in a genetic screening program or twenty thousand in need of inoculations? [43]

The proportionality question is a difficult one. In particular transplant decisions the answer frequently is not at all obvious, and when the question is raised to the societal level it becomes even more problematic. Many transplant surgeons and researchers claim that what has been learned from these procedures already has paid off in better care for *all* patients suffering from kidney and heart diseases. Others are less sure. In any event, it seems wise to continue work on those types of transplants which are still very experimental (e.g., heart and lung) in the hope of further sophistication and less costly procedures. But proportionality would dictate that such work be done on a relatively small scale at only a few major transplant centers in order that public resources not be drained from the more elementary and preventive medical needs.[44]

The Just End

The last great question from the classic just war tradition deals with the probability of success. Will the intended end, an increase of justice, most likely be achieved?

One rather obvious application is in *the assessment of risks* for both organ recipients and donors. We have seen some of the varied and interweaving types of risks — physical, psychological, interpersonal, and financial. In each of these we confront probabilities and not certainties, and statistical probabilities regarding physical risks constantly change with increased medical experience. For example by 1973 some transplant centers were indicating that the patient receiving a kidney from a relative had over 80 percent chance of having a functioning kidney two years after surgery, and 60 percent if the kidney came from a cadaver. With rapidly-improving techniques some physicians were indicating that a 95 percent success rate for related-donor kidneys and 80 percent for cadaver kidneys would be realized soon.

Risk assessments, however, are never confined to the juggling of medical statistics. They must always include careful assessment of the personal human factors. For example, will this man be able to cope with facial puffiness which might result from immunosuppressive therapy? Will this woman psychologically be able to cope with another person's heart inside her? Will members of the heart donor's family be able to adjust to the reality that the heart of their loved one is beating in the chest of another? Inexact as the varied judgments of risks must be, the moral quality of transplant decisions does depend upon a high probability of success.

An additional and crucially important moral calculation is part of the "just end" — *the selection of the organ recipient.* There is now, and there will be in the foreseeable future, serious competition for scarce organ resources. Only a fraction of those who could benefit by kidney transplants are now able to receive them; every major transplant center has its waiting list. In the face of such competition, the moral success of a transplant procedure hinges in some real measure upon the moral viability of the way recipients are selected.

Strictly medical judgments must be made at the outset, and these narrow the competitive field. A number of criteria must be brought into play.[45] How critical is the patient's need for the organ? Is there little reasonable hope for his survival without a transplant? Though he critically needs the organ is he sufficiently free from other medical complications so that he will likely survive the procedure? Not only does the blood type of the patient match that of the potential donor, but also is there a good "tissue match"? [46]

When organs become available for transplant, medical judgments will usually narrow but not eliminate patient competition for them. What then? Unfortunately, the ability to pay has become a factor. Transplant costs are prohibitive for most patients, even those with good private insurance, and public assistance is needed. But in recent years states have varied widely in their participation in federal programs designed for such assistance. The net result is that regional transplant centers increasingly have found themselves unable to absorb the financial strains of large unpaid bills and have had to reject patients from non-participating states who could not privately afford the expense.[47] Fortunately, new legislation effective in July 1973 greatly enlarges the scope of government assistance to kidney patients, who are by far the largest group of transplant candidates.[48] By minimizing the ability-to-pay factor for many more persons, this helps to democratize the selection process but once more increases the competition and the necessity for someone to make hard choices.

Some transplant choices have been made by selecting the patient whose surgery might prove of most value to medical science. In the more highly experimental procedures, this criterion has a certain validity, though it should not apply to more routine transplants. Its use carries with it all of the complex moral considerations surrounding any kind of human experimentation (see Chapter Four).

Two major possibilities remain: choosing on the basis of social utility and choosing by some method of random selection. The social usefulness criterion is frequently used. It seems to have much in its favor. After all, it would seem morally responsible to ask about the candidates such questions as these: who would probably contribute more to society? whose talents are most needed? who has more dependents? who probably has more useful time remaining following the transplant?

Yet, the difficulties with these social usefulness judgments are enormous.[49] Do we know with any kind of objectivity what really makes for social worth? Or what talents society will need in the future? Or whether we can successfully avoid reducing a person's transcendent worth to his social functions? We might take second thought about the social utility criterion if we listen to those who reviewed the utility-based decisions made for several years at the Seattle Artificial Kidney Center. They concluded that the selection committee's decisions looked like the bourgeoisie sparing the bourgeoisie, like the socially-respectable saving the socially-respectable. It appeared, they observed, that the Pacific Northwest is no place for a Henry David Thoreau if he has bad kidneys! [50]

What, then, of random selection? Shall we just draw straws or rely upon the principle of first-come-first-served? This may appear to be a surrender to irrationality and chance at the very time that courageous, rational, and responsible decision-making is called for. Yet, there are some compelling reasons for random choice.[51] For one, there is the psychological benefit for the rejected patient. At least he knows he was not rejected because someone had judged him less socially-useful than another candidate. There is the corresponding value of trust between patient and physician. The patient's confidence depends in no small measure upon his trust that the doctors will always treat him as a person and not simply as a social status or a social function.

In the final analysis, the method of random selection preserves something very important in personal dignity. Surely, in the normal day-by-day course of life people are rewarded with society's benefits and honors largely because of their social status and by their society's judgments of their worth. But in life-and-death decisions these precarious judgments of social worth ought to be radically relativized and even put aside. Each person's dignity ought to be respected regardless of social role, or achievement, or even promise. Surely such considerations as these in the selection process have something to do with the "just end" of an organ transplant.

The Future of Organ Transplants

Transplant technology of the last quarter of this century is unpredictable in its specifics, but a great deal of informed speculation exists.[52] Problems of tissue rejection may be largely modified if not eliminated. An International Tissue Registry for matching organs and recipients will probably come into being in the meantime. The use of cadaver organs may virtually replace that of living donors, and freezing techniques may make organ banks common. Some believe that widespread use of animal organs will be the wave of the future. Others anticipate that vastly more sophisticated synthetic organs will be the emphasis.

The brain transplant has been raised as a possibility. Some think that it is medically unlikely. Dr. Christiaan Barnard represents others, however, when he envisions the time when "a healthy brain from a dead body will be transplanted into a healthy body with a dead brain." [53] In actuality the term itself is grossly misleading. Were it to come, it should be called a "total body transplant." For hopefully obvious theological, psychological, and basically human reasons its moral feasibility should be rejected out-of-hand, regardless of any technical feasibility.

Short of that last unthinkable possibility, however, there are a host of emerging issues raised by transplant technology. Of them we shall have to raise the same kinds of questions which some persons have been raising for centuries in grappling with the limits of regrettable violence. The existence of a framework of questions supplied by the just war theory does not guarantee responsible transplant decisions any more than it has guaranteed responsible decisions about military violence. But of one thing we can be sure: irresponsible decisions will result when these questions are neglected. Certain persisting concerns about the way we choose our goals and evaluate the means used to reach them are part of our religious heritage. They can be useful in dealing with medical possibilities which our ancestors-in-faith never dreamed of.

CHAPTER EIGHT

Medical Care
for a More
Human Society

Cases

"The surgeon's behavior was routine. Bustling through rounds recently at a Manhattan teaching hospital, he ignored the questions of the young woman recovering from surgery, drew back the bedclothes and proceeded to explain her condition and the operation performed to correct it to his entourage of residents and interns. But there was nothing typical about the patient's angry reaction. She snatched the sheet out of the amazed doctor's hand and pulled it up to her chin. 'No peeking unless you answer my question,' she said. 'I'm a patient, damn it, not a case.' The surgeon finally complied." [1]

A Cornell engineering student was paralyzed for life by a tragic football injury. In addition to their personal suffering, his once comfortably affluent family has been financially devastated by the accident — $50,000 in five months and there is no end to the bills in sight. The irony is that the student's father is an insurance salesman who carried the best health policy offered by his company.[2]

A mother described the plight of her child: "Poverty is having a child with eye trouble and watching it grow worse every day, while the welfare officials send you to the private agencies, and the private agencies send you back to the welfare, and when you ask the welfare officials to refer you to this special hospital, they say they can't — and then when you say it is prejudice because you are a Negro they deny it flatly — and they shout at you: 'Name one white child we have referred there.' And when you name twenty-five they finally refer you, but it is too late. . . ." By the time her child had been seen by the specialists he had lost 80 percent of his vision. The doctors told her that they could have preserved his vision — if she had only gotten the child to them a month earlier when she first made the inquiry about the film over his eyes.[3]

A Health Care Crisis?

Less than a hundred years ago the physician carried in his head and in his hands virtually all that he needed by the standards of that day to treat his patients. His charges were about 25c for an office call (usually including medicine) and 50c to 75c for a house call. An obstretrics case brought the princely sum of five dollars. Hospital admissions were uncomplicated, and treatment within the hospital was usually handled by the single physician.

The complexity of the medical delivery system today, obviously, is vastly increased as are the costs for treatment. Consider the components of the American medical system.[4] Physicians and their supporting professionals have taken on varied forms of organization. In addition to the solo practitioner there are numerous group and clinic practices. An increasing number of "health maintenance organizations" (HMOs) guarantee the delivery of comprehensive medical care to a voluntarily-enrolled group of persons on the basis of fixed-price contracts. A host of types of public health agencies exist for purposes of service, education, and research, including medical schools and medical services for special populations (the medically-indigent, school children, the mentally ill, the military, alcoholics, etc). Beyond the public health agencies there are a plethora of voluntary medical agencies — associations for research and treatment in specific diseases, professional groups, coordinating agencies, and free clinics.

In addition to the groups of medical practitioners there are major supporting industries. Health insurance companies, which began in 1798, now provide about 85 percent of our population

with at least some coverage. The vital medical equipment industry, in the background for the consumer, illustrates the inter-
locking web of relationships through various types of federal
regulation of standards and through numerous forms of mutual
influence between the industry and associations of physicians
and hospital administrators. The pharmaceutical industry similarly is part of the whole network of research, production, and
massive influence. Finally, of course, are the hospitals, two-thirds
of them largely privately financed and a third publicly supported.
All together it is a gigantic medical-industrial complex. It is,
indeed, a system — whether it is a rational system delivering the
optimum in human medicine is another matter.

The last quarter century has brought rapid changes.[5] Prior to
World War II, the American health care system was built around
the solo practitioner. Most of the financial transactions were on
the basis of uninsured fee-for-service situations. The American
Medical Association was the virtually unchallenged voice of the
nation's physicians. The hospital of that day was primitive in its
internal organization and technology.

The post-war decades saw a shift in the center of gravity away
from the private practitioner to complex medical institutions.
According to the Health Policy Advisory Center, this shift "is
the result of three complementary forces: changes in technology,
changes in financing, and changes in the prestige structure of
the medical profession." [6] With the rapid growth in medical
sophistication and specialization doctors became more interdependent, and dependent upon the technology and personnel of hospitals as well. Rapidly growing insurance plans made
the hospitals independently viable institutions. At the same
time, however, physicians fearing a threat to their independence
resisted the very insurance schemes which would cover their own
costs. The result was that the physician became still more dependent upon the hospital, for persons needing expensive diagnostic
work and certain kinds of therapy increasingly were referred to
the hospitals where their insurance would cover at least a sizeable part of the bill. As the hospital began to replace the solo
practitioner as the center of medical practice, individual hospitals
became increasingly dependent upon medical schools and major
teaching hospitals where interns and residents, as well as large
public grants for research and complex equipment, were available. The rise of these medical empires thus has been coupled

with a decline in the power and prestige of both individual
practitioners and the A.M.A., which now counts fewer than half
of the nation's doctors as members. But the changes within the
system have not eliminated the health care crisis of which the
public is increasingly and vocally aware, a crisis centered largely
around three factors: the costs, the quality, and the accessibility
of medical care.

The costs of medical care have risen dramatically.[7] In two
decades, there was a 400 percent increase in medical expendi-
tures, from about $13 billion in 1950 to almost $70 billion in
1970. The 1960s saw an increase in the amount of the gross
national product spent on medical care from 5.3 percent to 7
percent. By the mid-seventies, the total figure could approach
$125 billion. Health care in recent years has been the fastest-
rising commodity in the cost of living. In the decade of the 1960s
the average personal medical expenditure rose from $145 annu-
ally to $324, an increase of over 150% compared to an overall
Consumer Price Index increase of 33% for the same period.
The trend in the early 1970s showed no abatement.

Hospital charges rose over twice as fast as other health care
prices. The average daily hospital charge in urban areas of well
over $100 in the early 1970s had a number of explanations. One
significant reason was the high cost of expensive new technology.
Another was the belated rise in the wages of hospital employees,
once among the most underpaid workers in the country. While
costs could be pared by more efficient management and hospital
linkage, little headway was made in this respect. Physicians,
frequently indifferent to economic considerations, continued to
dominate hospital policy-making. Competition among hospitals
in the same geographic area led to unnecessary duplication of
expensive equipment. And in spite of overcrowding and critical
shortages of beds in some places, other hospitals were under-
utilized.

The quality of medical care is a second dimension of the crisis.
The American medical system has been second to none in research and therapeutic developments. That this record does not
adequately carry over into the overall quality of health care,
however, is a source of national embarrassment. In spite of the
largest per capita expenditure on medical care and the highest
percentage of gross national product devoted to this end, the
current statistics are sobering. The United States ranks seventh

in maternal deaths resulting from childbirth, seventh in life expectancy for females, fourteenth in infant mortality, and eighteenth in life expectancy for males.[8] Effective quality control to minimize hospital errors has not been achieved. It is probable that unnecessary surgical procedures — particularly tonsillectomies, adenoidectomies, and appendectomies — have resulted in several thousands of deaths annually.[9] Beyond the specific quality problems has been the one large inescapable fact: our medical system has not placed a premium upon the practice of preventive medicine. The vast preponderance of resources are geared to the cure of disease. Relatively little is focused upon its prevention.

The distribution and accessibility of medical care is the third and related crucial issue. Paramount among the distribution problems is the cruel lack of adequate medical services for the poor and for members of racial and ethnic minorities.[10] While we have long known about the interdependence of poverty and illness — the poor are much more likely to be chronically ill and the chronically ill are much more likely to be poor — we have not fully faced up to this fact whether in the racial ghettoes and central cities of the urban North, in the shacks of the rural South, or on the Midwest reservations for the original Americans. The statistics are unmistakable. Infant mortality increases as family income decreases. Physical rejections by the armed forces are heavily weighted toward those coming from poverty environments. According to Rodger Hurley,

> The result of this typical situation is that the poor suffer to a staggering degree from almost every physical and emotional malady known to man. Among these conditions are cardiovascular disorders, rheumatic fever, heart disease, diabetes, cancer, prematurity, infant mortality, schizophrenia, dental disorders, arthritis, rheumatism, visual impairments, general mental disorders, and many others.[11]

Even if public funds were adequate and available for the health care of the poor, problems would remain. One is the accessibility of medical professionals to those who need them most. Opinions differ as to whether our society has a real doctor shortage or whether the distribution (both in geography and in medical focus) is the problem.[12] The experience of many, poor or not, seems to suggest an actual shortage of doctors: the virtual lack of physicians in many rural and inner city areas, long waits for appointments for routine services, hours spent in waiting rooms, hurried attention when a patient finally sees the doctor, difficulties in reaching a physician on weekends or in evenings.

In spite of the profession's fears of oversupply, however, the number of physicians has grown proportionately more rapidly than population growth in the last quarter century. Even so, the distribution problems are actually increasing. In medical focus, a third of all physicians are now involved in research, teaching, industry, administration, and health-related institutions — all important activities. But the number of physicians actually caring for private patients actually declined by 10 percent relative to the population between 1950 and 1965. Specialization has taken an additional number away from family care. In some areas there are many more surgeons than are needed while general practitioners and internists are overworked. And the problems of geographical distribution are increasing. Numerous small communities throughout the country lack physicians. At the end of the last decade the state of New York had two hundred physicians caring for every 100,000 residents, while Mississippi had only sixty-nine to serve the same population number.

In addition to the poverty and distribution problems there are other systemic difficulties built into the accessibility of medical care. According to the Health Policy Advisory Center, three million persons in our society go out searching for medical assistance each day (and several times that many need care but do not search for it because they are not healthy enough, wealthy enough, or enterprising enough to try). The first problem they face is finding the place where the kind of medical care they need is available at a reasonable price. Related to this is the difficulty in simply finding one's way in the maze of available types of medical care. Beyond this, the patient frequently has trouble finding out exactly what is being done to him. A further problem is knowing how to participate in the evaluation of his own medical needs and the treatment options which are open to him. And, if things do not seem to go right in the treatment, there is the problem of getting a hearing. Pervading all of this for those who do not belong to the dominant power group in our society — white males — is the problem of overcoming the racism and sexism which are built into most parts of our medical system.[13]

The Proposed Solutions

If these factors of cost, quality, and accessibility point to major dimensions of the health care crisis, we need to consider and evaluate the solutions now being proposed.[14] Some advocate *the increase in medical manpower* as the solution. It is commonly said that our country needs another fifty thousand physicians. Early in the decade of the seventies the federal government embarked upon new aid to medical schools for their expansion. New programs for para-medicals — nurses, mid-wives, physician assistants — have been instituted in order to relieve physicians of duties which others can handle competently. Some medical schools have shortened their curricula in order to produce more graduates. Encouragement has been given to large numbers of physicians from abroad to practice in this country (to the detriment of medical care in their own countries).

Yet, the increase in physicians is not the single answer. Indeed, the number has been growing rapidly for several years. In 1965 there were 292,000 doctors or one for every 682 Americans; by the end of 1972 the figures had increased to 344,000 or one for every 630 persons. Estimates for 1975 range from 369,000 to 382,000 physicians, an increase which will keep pace with population growth.[15] While the demands for medical services will continue to increase with expanding health consciousness and augmented purchasing power, America already has one of the highest physician-patient ratios in the world — much higher, indeed, than some nations which have superior indications of health. Physician increases will mean little unless problems of distribution in medical focus and geography are worked out: the San Francisco Bay area already boasts more neurosurgeons than it needs, a larger number than in the whole of the British Isles. The Health Manpower Commission declares that "if additional personnel are employed in the present manner and within the present patterns and 'systems' of medical care, they will not avert, or perhaps even alleviate, the crisis. *Unless we improve the system* through which health care is provided, care will continue to become less satisfactory." [16]

Various programs of financing medical care are offered as the second type of remedy. In 1971 a number of bills were introduced in Congress, each promising a financial solution to the health care crisis primarily through significant expansions of the federal government's role in medical insurance. If the first solution was based upon the assumption that the core problem was lack of medical personnel, the second assumes the central issue to be the individual's inability to pay for proper treatment.

The debate over national health insurance is not new. It has been on the scene for at least sixty years. What is new, however, is the degree of public interest in the subject. Reasons are not difficult to discover. The apparently uncontrollable rise in medical costs threatens not only consumers but also the viability of our major medical institutions. Private health insurance carriers are having difficulty maintaining present levels of benefits, not to mention improving coverage. Medicare has been generally popular. Medicaid has had grossly uneven state participation and, consequently, grossly uneven results among those for whom it was intended.[17]

The major current proposals fall into three general categories. One type envisions a program covering all or most of the population with broad medical benefits, financed by both payroll taxes and general federal taxes and administered by the federal government. At the other end of the continuum are those proposals which would make minimal changes in our financing system: the federal government would give income tax credits to taxpayers and vouchers to nontaxpayers to assist them in purchasing private health insurance with more restricted benefits. The third group of proposals falls in between with some characteristics of each of the other types.[18]

To the extent that financing solutions will help to answer the present crisis, the broad-coverage proposals financed and administered by the federal government are the most persuasive. They could help correct a number of the present problems in our system. More persons are now hospitalized than necessary because such charges are covered by insurance plans but office visits are not. Physicians who specialize are now rewarded with higher salaries and, often, shorter working hours; hence we have shortages in general and family practitioners. Private hospitals, which cannot afford to treat persons without insurance, restrict their services to the relatively affluent leaving public hospitals swamped by the poor financial risks. And, because private companies market health insurance primarily for good health risks, numerous and fragmented government programs have been established to cover the poor risks and special disease problems.[19]

Each of these problems could be alleviated by an inclusive government insurance program, argue its proponents.

Undeniably, part of the current health care problem is financial. Insurance alone, however, is only a partial solution and in some ways augments the problem. Health insurance in its present form is actually sickness insurance. It provides no built-in incentives for medical professionals to keep their patients healthy; indeed, they profit from illness. Private policies and the government programs of Medicare and Medicaid reimburse doctors on a fee-for-service and hospitals on a cost-plus basis, but the system of *delivering* health care is not changed. Further, both private and public insurance programs now motivate over-utilization of medical services by some people and constrain others who need more services than their policies offer. Since third-party insurers tend to pay medical providers with little examination of the service rendered or the charges made, there is an open invitation to rising costs and inefficient use of medical facilities.[20] Broad health coverage and prepayment of medical costs are needed, to be sure. But financial solutions alone will not significantly change the pattern of health care delivery.

The third type of proposal for meeting the current crisis deals much more directly with *the system of delivery*. Inasmuch as the United States now spends more money per person and a larger percentage of its gross national product on health care than does any other nation and still has a poorer health record than many, something appears to be wrong with the system itself. The change which holds greatest promise is the health maintenance organization (HMO), a plan encouraged by some of the insurance proposals in recent years.[21]

The HMO, as we saw earlier, is an organized system of health care which provides the full range of health maintenance and treatment services to an enrolled group of persons who pay a fixed fee in advance. Several characteristics distinguish the HMO from most parts of our present medical system. First, the prepayment for all basic medical services gives the medical professional an economic incentive for maintaining the health of his patients and practicing preventive medicine. Further, the full range of medical services is guaranteed to the member. Present insurance plans guarantee reimbursement for services if the patient can find them; the HMO guarantees the service itself. The HMO is organized either by a non-profit agency (e.g., a public hospital or university medical school) or by a profit-making group. In either case its physicians are on fixed salaries, though in the latter instance they might also share in the organization's annual profits. Since the HMO coordinates a whole range of professional specializations, equipment, and facilities (often including its own hospitals), it has the additional advantage of economies which result from coordinated planning.

Already those HMOs which now exist have demonstrated their viability through three impressive measures. First, they have shown higher success rates than the national averages in actually maintaining health, evidenced by lower infant mortality rates, increased longevity of members, and the need for fewer surgical procedures. They have, second, required a lower proportion of physicians per population unit and have required less frequent and shorter hospital use. Finally, their annual costs to members have been lower than the national average under traditional arrangements.

The Kaiser Foundation operates the largest and oldest HMO in America. Beginning in the late 1930s, it now has over two million members and its own network of clinics and hospitals in California, Oregon, and Hawaii. Access to the whole range of specialized as well as general medical services is easy for members. Kaiser-Permanente doctors receive fixed incomes which match those of private practitioners. While there is no limit to the number of doctor visits for any member, the accent on preventive medicine results in slightly fewer calls. The most dramatic savings, however, come through the elimination of unnecessary hospitalization. The average Kaiser member spends about 30 percent less time in the hospital than does the non-member in the same geographic region.

Critics claim that HMOs are impersonal and limit the individual's choice of a doctor. Proponents of the Kaiser program, however, maintain that actually a more educated choice is possible when one relates to a large clinic where he is in a position to compare physicians and then make his choice. Further, peer review is inherent in the HMO. An incompetent doctor is quickly discovered by his colleagues, whereas in private practice incompetence frequently goes undetected and indeed is often financially rewarded.

Health maintenance organizations presently serve a tiny fraction of the American public. New HMOs, however, are being organized by insurance companies, publicly-supported general hospitals, universities, business corporations, labor unions, county medical societies, and private entrepreneurs. The HMO's ability to meet the cost and quality factors in the health care crisis appears impressive, though admittedly some of the data reflect the selectivity of members in certain plans. Nevertheless, the efficiencies of the HMO and its incentives for preventive medicine are demonstrable and persuasive.

Distribution and accessibility of health care is the third major ingredient of our present problem. Could and would sufficient numbers of HMOs be established to care for the health of those groups and geographic areas now suffering from grossly inadequate care? Government incentives and regulation would be necessary. Requirements for adequate structures and resources, for public reporting of medical performance, and for accepting the old and the poor would go far toward providing quality group health care to the medically dispossessed. Financial incentives to establish HMOs in needy geographical areas would be necessary but also eminently feasible. While the magnitude of our national health care problem admits of no single solution, those answers which do not take seriously the need for systemic change in health care delivery will fail to meet our present malaise. That the HMO concept does this and that it has in some measure already proven its worth are signs of hope.

The Right to Health Care

The distinguished *New England Journal of Medicine* printed an article entitled "Medical Care as a Right: A Refutation." Its physician-author argued:

> The concept of medical care as the patient's right is immoral because it denies the most fundamental of all rights, that of a man to his own life and the freedom of action to support it. Medical care is neither a right nor a privilege: it is a service that is provided by doctors and others to people who wish to purchase it.[22]

The real right, maintained Dr. Robert M. Sade, is the freedom of a person (in this case the physician) to support his life by selling his services in the manner and to whom he chooses. When this "natural right" is abrogated or qualified by government intervention, doctors and others will become mere chattels of a coercive state and the quality of medical care will become moribund.

The letters received by the *Journal* in criticism of Sade's position were numerous and pointed.[23] Sade has forgotten, some said, that today's physician is not a rugged individualist. On the contrary, the public has given him a helping hand at every step, subsidizing his education, his research, the hospitals he practices in. Further, the skills of the physician are demeaned when they are equated with a commodity to be bartered. And what bargaining power does the inner-city black mother have when she brings her acutely ill child to the public hospital? Moreover, government's sole purpose is not that of protecting the rights of entrepreneurs; it is obligated to protect the well-being of all of its citizens. In short, said some of the respondents, of course medical care is a right — it follows directly from the right to live.

The *Journal's* editor sided with the views of these respondents in finding Sade's "Ayn Rand brand of objectivism and libertarianism morally unacceptable." But, he noted, although the protests to this article had been anticipated, what was not foreseen were the intensity and volume of the *positive* response. "What does this mean? Dr. Sade has obviously tapped a strong undercurrent of medical opinion that not only opposes but resents the doctrine of health care as a right." [24] If, the editor reasoned, the surprisingly voluminous positive response to Sade's position is representative of a large body of medical opinion, then this constitutes "a major but rarely emphasized ingredient in our much lamented health-care crisis — namely, the huge ideologic gap that separates society and its leaders on one hand from large segments of the medical profession on the other." [25]

The assumption that adequate health care is a human right, and not simply a privilege for those who can afford to purchase it, has been implicit throughout this book. If the scarcity and primitive quality of medical care in previous centuries made such talk remote and speculative, that is no longer true today. But what is a "right"? Ethically speaking, a right is a power reserved to the person such that he can morally demand of others that it not be interfered with or taken from him.[26] As to the source of human rights, there are different answers. Utilitarians say that individual rights are derived from what is good for society. Totalitarian theories hold that the individual has only those rights which the state chooses to grant him. Others believe that certain rights inhere in natural law; they are just there, given by nature or nature's God.

Christian affirmations often find affinity with those of natural law. Beyond any static categories, however, many of us affirm that human rights are based upon God's humanizing intentions for persons. Such intentions are dynamically related to the possibilities available for human fulfillment. Thus it makes sense to consider freedom from smallpox part of every person's basic right to health today, for that freedom is now eminently possible. In an earlier stage of medical development such an assertion would have been meaningless.

Though a person's health as a state of physical and emotional well-being is not the whole of that individual's *humanum*, surely it is a meaningful part and prerequisite for it. All rights have corresponding obligations and duties. Precisely because our society does have the capacity both in medical knowledge and economic resources to defend the right to good health care for every citizen, we can claim this as society's obligation. While Christians may argue this case out of their own theological convictions, it is not a narrowly sectarian issue. The rights and duties of health care can be defended on the basis of widely-shared claims expressed in the founding documents of our nation. Beyond our society's charters lie the opinions of humankind to which we owe a decent respect. The charter of the World Health Organization thus clams that health should be regarded as a human and civic right.

Only belatedly and somewhat reluctantly have leaders of organized medicine in America recognized the fact that most people do regard decent health care as a basic right. That large segments of the medical profession still do not agree probably has several explanations. One answer lies simply in the social background and education of many physicians, especially the middle-aged and older. While the complexion of medical school student bodies is gradually changing, the overwhelming majority of doctors are white males who grow up and eventually practice in the middle and upper classes. Further, most of our present physicians were college science majors, and until recently few had been exposed in depth to the humanities and the arts. "Thus it is difficult for most practicing physicians to appreciate the arguments of their critical colleagues — or even to understand what they are talking about." [27]

Related to these factors is the ideology which has permeated much of the upper and middle classes in recent decades. Federal health plans have been equated with socialism, and socialism with the loss of individual freedom. Freedom, in this view, is not primarily the capacity of interdependent persons to realize their fullest humanity; rather, freedom is defined (and this from the viewpoint of the privileged person) as the absence of external constraints. As Richard Lichtman aptly puts it, however, such freedom from the standpoint of the less-privileged "is simply the freedom to suffer physical misery and humiliation in the face of illness." [28]

A Christian perception of sin is crucial at this point. Sin is universal and ubiquitous among and within us. Constrained by the narrow confines of our social backgrounds, limited in understanding the situations of those unlike us, and prone as we are to self-justification, we tend to absolutize our own interpretations of social reality and to elevate our estimates of our own virtue. And sin is social as well as individual. Our distortions of reality and our dehumanizing practices become embedded in our institutional systems. Added to all of this, those of us in positions of power and privilege seldom give up our perceived advantages voluntarily.

The large majority of physicians are conscientious and dedicated professionals. They are dedicated to the best possible care for their own patients, and most of them work unusually hard in this demanding responsibility. It is understandable why many doctors react with indignation in the face of criticism. But they, no less than any of us, can and do become unwitting victims of narrowness of vision and assumptions of virtue. They can become victimized because the demands of a busy practice keep them preoccupied with those patients immediately before them, because their willingness to adjust and even cancel fees for the poor has convinced them of their own goodness, and because they have been shaped professionally by a system which perpetuates inefficiencies and rewards the cure of disease far more than it rewards the maintenance of human health.

The Movement for Change

Yet, the times, indeed, are changing, and much of the impetus is coming from segments within the medical profession itself. Dr.

Victor W. Sidel observes that three closely-interrelated influences have led to the health professional's increasing concern about political and social change.[29] One is the broader concept of health, meaning not just the absence of disease but, as the World Health Organization puts it, "a state of complete physical, mental, and social well-being." Another influence is the changing technology of medical care and disease prevention. Unlike earlier days, we now have a wide range of effective techniques, from immunization and fluoridation to genetic screening, for early detection, treatment, and prevention of disease. But the effective use of these techniques involves community-wide (and hence political) action. A third factor is the growing awareness that the maldistribution of power and resources, bringing with it the defilement of our environment, is in itself a major cause of poor health both within and among nations.

The most vocal change advocates have been members of several groups of the radical health movement.[30] The Student Health Organization was founded in 1965 by students from schools of medicine, nursing, dentistry, and social work. After several summers of health projects in poverty areas, the SHO turned its attention to protest and activism aimed at the larger structures of the health professions. In December 1967, a hundred students interrupted an A.M.A. conference in Chicago — an unprecedented act — accusing the organization of plotting to "silence the anguished cries of the poor."

Also founded in the mid-sixties was the Medical Committee for Human Rights. At first it was largely young, white, male doctors who were organizing in support of the civil rights movement. Later as the MCHR broadened its scope of advocacy and began to attack the health establishment itself, it lost some of its physician members but picked up others among medical students, nurses, and laboratory technicians. The MCHR's charges have been typical of others in the radical health movement: profit and power have taken precedence over prevention of illness; doctors have guarded their knowledge in an atmosphere of "mystique," leaving patients confused and dependent; hospital medical centers have invested in expensive and fashionable equipment for exotic medical procedures while neglecting less interesting but more basic medical needs.

Beginning in the late 1960s "free clinics" were established in cities across the country. They attempted to give visible expression to the radical platform of demystifying the medical art, giving direct control of health institutions to the local community, and making basic health care available to everyone. Charging either no fees or nominal ones, the free clinics attempt to give decentralized, neighborhood-based health care in a way which encourages the patient to participate actively in the choice of therapy and in the learning of health care skills. Among the liberals in the health establishment the clinics have both defenders and critics. Some say the free clinics are a conscience for modern medicine. Others, however, charge them with constructing an unworkable professional model and "playing house" without meeting the real needs for systemic change.

The radical health movement has enlisted only a small fraction of medical professionals. Like most other radical movements it has its own internal ideological disputes, and its achievements fall short of its rhetoric. Nevertheless, in authentic radical fashion it has gone to the roots of the health care system and has raised basic and important questions. It has struck responsive chords with many medical liberals in questioning priorities and in calling for a more person-centered and equitable health care delivery system. Indeed, such a welcome development as the Patient's Bill of Rights, issued by the American Hospital Association in 1972, may owe its appearance in part to the radical critique. That list of patients' rights is not startling to anyone in the medical profession. But if the health professionals have known about these long-established principles, the majority of patients have not. That they are now publicly affirmed is both an indication of increasing sensitivity within established medicine and a spur to greater accountability.[31]

Responsible Human Medicine

What might a Christian interpretation of responsibility have to say to medicine? According to H. Richard Niebuhr, "Responsibility affirms: 'God is acting in all actions upon you. So respond to all actions upon you as to respond to his action.' " [32] And what is this "action," this divine intentionality or purpose in the midst of our existence? Paul Lehmann puts it in these words: "God has always been and is contemporaneously doing what it takes to make and to keep human life human." [33] Responsibility, then, is indeed response-ability, the ability to respond to that in the midst of our relationships which is ultimately real and worthwhile. In a Christian perception it points to a manner of responding to our fellow beings so that our relationships with them express our openness to the one in our midst who is our Creator, Judge, and Redeemer, the living Spirit who is the source of whatever authentic humanness we might experience with our companions.

What marks the responsible relationship between the physician and the patient? Robert M. Veatch suggests that several varied models are common today.[34] Nurtured by the biological revolution, some physicians behave like the applied scientist, attempting to eliminate all ethical and value considerations from their relationships with patients and simply applying medical techniques. Revolted by this engineering model, which makes the patient into a case and the physician into a plumber, some go to the opposite extreme and see themselves in a priestly role. This perhaps is the more common model. The difficulty is, however, that the physician-priest transfers his rightful expertise in the technical aspects of medicine into an unwarranted expertise in making moral and human decisions on behalf of his patient. But the patient is deprived of human dignity by priestly paternalism, however well-intended it may be.

To avoid dominating their patients some doctors attempt to use a collegial model. Here the professional and the patient participate as equals in the process of maintaining health and treating illness. Here decisions are mutually shared as an expression of the equality of dignity and respect among persons. The problem is that collegial assumptions, however admirable, are utopian and unworkable. The doctor does, in fact, know a great deal more about some things than the patient does, and there are some decisions that he alone can and should make.

A more adequate approximation of responsibility is in a contractual or, better, covenantal model. Patient and professional relate in ways which affirm their full human equality, but in ways which recognize realistically their functional differences. Trust and confidence are enhanced because the physician neither abdicates his moral responsibility for the patient, nor does the patient abdicate his freedom in significant choices which will affect his life. The doctor sees himself as part of the health care team. He has a crucial role in this caring community, but he does not direct all of its decisions. There are other members on the team as well — the patient's family, his minister or chaplain, nurses and other health professionals, and, of course the patient himself for he is not an object of manipulation by others but a key participant in the process.

Responsibility involves duties as well as rights. Booklets on patients' rights now appearing in hospitals and free clinics appropriately include sections on patients' obligations, too. If the patient has a right to truthfulness from the medical professional, the patient has a corresponding obligation to such integrity. Correlative patient obligations follow other rights — the duty to try to understand the possible therapies, to follow faithfully the treatment plan agreed upon, and in general to be responsible in caring for one's own health.

Covenantal relationships admittedly take more time than many doctors now realistically can afford. A significant part of the time problem, however, lies in the inefficiencies and fragmented character of our present health delivery system. In addition to systemic changes for which we can hope, some important shifts in medical care patterns almost certainly will be wrought by the increasing use of automation and computers. The mere suggestion of such technology raises understandable anxiety about more depersonalization. But the danger is not inevitable. Considerable diagnostic use of computers can free the physician for greater time to be spent in the art of caring for the patient.[35]

Responsible relationships in medicine, of course, extend beyond the immediate covenant of caring. Responsibility is an expression of love, and love always calls for justice in the common life.

In its narrowest sense justice is often perceived as simple conformity to law. But the biblical notion — and that of wise persons in every culture — goes beyond that to press toward *distributive* justice. Of the present norms governing the distribution of health care benefits, responsibility asks the question, are they fair and humanizing? How shall we allocate our scarce medical resources for a more human society? How much, for example, shall we invest in additional heart transplants and genetic research over and against inoculation programs and child health care among the poor? Distributive justice also presses us toward *compensatory* justice. Those against whom the dominant groups in society have discriminated now ought to have special claims upon us. Theirs is the just priority.

Justice under the impetus of love thus presses toward *creative* justice. Distributive justice gives to a person what is due to him. Compensatory justice makes amends for past unfairness. Paul Tillich reminds us that justice goes beyond even these quantitative measurements, necessary though they be:

> What is the criterion of creative justice? In order to answer this question one must ask which is the ultimate intrinsic claim for justice in a being? The answer is: Fulfillment within the unity of universal fulfillment. The religious symbol for this is the kingdom of God.[36]

Seen in this manner, creative justice is a form of reuniting love. It unites us with that to which we are essentially bound but from which we have in fact become estranged.

Truly human medicine is an instrument of such reuniting love. Caring for human health does involve careful judgments about the use of medical technologies and the distribution of medical resources. Beyond these it moves toward the transformation and healing of those conditions, both personal and social, which undermine health. Those of us privileged to read and write books about medical ethics doubtless need not go to bed tonight worrying about the rats or about the peeling paint and lead poisoning. Nor will we awake in the morning to experience the malnutrition which is part of daily life for many in this global village. But we can become more sensitive to both the perplexities and the great possibilities of truly human medicine.

While health is not the totality of human wholeness, it is a basic component. While physical healing is not the same as personal healing, it is intrinsically related. And while creative medicine will not usher in the kingdom of God, it can contribute significantly to that fuller realization of our common humanity, which is both a gift and an achievement.

NOTES

Preface

1. Constance Holden, "Ethics: Biomedical Advances Confront Public and Politicians as Well as Professionals with New Issues," *Science*, Vol. 175 (January 7, 1972), p. 40.

Chapter One

1. John Noble Wilford, "Navajo Healers Successful Where Medicine Falls Short," *The New York Times*, July 7, 1972, p. 27.
2. *Ibid.*
3. James N. Lapsley, *Salvation and Health* (Philadelphia: The Westminster Press, 1972), p. 38. Cf. Cecil A. Sherman, "An Ancient Relationship," in Claude A. Frazier, *Should Doctors Play God?* (Nashville: Broadman Press, 1971).
4. Lapsley, *Salvation and Health*, Chap. 2. Cf. United Presbyterian Church, U.S.A.: *The Relation of Christian Faith to Health* (New York: U.P.U.S.A., 1960).
5. Robert B. Reeves, Jr., "How to Put Man Together Again?" (Address to the American Medical Association Committee on Medicine and Religion, June 20, 1971). Cf. Sherman, "Ancient Relationship," pp. 21ff.
6. *Webster's New World Dictionary of the American Language* (New York: The World Publishing Company, 1970), p. 645.
7. See Seward Hiltner, "The Bible Speaks to the Health of Man," in Dale White (ed.), *Dialogue in Medicine and Theology* (Nashville: Abingdon Press, 1967, 1968).

8. Paul Tillich, "The Meaning of Health," in David Belgum (ed.), *Religion and Medicine* (Ames: Iowa State University Press, 1967).

9. Paul L. Lehmann, *Ethics in a Christian Context* (New York: Harper & Row, 1963), p. 85.

10. Helmut Thielicke, "The Doctor as Judge of Who Shall Live and Who Shall Die," in Kenneth Vaux (ed.), *Who Shall Live?* (Philadelphia: Fortress Press, 1970), pp. 148f.

11. Daniel Callahan, *Abortion: Law, Choice and Morality* (New York: The Macmillan Company, 1970), Chap. 11.

12. See, for example, James M. Gustafson, *Christian Ethics and the Community* (Philadelphia and Boston: Pilgrim Press, 1971), esp. Chap. 9; Joseph Fletcher, "Indicators of Humanhood: A Tentative Profile of Man," *The Hastings Center Report*, Vol. 2, No. 5 (Nov. 1972), pp. 1-4; W. Norman Pittenger, *Making Sexuality Human* (Philadelphia and Boston: Pilgrim Press, 1970), Chap. 2.

13. Reinhold Niebuhr, *The Nature and Destiny of Man* (New York: Charles Scribner's Sons, 1941, 1943). See Vol. I, esp. Chaps. 6 through 8.

14. For a more fully-developed argument on this point see my *Moral Nexus: Ethics of Christian Identity and Community* (Philadelphia: The Westminster Press, 1971), esp. pp. 31-35, 113-116.

15. Victor E. Frankl, "The Significance of Meaning for Health," in Belgum, *Religion and Medicine.*

16. Rollo May, *Love and Will* (New York: W. W. Norton & Company, 1969), p. 230.

17. See Callahan, *Abortion*, Chap. 9; and Callahan, "The Sanctity of Life," in Donald R. Cutler (ed.), *Updating Life and Death* (Boston: Beacon Press, 1968, 1969).

18. Edward Shils, quoted by Callahan, *Abortion*, p. 313.

19. The most perceptive reflection on faith and valuing in contemporary Protestant ethics has been done by H. Richard Niebuhr. See especially his essay "The Center of Value," in *Radical Monotheism and Western Culture* (New York: Harper & Brothers, 1960).

20. Callahan, *Abortion*, pp. 328ff.

21. The style of ethics reflected in this paragraph and its manner of formulation owes much to H. Richard Niebuhr and James M. Gustafson. See Niebuhr, *The Responsible Self* (New York: Harper & Row, 1963); Gustafson, *Christian Ethics*, and "Basic Ethical Issues in the Bio-medical Fields," *Soundings*, Vol. LIII, No. 2 (Summer 1970).

22. Michael Wilson, "Violence and Nonviolence in the Cure of Disease and the Healing of Patients," *The Christian Century*, June 17, 1970, p. 757. I am indebted to Wilson's lucid interpretation of the parable referred to in this section.

23. May, *Love and Will*, p. 289.

24. Milton Mayeroff, *On Caring* (New York: Harper & Row, 1971) p. 1.

25. *Ibid.*, p. 2.

26. While Mayeroff, on whose insightful and almost lyrical description of caring I have drawn in this section, does not relate this to a Christian perspective, his analysis has all the marks of the gospel's analysis of love, except it remains to be said that the source and possibility of both care and love are in God.

27. Abraham Kaplan, "Social Ethics and the Sanctity of Life," in Daniel H. Labby (ed.), *Life or Death: Ethics and Options* (Portland: Reed College; and Seattle: University of Washington Press, 1968), p. 154.

Chapter Two

1. Tilda Norberg, "Female Anguish and Abortion," in *Abortion: A Human Choice* (Washington, D.C.: Board of Christian Social Concerns, The United Methodist Church, 1971), p. 1.
2. The details of this case are the alleged facts of "Mary Doe" (pseudonym) in the Supreme Court case challenging the Georgia abortion statute, *Doe v. Bolton*, 93 S. Ct. 739 (1973), *Supreme Court Reporter* (St. Paul: West Publishing Co.), February 15, 1973, p. 744.
3. I have taken these statistics from Daniel Callahan, *Abortion: Law, Choice, and Morality* (New York: The Macmillan Company, 1970), pp. 129 and 132ff.; Robert E. Cooke, *et al., The Terrible Choice: The Abortion Dilemma* (New York: Bantam Books, Inc., 1968), Chap. 4; and *The Minneapolis Tribune*, Nov. 22, 1971.
4. *Medical World News*, October 22, 1965, p. 70, as quoted in Frederick K. Wentz and Robert H. Witmer, *The Problem of Abortion* (Lutheran Church in America, 1967), p. 1.
5. Helpful historical summaries upon which I have drawn in this section are Julia and Harry Abrahamson, *Who Shall Live?* (New York: Hill and Wang, 1970), pp. 18f.; David Granfield, *The Abortion Decision* (Garden City, N.J.: Doubleday & Company, Inc., 1969), Chap. 2; David R. Mace, *Abortion: The Agonizing Decision* (Nashville: Abingdon Press, 1972), pp. 52ff.; Allen J. Moore, "Abortion: A Human Choice," in United Methodist Church, *Human Choice;* Harmon L. Smith, *Ethics and the New Medicine* (Nashville: Abingdon Press, 1970), pp. 26ff.; and, John T. Noonan, Jr., "An Almost Absolute Value in History," in Noonan (ed.), *The Morality of Abortion* (Cambridge: Harvard University Press, 1970).
6. See for example Pius XII, "Allocution to the Association of Large Families," (November 26, 1951).
7. Walter M. Abbott (gen. ed.), *The Documents of Vatican II* (New York: Guild Press, 1966), p. 256.
8. See Ralph B. Potter, Jr., "The Abortion Debate," in Donald R. Cutler (ed.), *Updating Life and Death* (Boston: Beacon Press, 1968, 1969), esp. pp. 88ff. Cf. Wilson Yates, *Family Planning on a Crowded Planet* (Minneapolis: Augsburg Publishing House, 1971), Chap. 4 and 5, for an excellent treatment of individual and social values as they affect the family planning issue.
9. Eighth General Synod, United Church of Christ, "Freedom of Choice Concerning Abortion," *Social Action*, Vol. XXXVIII, No. 1 (September 1971), p. 11.
10. Summaries of these scientific data to which I am indebted in this section will be found in Cooke, et al., *Terrible Choice*, Chap. 3; Abrahamson and Abrahamson, *Who Shall Live?*, pp. 19ff.; Mace, *Agonizing Decision*, pp. 34ff.; and Callahan, *Abortion*, pp. 31ff.
11. The data summarized in this section are taken largely from Callahan, *Abortion*, Sec. I.

12. *Ibid.,* pp. 79f.
13. *Ibid.,* p. 91.
14. Sources for much of the information included in this section are Callahan, *Abortion,* Sec. II; Mace, *Agonizing Decision,* pp. 70ff.; Cooke, et al., *Terrible Choice,* Chap. 5; Abrahamson and Abrahamson, *Who Shall Live?,* pp. 22ff.; and *Roe v. Wade,* 93 S. Ct. 705 (1973), *Supreme Court Reporter* (St. Paul: West Publishing Co.), February 15, 1973.
15. Callahan, *Abortion,* p. 184.
16. *Roe v. Wade,* p. 731.
17. *Ibid.,* p. 732.
18. *Ibid.*
19. *Ibid.* Note, however, that physicians generally consider the fetus viable much earlier than the last ten weeks of pregnancy.
20. *Doe v. Bolton,* p. 741.
21. In addition to Callahan, *Abortion,* Sec. II, see his "Abortion: Thinking and Experiencing," *Christianity and Crisis,* Vol. 32, No. 23 (January 8, 1973), pp. 296f.
22. Helmut Thielicke, *The Ethics of Sex,* trans. John W. Doberstein (New York: Harper and Row, 1954), p. 228.
23. Dietrich Bonhoeffer, *Ethics,* trans. N. H. Smith (New York: The Macmillan Co., 1955), pp. 130f.
24. Paul Ramsey, "The Morality of Abortion," in Daniel H. Labby (ed.), *Life or Death: Ethics and Options* (Portland and Seattle: Reed College and University of Washington Press, 1968), p. 72. For a helpful and more detailed discussion of the positions of several major Protestant theologians see Smith, *New Medicine,* pp. 35ff.
25. Michael V. Viola, "Abortion: A Catholic View," in E. Fuller Torrey (ed.), *Ethical Issues in Medicine* (Boston: Little, Brown and Company, 1968), pp. 100f.
26. A. Hellegers, quoted in Viola, *ibid.,* p. 92.
27. Potter gives a helpful portrayal of this argument, "Abortion Debate," pp. 101f.
28. Granfield, *Abortion Decision,* p. 134.
29. Ramsey, "The Morality of Abortion," p. 79.
30. Granfield, *Abortion Decision,* p. 135.
31. James M. Gustafson, "A Protestant Ethical Approach," in Noonan, *Morality of Abortion,* pp. 102ff.
32. *Roe v. Wade,* p. 735.
33. Rachel Conrad Wahlberg, "The Woman and the Fetus: 'One Flesh'?" *The Christian Century,* September 8, 1971, pp. 1045ff.
34. Norberg, "Female Anguish," pp. 6f.
35. Garrett Hardin, "Abortion — or Compulsory Pregnancy?" *Journal of Marriage and the Family,* Vol. XXX, No. 2 (May 1968), p. 249.
36. Callahan, *Abortion,* p. 450; Potter, "Abortion Debate," p. 94.
37. Quoted in Potter, *"Abortion Debate,"* p. 94.
38. See H. Richard Niebuhr, *Radical Monotheism and Western Culture* (New York: Harper & Brothers, 1943, 1952, 1955, 1960), pp. 102ff.
39. Potter, "Abortion Debate," pp. 118f.
40. Callahan, *Abortion,* p. 456. Some studies indicate that very high percentages of women emotionally reject their pregnancies at some stage.

41. John Moore and John Pamperin, "Abortion and the Church, *The Christian Century*, May 20, 1970, p. 630.
42. Callahan's treatment of this issue is most persuasive. See *Abortion,* pp. 451ff., upon which I have drawn in these paragraphs.
43. Cf. J. Claude Evans, "The Abortion Decision: A Balancing of Rights," *The Christian Century*, (February 14, 1973), pp. 196f.; Editorial, *The New York Times,* January 24, 1973.
44. Justice Blackmun, writing for the majority, attempted to steer a middle ground between opposing theological views on the question of when human life begins. "We need not resolve the difficult question of when life begins. When those trained in the respective disciplines of medicine, philosophy, and theology are unable to arrive at any consensus, the judiciary, at this point in the development of man's knowledge, is not in a position to speculate as to the answer." *Roe v. Wade,* p. 730. He then attempted to steer a middle ground between opposing theological views by espousing a somewhat loosely-framed developmentalist position. Unfortunately, Blackmun's language is imprecise. There is obviously "life" in the fetus. The question is when is that life distinctly human in such a way that it makes moral claims upon us which deserve the protection of law.
45. Howard Moody, "Church, State and the Rights of Conscience," *Christianity and Crisis*, Vol. 32, No. 23 (January 8, 1973). See also Margaret Mead, "Rights to Life," and John C. Bennett, "Avoid Oppressive Laws!" in the same journal issue.
46. Moore and Pamperin, "Abortion and the Church," p. 631.

Chapter Three

1. This case is described in Charles P. Kindregan, *The Quality of Life: Reflections on the Moral Values of American Law* (Milwaukee: Bruce Publishing Co., 1969), pp. 7ff.
2. Wilfred J. Finegold, "Artificial Insemination," in E. Fuller Torrey, *Ethical Issues in Medicine* (Boston: Little, Brown, and Company, 1968), p. 56.
3. *Ibid.*
4. Norman St. John-Stevas, *Life, Death and the Law* (Bloomington: Indiana University Press, 1961), p. 117.
5. See the statistics quoted by Harmon L. Smith, *Ethics and the New Medicine* (Nashville: Abingdon Press, 1970), pp. 57f.; and by Paul Ramsey, *Fabricated Man* (New Haven: Yale University Press, 1970), p. 128.
6. J. K. Sherman, "Research on Frozen Human Semen," *Fertility and Sterility*, Vol. 15, No. 5 (1964), pp. 485ff.; also Genetic Laboratories, Inc., "Facts about the History, Techniques and Reasons for Freezing and Storing Human Semen," (St. Paul: Genetic Laboratories, Inc., n.d.).
7. Quoted in Genetic Laboratories, Inc., "Freezing and Storing."
8. Sherman, "Frozen Human Semen"; Genetic Laboratories, Inc., "Freezing and Storing."
9. Reported in *The Minneapolis Tribune*, March 12, 1972.
10. *The Minneapolis Tribune,* September 20, 1971.
11. St. Johns-Stevas, *Life, Death and the Law,* p. 121.

12. On the legal problems involving AID I am indebted to several sources for information and insight: St. Johns-Stevas, *ibid.,* pp. 128ff.; Finegold, "Artificial Insemination," pp. 68ff.; Kindregan, *Quality of Life,* pp. 7ff.; Smith, *New Medicine,* pp. 58ff.; Joseph Fletcher, *Morals and Medicine* (Boston: Beacon Press, 1954) pp. 135ff.; Vincent Edmunds and G. Gordon Scorer, *Ethical Responsibility in Medicine* (Edinburgh and London: E. & S. Livingstone, Ltd., 1967), p. 82; and John B. Gordon: "Artificial Insemination Donor: Some Legal Considerations," *Soundings,* Vol. LIV, No. 3 (Fall 1971), pp. 308ff.

13. Gordon, "Legal Considerations," p. 309.

14. Quoted by St. John-Stevas, *Life, Death and the Law,* p. 131.

15. Oklahoma Stat. Art. 10, sec. 534 (1966) *Artificial Insemination,* quoted in Gordon, "Legal Considerations," p. 313.

16. See John Marshall, "A.I.D.: An Occasion for Creative Law Making," *Soundings,* Vol. LIV, No. 3 (Fall 1971), pp. 326ff.

17. Anonymous, "Sterility: A Husband's Story," *Good Housekeeping,* Vol. 176, No. 1 (January 1973), p. 129.

18. This study is described in Finegold, "Artificial Insemination," pp. 62f.

19. Karl Ostrom, "Psychological Considerations in Evaluating A.I.D.," *Soundings,* Vol. LIV, No. 3 (Fall 1971), p. 296.

20. Deutsch's study is described by Finegold, "Artificial Insemination," p. 61.

21. Fletcher, *Morals and Medicine,* p. 129.

22. As reported by Henry Clark, "Fate, the 'Experts,' and Individual Choice," *Soundings,* Vol. LIV. No. 3 (Fall 1971), p. 336.

23. Fletcher, *Morals and Medicine,* pp. 129f.

24. Joan Holland, "Adoption and Artificial Insemination," *Soundings,* Vol. LIV, No. 3 (Fall 1971), pp. 302ff.

25. See Gerald Kelly, *Medico-Moral Problems* (St. Louis: The Catholic Hospital Association, 1958), pp. 228ff. Cf. Richard P. Richards, "Artificial Insemination Donor: Ethical and Theological Aspects," *Soundings,* Vol. LIV, No. 3 (Fall 1971), p. 316.

26. Finegold, "Artificial Insemination," p. 66.

27. Ramsey, *Fabricated Man,* p. 131.

28. *Ibid.,* p. 136.

29. Fletcher, *Morals and Medicine,* p. 139. Cf. his *Situation Ethics* (Philadelphia: The Westminster Press, 1966) for his detailed argument on love as the only norm.

30. Charles E. Curran, *Absolutes in Moral Theology?* (Washington: Corpus Books, 1968), p. 111; cf. Curran's *A New Look at Christian Morality* (Notre Dame, Ind.: Fides Publishers, Inc., 1968), Chap. 8.

31. Helmut Thielicke, *The Ethics of Sex,* trans. John W. Doberstein (New York: Harper & Row, 1964), p. 262.

32. Clark, "Individual Choice," p. 339.

33. Smith, *New Medicine,* p. 74.

Chapter Four

1. Philip R. Sullivan, "Morals and Medical Research," *Christianity and Crisis,* Vol. 27, No. 10 (June 26, 1967), p. 151.

2. *The Minneapolis Tribune,* November 10, 1971.

3. Robert M. Veatch, " 'Experimental' Pregnancy," *The Hastings Center Report,* No. 1 (June 1971) , p. 2.
4. Geoffrey Edsall, "A Positive Approach to the Problem of Human Experimentation," *Daedalus,* Vol. 98, No. 2 (Spring 1969) , p. 465.
5. *Ibid.,* p. 466.
6. Henry K. Beecher, *Research and the Individual* (Boston: Little, Brown and Company, 1970) , p. 15; William J. Curran, "Governmental Regulation of the Use of Human Subjects in Medical Research: The Approach of Two Federal Agencies," *Daedalus,* Vol. 98, No. 2 (Spring 1969) , p. 542.
7. Henry K. Beecher, "Ethics and Clinical Research," *The New England Journal of Medicine,* Vol. 274, No. 24 (June 16, 1966) , p. 1355. While in the early 1970s the federal government was cutting back its support of medical research, the overall quantity and research ethos were still markedly different than that which had existed just a decade or two earlier.
8. Thomas Anderson, *et al., As a Patient You Have Rights* (Minneapolis: Model Cities Communications Center, Inc., 1972) , p. 6.
9. Beecher, "Clinical Research," p. 1355.
10. "The Declaration of Helsinki" and "The A.M.A. Ethical Guidelines for Clinical Investigation" are published together in pamphlet form by the American Medical Association, 535 North Dearborn Street, Chicago, Illinois 60610. All quotations from these two statements are taken from this publication.
11. Quoted by Henry K. Beecher, "Medical Research and the Individual," in Daniel H. Labby (ed.) , *Life or Death: Ethics and Options* (Portland and Seattle: Reed College and University of Washington Press, 1968) , p. 128.
12. Otto E. Guttentag, "Ethical Problems in Human Experimentation," in E. Fuller Torrey, *Ethical Issues in Medicine* (Boston: Little, Brown and Company, 1968) , pp. 198ff.
13. Catherine Lyons, *Organ Transplants: The Moral Issues* (Philadelphia: The Westminster Press, 1970) , pp. 28ff., states this point well.
14. Guttentag, "Ethical Problems," pp. 199f.
15. Paul Ramsey, *The Patient as Person* (New Haven: Yale University Press, 1970) , pp. 6f.
16. John Fletcher, "Human Experimentation: Ethics in the Consent Situation," in Paul T. Jersild and Dale A. Johnson (eds.) : *Moral Issues and Christian Response* (New York: Holt, Rinehart and Winston, Inc., 1971) , pp. 444f.
17. M. H. Pappworth, "Ethical Issues in Experimental Medicine," in Donald E. Cutler (ed.) , *Updating Life and Death* (Boston: Beacon Press, 1968, 1969) , p. 69.
18. Guttentag, "Ethical Problems," p. 204.
19. Beecher, *Research and the Individual,* p. 69.
20. *Ibid.,* pp. 76f.
21. Ramsey, *Patient as Person,* Chap. 1.
22. Beecher, *Research and the Individual,* pp. 68f.
23. Guttentag, "Ethical Problems," p. 206.
24. Hans Jonas, "Philosophical Reflections on Experimenting with Human Subjects," *Daedalus,* Vol. 98, No. 2 (Spring 1969) , p. 237.

25. John Fletcher, "Consent Situation," p. 450.
26. I am indebted to Chaplain Lloyd Beebe, Hennepin County General Hospital, Minneapolis, for these insights.
27. Guttentag, "Ethical Problems," pp. 206f.
28. The Nuremberg Code is included as an appendix to Guttentag, "Ethical Problems," pp. 214f.
29. *Ibid.*, p. 208.
30. John Fletcher, "Consent Situation," pp. 454f.
31. Beecher, "Medical Research and the Individual," p. 127.
32. Pappworth, "Ethical Issues," p. 70.
33. Paul A. Freund, "Ethical Problems in Human Experimentation," *The New England Journal of Medicine*, Vol. 273, No. 13 (Sept. 23, 1965), p. 692.
34. *The Minneapolis Tribune*, July 30, 1972; *Commission News*, The Commission for Racial Justice, the United Church of Christ, Vol. 2, No. 12 (September 30, 1972), p. 3.
35. Beecher, "Ethics and Clinical Research," p. 1360.
36. A thorough description of the development of regulatory law in the F.D.A., the P.H.S., and the N.I.H. is found in Curran, "Governmental Regulation," pp. 542-594.
37. Freund, "Ethical Problems," p. 689.
38. Beecher, "Medical Research and the Individual," p. 135.
39. Langdon Gilkey, *Religion and the Scientific Future* (New York: Harper and Row, 1970), Chap. 3; Paul Ramsey, "The Ethics of a Cottage Industry in an Age of Community and Research Medicine," *The New England Journal of Medicine*, Vol. 284 (April 1, 1971), pp. 700ff.
40. James M. Gustafson, "Basic Ethical Issues in the Bio-Medical Fields," *Soundings*, Vol. LIII, No. 2 (Summer 1970), pp. 151ff.

Chapter Five

1. Leroy Augenstein, *Come, Let Us Play God* (New York: Harper & Row, 1969), p. 17.
2. "Man into Superman," *Time*, April 19, 1971, p. 51.
3. David M. Rorvik, *Brave New Baby* (Garden City, N.J.: Doubleday & Company, Inc., 1971), pp. 26f.
4. For useful descriptions of the current genetic situation see Augenstein, *Play God*, pp. 31ff.; *Time*, pp. 33ff.; Paul Ramsey, *Fabricated Man* (New Haven: Yale University Press, 1970), Chap. 1.
5. Quoted in *Time*, p. 33.
6. Ramsey, *Fabricated Man*, p. 5.
7. Bruce Hilton, "Will the Baby Be Normal?...And What Is the Cost of Knowing?" *The Hastings Center Report*, Vol. 2, No. 3 (June 1972), p. 8.
8. Hilton, "Will the Baby Be Normal?" pp. 8f.; Daniel Callahan, "Ethics, Law, and Genetic Counseling," *Science*, Vol. 176 (April 14, 1972), pp. 197ff.; Marc Lappé, "Risk-taking for the Unborn," *The Hastings Center Report*, Vol. 2, No. 1 (February 1972), pp. 1ff.; Lappé "The Genetic Counselor: Responsible to Whom?" *The Hastings Center Report*, Vol. 1, No. 2 (September 1971), pp. 6ff.; Lappé, "Genetic Counseling and Genetic

Engineering," *The Hastings Center Report*, Vol. 1, No. 3 (December 1971), pp. 13f.; and Ramsey, *Fabricated Man*, pp. 98ff.

9. Lappé, "The Genetic Counselor: Responsible to Whom?", p. 6.
10. Quoted in Hilton, "Will the Baby Be Normal?", p. 9.
11. Ramsey, *Fabricated Man*, p. 97.
12. Callahan, "Genetic Counseling," p. 199.
13. See Hilton, "Will the Baby Be Normal?" p. 9; Augenstein, *Play God*, pp. 33ff., Ramsey, *Fabricated Man*, pp. 97f.
14. Callahan, "Genetic Counseling," p. 198.
15. P. B. Medewar, "Genetic Options: An Examination of Current Fallacies," in Daniel H. Labby (ed.): *Life or Death: Ethics and Options* (Portland and Seattle: Reed College and University of Washington Press, 1968), p. 109.
16. Hilton, "Will the Baby Be Normal?" p. 9.
17. Ramsey, *Fabricated Man*, p. 59.
18. I am particularly indebted in this section to Marc Lappé, James M. Gustafson, and Richard Roblin, "Ethical and Social Issues in Screening for Genetic Disease," *The New England Journal of Medicine*, Vol. 286, No. 21 (May 25, 1972), pp. 1129ff.; and Robert F. Murray, Jr., "Problems Behind the Promise: Ethical Issues in Mass Genetic Screening," *The Hastings Center Report*, Vol. 2, No. 2 (April 1972), pp. 10ff.
19. Lappé, Gustafson, and Roblin, "Screening for Genetic Disease," pp. 1129.
20. The means here discussed follow the guidelines set out by the Research Group of the Institute of Society, Ethics, and the Life Sciences; see *ibid*, pp. 1130ff.
21. Samuel P. Bessman and Judith P. Swazey, "Phenylketonuria: A Study of Biomedical Legislation," in Everett Mendelsohn, *et al.*, *Human Aspects of Biomedical Innovation* (Cambridge: Harvard University Press, 1971), pp. 49ff.
22. W. French Anderson, "Genetic Therapy," in Michael P. Hamilton (ed.), *The New Genetics and the Future of Man* (Grand Rapids: William B. Eerdmans Publishing Company, 1972), p. 110.
23. See the varying opinions expressed by Arno G. Motulsky, "Genetic Therapy: A Clinical Geneticist's Response," in Hamilton, *ibid.*, pp. 125ff.; Augenstein, *Play God*, pp. 20ff.; E. Fuller Torrey, "Ethical Issues in Medicine: The Future," in Torrey (ed.), *Ethical Issues in Medicine* (Boston, Little, Brown and Company, 1968), pp. 386f.
24. See Rorvick, *Brave New Baby*, Chap. 4.
25. Ramsey, *Fabricated Man*, pp. 44f., 101f., and 115f.
26. Augenstein, *Play God*, pp. 103f.
27. Hermann J. Muller, "Genetic Progress by Voluntarily Conducted Germinal Choice," in Paul T. Jersild and Dale A. Johnson (eds.), *Moral Issues and Christian Response* (New York: Holt, Rinehart and Winston, Inc., 1971), pp. 422ff.
28. *Ibid.*, p. 432.
29. Ramsey, *Fabricated Man*, pp. 49f.
30. Quoted in Roger L. Shinn, "Christian Ethical Methodology and Questions Relating to Genetics" (Paper delivered at the Tenth Annual Meeting of the American Society of Christian Ethics, Washington, D.C., January 25, 1969), p. 5.

31. Ramsey, *Fabricated Man*, p. 49.
32. Quoted in Shinn, "Christian Ethical Methodology," p. 6.
33. Ramsey, *Fabricated Man*, p. 61.
34. Leon R. Kass, "New Beginnings in Life," in Hamilton, *The New Genetics*, p. 42.
35. Kass, "New Beginnings," pp. 44f.; Rorvick, *Brave New Baby*, pp. 115ff.
36. Joseph Fletcher, "New Beginnings in Life: A Theologian's Response," in Hamilton, *The New Genetics*, p. 84.
37. Ramsey, *Fabricated Man*, pp. 73ff.; Kass, "New Beginnings," pp. 45ff.
38. Torrey, "The Future," pp. 380f.
39. Gerald Leach, *The Biocrats* (New York: McGraw-Hill Book Company, 1970), pp. 84ff.; Rorvick, *Brave New Baby*, pp. 34ff.
40. Leach, *The Biocrats*, pp. 86f.
41. Kass, "New Beginnings," pp. 26f. Italics added.
42. *Ibid.*, p. 27.
43. Paul Ramsey, "Shall We 'Reproduce'? I. The Medical Ethics of In Vitro Fertilization," *Journal of the American Medical Association*, Vol. 220, No. 10 (June 5, 1972), p. 1347.
44. Marc Lappé, "Risk-Taking for the Unborn," *The Hastings Center Report*, Vol. 2, No. 1 (February 1972), pp. 2f.
45. Kass, "New Beginnings," p. 36.
46. Paul Ramsey, "Shall We 'Reproduce'? II. Rejoinders and Future Forecast," *Journal of the American Medical Association*, Vol. 220, No. 11 (June 12, 1972), p. 1481.
47. Shinn, "Christian Ethical Methodology," p. 1.
48. Donald Fleming, "On Living in a Biological Revolution," in Jersild and Johnson, *Moral Issues*, p. 415.
49. Medewar, "Genetic Options," p. 106.
50. James M. Gustafson, "Basic Ethical Issues in the Bio-Medical Fields," *Soundings*, Vol. LIII, No. 2 (Summer 1970), pp. 153ff.
51. Ramsey, *Fabricated Man*, pp. 92ff.; Shinn, "Christian Ethical Methodology," pp. 7f.
52. Quoted in Shinn, *ibid.*
53. See Charles E. Curran, *Contemporary Problems in Moral Theology* (Notre Dame, Ind.: Fides Publishers, Inc., 1970), pp. 198f.
54. Gustafson, "Basic Ethical Issues," pp. 176ff.; Callahan, "Genetic Counseling," pp. 198f.; Christopher Lasch, "Birth, Death and Technology: The Limits of Cultural Laissez-Faire," *The Hastings Center Report*, Vol. 2, No. 3 (June 1972), pp. 1ff.; Robert L. Sinsheimer, "Ambush or Opportunity?" *The Hastings Center Report*, Vol. 2, No. 4 (September 1972), p. 7.

Chapter Six

1. *The Minneapolis Star*, November 8, 1971.
2. *U.S. News & World Report*, May 22, 1972, p. 45.
3. Joseph Fletcher, "Elective Death," in E. Fuller Torrey, *Ethical Issues in Medicine* (Boston: Little, Brown and Company, 1968) pp. 141f.
4. See Merle Longwood's discussion of Gorer, "Ethical Reflections on the Meaning of Death," *Dialog*, Vol. 11, No. 3 (Summer 1972), pp. 195f.

5. Joseph Fletcher, *Moral Responsibility* (Philadelphia: The Westminster Press, 1967), p. 145.
6. This translation of the Hippocratic Oath is that used in Michael Gelfand, *Philosophy and Ethics of Medicine* (Edinburgh: Livingstone, 1968), pp. 107f.
7. Frank J. Ayd, Jr., "What Is Death?" (Paper delivered to the Second National Congress on Medical Ethics, Chicago, Illinois, October 5-6, 1968). Cf. Catherine Lyons, *Organ Transplants: The Moral Issues* (Philadelphia: The Westminster Press, 1970), Chap. 2.
8. Paul Ramsey, *The Patient as Person* (New Haven: Yale University Press, 1970), pp. 64ff. Cf. Lyons, *Organ Transplants*, pp. 6off.
9. Henry K. Beecher, et al., "A Definition of Irreversible Coma," in Donald R. Cutler (ed.), *Updating Life and Death* (Boston: Beacon Press, 1968, 1969), pp. 56ff. Many physicians are quick to insist that the EEG machine does not itself register death. A flat EEG can also be caused by sedatives, intoxication, and profound hypothermia (lowering of the bodily temperature).
10. Dr. Henry K. Beecher says, "The moment of death can only be approximated; it is an imprecise term. That is the principal reason why the Harvard Committee chose to give a definition of irreversible coma... rather than to attempt a definition of death." Beecher, *Research and the Individual* (Boston: Little, Brown and Company, 1970), p. 153. Cf. Ramsey, *Patient as Person*, Chap. 2.
11. Robert S. Morison, "Death: Process or Event?" and Leon R. Kass, "Death as an Event: A Commentary on Robert Morison," *Science*, Vol. 173 (August 20, 1971).
12. Morison, "Process or Event?", p. 696.
13. Kass, "Death as an Event," p. 699.
14. *Ibid.*, p. 700.
15. Ramsey, *Patient as Person*, p. 63.
16. Daniel Callahan, *Abortion: Law, Choice and Morality* (New York: The Macmillan Company, 1970), pp. 387f. Cf. Harmon L. Smith, *Ethics and the New Medicine* (Nashville: Abingdon Press, 1970), p. 129.
17. Morris A. Wessel, "To Comfort Always," *Yale Alumni Magazine*, Vol. XXXV, No. 9 (June 1972), p. 17.
18. *Ibid.*
19. *Ibid.*, p. 18.
20. Paul Ramsey's discussion of these terms is particularly helpful; see *Patient as Person*, pp. 118ff. Cf. Smith, *New Medicine*, pp. 144ff; and Longwood, "Meaning of Death," pp. 199f.
21. Smith, *New Medicine*, p. 145.
22. Quoted in Longwood, "Meaning of Death," p. 199.
23. *St. Paul Sunday Pioneer Press*, April 2, 1972.
24. Edward H. Rynearson, "Should We Use Extraordinary Measures to Prolong the Life of a Patient Dying of Untreatable Cancer?" (Address to the American Medical Association, Chicago, Illinois, June 28, 1962), p. 5.
25. Fletcher, "Elective Death," p. 143.
26. Brian Whitlow, "Extreme Measures to Prolong Life," in D. Wayne Montgomery (ed), *Healing and Wholeness* (Richmond: John Knox Press, 1971), p. 124.

27. Fletcher, "Elective Death," p. 148.
28. Fletcher, *Moral Responsibility*, p. 150.
29. Ramsey, *Patient as Person*, p. 151.
30. See, for example, Lucy Griscom Morgan's poignant essay which suggests this metaphor, "On Drinking the Hemlock," *The Hastings Center Report*, Vol. 1, No. 3 (December 1971), pp. 4f.
31. More elaborated responses to the objections may be found in Joseph Fletcher, *Morals and Medicine* (Boston: Beacon Press, 1960), Chap. 6; Glanville Williams, *The Sanctity of Life and the Criminal Law* (New York: Alfred A. Knopf, 1957), Chap. 8; A. B. Downing (ed.) *Euthanasia and the Right to Die* (London: Peter Owen, 1969); and "The Right to Die," (Statement adopted by the Council for Christian Social Action, United Church of Christ, February 17, 1973).
32. The legal considerations for recognized social approval of euthanasia under carefully-wrought procedures are weighty ones but certainly feasible. Euthanasia societies in both America and Britain have studied this for years. For information on England's Voluntary Euthanasia Society see the appendix to Downing, *Euthanasia and the Right to Die*, pp. 197ff. For the American group's work contact the Euthanasia Educational Council, 250 West 57th Street, New York, N.Y. 10019.
33. Fletcher, "Elective Death," p. 151.
34. David H. Smith, "Euthanasia: Can Killing Be an Act of Love for the Dying?" (Paper delivered at the Society for Religion in Higher Education, Collegeville, Minnesota, August 1972), p. 24. Smith's perceptive paper makes the distinction between the "consumer" perspective on euthanasia (that of those removed from the immediate situation). He argues that neither perspective may be fully adequate, for the consumer may not be in position to make a rational choice and the administrator (the ethicist, for example) may be reasoning abstractedly apart from those specific relationships which should be part of the moral judgment in a given case.
35. As related in James T. Stephens and Edward LeRoy Long, Jr., *The Christian as Doctor* (New York: Association Press, 1960), p. 109.
36. George P. Fletcher, "Legal Aspects of the Decision Not to Prolong Life," in Montgomery, *Healing and Wholeness*, p. 136. Other sources indicate, however, that of the eleven American court cases for mercy killing, nine defendants were acquitted and two (presumably not physicians) were convicted.
37. *Ibid*, pp. 135ff.
38. *Ibid.*, p. 140. Italics added.
39. Quoted in Ian McColl Kennedy, "The Kansas Statute on Death — An Appraisal," *The New England Journal of Medicine*, Vol. 285, No. 17 (Oct. 21, 1971), p. 946.
40. *Ibid.*
41. Don Harper Mills, "The Kansas Death Statute: Bold and Innovative," *The New England Journal of Medicine*, Vol. 285, No. 17 (Oct. 21, 1971).
42. Robert M. Veatch, "Allowing the Dying Patient to Die: An Ethical Analysis of New Policy Proposals," (unpublished paper, n.d.), p. 7.
43. Jonas B. Robitscher, "The Right to Die," *The Hastings Center Report*, Vol. 2, No. 4 (September 1972), pp. 11ff.
44. Veatch, "Allowing the Dying Patient to Die," pp. 14ff.

Notes 203

45. *Ibid.*, p. 16.
46. *Ibid.*, p. 19. I am also indebted to Chaplain Lloyd Beebe, Hennepin County General Hospital, Minneapolis, and to Dr. James Maddock and Dr. Theodore Cole, University of Minnesota Medical School, for their insights about such shared decision-making.
47. *Ibid.*, p. 29.
48. Bayless Manning, "Legal and Policy Issues in the Allocation of Death," in Orville G. Brim, Jr., et al., (eds.), *The Dying Patient* (New York: Russell Sage Foundation, 1970), pp. 271ff.
49. Veatch, "Allowing the Patient to Die," p. 16.
50. Joseph Fletcher, *Morals and Medicine,* Chap. 2, makes this point strongly.
51. James T. Laney, "Ethics and Death," in Liston O. Mills, (ed.), *Perspectives on Death* (Nashville: Abingdon Press, 1969), p. 243. Other particularly helpful discussions of truth as relationship are found in Dietrich Bonhoeffer, *Ethics,* Eberhard Bethge (ed.) (New York: The Macmillan Company, 1955), pp. 326ff.; and Paul L. Lehmann, *Ethics in a Christian Context* (New York: Harper & Row 1963), pp. 159ff. and 192ff.
52. Ramsey, *Patient as Person,* Chap. 3.
53. Robitscher, "The Right to Die," p. 13.
54. Ramsey, *Patient as Person,* p. 135.
55. Robert E. Neale, "A Place to Live, A Place to Die," *The Hastings Center Report,* Vol. 2, No. 3 (June 1972), pp. 12ff.
56. William F. May, "On Not Facing Death Alone," *The Hastings Center Report,* Vol. 1, No. 1 (June 1971).
57. Elisabeth Kübler-Ross, *On Death and Dying* (New York: The Macmillan Company, 1969), Chaps. 3-7.
58. Laney, "Ethics and Death," pp. 238f. Laney is here drawing upon the terms used by Gabriel Marcel.

Chapter Seven

1. William A. Nolen, *Spare Parts for the Human Body* (New York: Random House, 1971), p. 6.
2. Harmon L. Smith, *Ethics and the New Medicine* (Nashville: Abingdon Press, 1970), p. 106.
3. Based upon an actual case, with name and circumstances disguised.
4. I am indebted to the historical interpretations of transplant procedures in Henry K. Beecher, *Research and the Individual* (Boston: Little, Brown and Company, 1970) Chap. 5; Gerald Leach, *The Biocrats* (New York: McGraw-Hill Book Company, 1970), Chap. 10; Catherine Lyons, *Organ Transplants: The Moral Issues* (Philadelphia: The Westminster Press, 1970), Chap. 1; and Smith, *New Medicine,* pp. 90ff.
5. Beecher, *Research and the Individual,* p. 132.
6. Cf. my article "Organ Transplants and the Just War," *Theological Markings,* Vol. 2, No. 1 (Spring 1972), from which I have drawn in this chapter.
7. Paul Ramsey, *War and the Christian Conscience* (Durham: Duke University Press, 1961), p. xxiii. Cf. Edward LeRoy Long, Jr.: *War and Conscience in America* (Philadelphia: The Westminster Press, 1968).

204 *Notes*

8. St. Augustine, *The City of God* (New York: The Modern Library, 1950),
   pp. 683ff.
9. "Guidelines for Organ Transplantation," *Journal of the American Medical
   Association,* Vol. 205, No. 6 (August 5, 1968), p. 90.
10. Harry S. Abram and J. F. Childress, "The Artificial Kidney and Its Moral
    Dilemmas," in Claude A. Frazier (ed.), *Should Doctors Play God?* (Nash-
    ville: Broadman Press, 1971), p. 43.
11. "Guidelines for Organ Transplantation," p. 90.
12. *U.S. News and World Report,* May 22, 1972, p. 46.
13. Smith, *New Medicine,* p. 106.
14. Beecher, *Research and the Individual,* p. 145.
15. Roberta G. Simmons and Richard L. Simmons, "Organ-Transplantation:
    A Societal Problem," *Social Problems,* Vol. 19, No. 1 (Summer 1971),
    pp. 50ff.
16. Paul Ramsey, *The Patient as Person* (New Haven: Yale University Press,
    1970), Chap. 4, provides a good discussion of these issues.
17. Pius XI, *Casti Connubi,* in Anne Fremantle (ed.), *The Papal Encyclicals
    in Their Historical Context* (New York: The New American Library,
    1956, 1963), p. 242.
18. Quoted by Martin Nolan, "The Principle of Totality in Moral Theology,"
    in Charles E. Curran (ed.), *Absolutes in Moral Theology?* (Washington:
    Corpus Books, 1968), p. 237.
19. *Ibid.,* p. 240.
20. John J. Lynch, S.J., "Ethical Implications of Renal Transplants," in D.
    Wayne Montgomery (ed.), *Healing and Wholeness* (Richmond: John
    Knox Press, 1971), p. 221.
21. Ramsey, *Patient as Person,* p. 187.
22. "The Gift of Life" (St. Paul: Kidney Foundation of the Upper Midwest,
    Inc., n.d.)
23. Joseph Fletcher, "Our Shameful Waste of Human Tissue," in Donald R.
    Cutler (ed.), *Updating Life and Death* (Boston: Beacon Press, 1969), p. 3.
24. Leach, *The Biocrats,* pp. 274f.
25. Simmons and Simmons, "Organ-Transplantation," p. 47.
26. Lyons, *Organ Transplants,* pp. 86ff.
27. Simmons and Simmons, "Organ-Transplantation," p. 48.
28. See Lyons, *Organ Transplants,* pp. 87f.; and Ramsey, *Patient as Person,*
    pp. 209f.
29. Simmons and Simmons, "Organ-Transplantation," p. 47.
30. Fletcher, "Our Shameful Waste," p. 25.
31. Keith Reemtsma, "Ethical Problems with Artificial and Transplanted
    Organs," in E. Fuller Torrey (ed.), *Ethical Issues in Medicine* (Boston:
    Little, Brown and Company, 1968), p. 252. Italics added.
32. Quoted by Leach, *The Biocrats,* p. 262. Italics added.
33. Beecher, *Research and the Individual,* pp. 157f.; Ramsey, *Patient as
    Person,* pp. 235ff.
34. Chad H. Calland, "Iatrogenic Problems in End-Stage Renal Failure," *The
    New England Journal of Medicine,* Vol. 287, No. 7 (Aug. 17, 1972), p. 334.
35. *Ibid.,* p. 335.
36. Leach, *The Biocrats,* p. 264.

37. Dieter Walther, "Theological and Ethical Aspects of a Heart Transplantation," in Paul T. Jersild and Dale A. Johnson (eds.), *Moral Issues and Christian Response* (New York: Holt, Rinehart and Winston, Inc., 1971), p. 463.

38. Simmons and Simmons, "Organ-Transplantation," p. 49.

39. Long, *War and Conscience*, p. 27.

40. "Guidelines for Organ Transplantation."

41. Smith, *New Medicine*, p. 102f.

42. Leroy Augenstein, *Come, Let Us Play God* (New York: Harper & Row, 1969), p. 42.

43. The comparison is adapted from Nolen, *Spare Parts*, p. 97.

44. Cf. L. Harold DeWolf, *Responsible Freedom* (New York: Harper & Row, 1971), p. 298.

45. Lyons, *Organ Transplants*, pp. 92ff.

46. Tissue typing and matching has become in recent years a technique of great importance for transplant success. Recipients whose tissues identically or nearly match the tissue types of their donors have a much lower rate of rejection problems with the new organ. Regional centers utilizing computers and teletype equipment to gather and quickly sort information about tissue compatibility have arisen in both Europe and the United States, thus facilitating the matching of cadaver organs with appropriate patients.

47. Simmons and Simmons, "Organ-Transplantation," p. 43.

48. This is the "Renal Amendment to the Medicare Bill," passed in 1972. It makes all persons covered by Social Security eligible for major renal transplant costs as well as for kidney dialysis.

49. Abram and Childress, "The Artificial Kidney," pp. 41ff.; James F. Childress, "Who Shall Live When Not All Can Live?" *Soundings,* Vol. LIII, No. 4 (Winter 1970).

50. Ramsey, *Patient as Person*, p. 248; Childress, "Who Shall Live?" p. 345.

51. Abram and Childress, "The Artificial Kidney," pp. 43ff.; Childress, "Who Shall Live?" pp. 347ff. For a critique of random selection see Frederic B. Westervelt, Jr., "The Selection Process as Viewed from Within," *Soundings,* Vol. LIII, No. 4 (Winter 1970).

52. E. Fuller Torrey, "Ethical Issues in Medicine: The Future," in Torrey, *Ethical Issues*, pp. 391ff.; Nolen, *Spare Parts*, Chap. 13.

53. Quoted in Walther, "Heart Transplantation," p. 465.

Chapter Eight

1. *Time,* January 15, 1973, pp. 51f.

2. Edward M. Kennedy, "A Crisis in Compassion," *Social Action,* Vol. XXXVIII, No. 2 (October 1971), p. 7.

3. Rodger Hurley, "The Health Care Crisis of the Poor," in Hans Peter Dreitzel, *Social Organization of Health* (New York: The Macmillan Company, 1971), p. 83.

4. Rodney M. Coe, *Sociology of Medicine* (New York: McGraw-Hill Book Company, 1970), Chaps. 12 and 13.

5. Barbara and John Ehrenreich, *The American Health Empire* (New York: Random House, 1970), Chap. 2.
6. *Ibid.*, p. 31.
7. For figures and interpretations in this section I have drawn upon the following sources: David Mazie, "The Rising Cost of Medical Care," *Britannica Book of the Year 1972* (Chicago: Encyclopedia Britannica, Inc., 1972), pp. 463f.; Paul M. Ellwood, Jr., and Earl J. Hoagberg, "The Health Maintenance Organization: Shape of Things to Come in Health Care," *Commercial West*, April 17, 1971, pp. 36ff.; Edmund K. Faltermayer, "Better Care at Less Cost Without Miracles," *Fortune*, January 1970, pp. 80ff.; John M. Meeklin, "Hospitals Need Management Even More Than Money," *Fortune*, January 1970, pp. 96ff.; George A. Silver, "National Health Insurance, National Health Policy, and the National Health," *American Journal of Nursing*, Vol. 71, No. 9 (September 1971), pp. 1730ff.; *The New York Times*, June 25, 1972; and *The Minneapolis Tribune*, April 17, 1972; November 29, 1972; January 14, 1973; and January 18, 1973.
8. Ellwood and Hoagberg, "The Health Maintenance Organization," p. 37; Charles Lerrigo, "The Delivery of Health Care — Taking on Crisis Proportions," *JSAC Grapevine*, Vol. 3, No. 9 (April 1972), p. 1.
9. *The Minneapolis Tribune*, December 17, 1971.
10. Hurley, "Crisis of the Poor," pp. 83ff.; Bonnie Bullough and Vern L. Bullough, *Poverty, Ethnic Identity, and Health Care* (New York: Appleton-Century Crofts, 1972).
11. Hurley, "Crisis of the Poor," p. 86.
12. Dan Cordtz, "Change Begins in the Doctor's Office," in Dreitzel, *Social Organization*, pp. 219ff.
13. Ehrenreich and Ehrenreich, *American Health Empire*, Chap. I.
14. In addition to the sources cited in this section, I am indebted to the insights of Mr. Earl Hoagburg, staff specialist in health care of the Institute for Interdisciplinary Studies, Minneapolis, and Dr. Vernon Weckworth of the University of Minnesota Medical School.
15. John H. Knowles, "Notes on Medical Manpower," in Everett Mendelsohn, et al., *Human Aspects of Biomedical Innovation* (Cambridge: Harvard University Press, 1971), pp. 188f.; *The Minneapolis Tribune*, January 3, 1972.
16. Cordtz, "Doctor's Office," p. 223.
17. Anne R. Somers, *Health Care in Transition: Directions for the Future* (Chicago Hospital Research and Educational Trust, 1971), p. 127.
18. *Ibid.*, pp. 129ff.
19. Kennedy, "A Crisis in Compassion," p. 9.
20. Ellwood and Hoagburg, "The Health Maintenance Organization," p. 37.
21. For the particular data on HMOs I am indebted to Ellwood and Hoagburg, "The Health Maintenance Organization"; Paul M. Ellwood, Jr., et al., "Health Maintenance Strategy," *Medical Care*, Vol. 9, No. 3 (May-June 1971); Faltermeyer, "Better Care"; Clark C. Havighurst, *Health Maintenance Organizations and the Market for Health Services* (Minneapolis: Institute for Interdisciplinary Studies, 1971); and *Hospitals (Journal of the American Hospital Association)*, Vol. 45 (March 16, 1971), which is devoted to this subject.

22. Robert M. Sade, "Medical Care as a Right: A Refutation," *The New England Journal of Medicine,* Vol. 285, No. 23 (December 2, 1971), p. 1289.
23. "Correspondence," *The New England Journal of Medicine,* Vol. 286, No. 9 (March 2, 1972), pp. 488ff.
24. F. J. Ingelfinger, "Rights of Authors and of Patients" (editorial), *The New England Journal of Medicine,* Vol. 286, No. 9 (March 2, 1972), p. 487.
25. *Ibid.*
26. John E. Smith, "Rights," in John Macquarrie, *Dictionary of Christian Ethics* (Philadelphia: The Westminster Press, 1967), pp. 300f.
27. Cordtz, "Doctor's Office," p. 232. As recently as 1968, 41 percent of all medical students still came from homes with incomes above $15,000 (the wealthiest eighth of the nation). The next 22 percent were from families with incomes between $10,000 and $15,000.
28. Richard Lichtman, "The Political Economy of Medical Care," in Dreitzel, *Social Organization,* p. 266.
29. Victor W. Sidel, "Medical Ethics and Socio-political Change," *The Hastings Center Report,* Vol. 2, No. 4 (September 1972), pp. 8ff.
30. Robert J. Bazell, "Health Radicals: Crusade to Shift Medical Power to the People," *Science,* Vol. 173 (August 6, 1971), pp. 506ff.; Michael G. Michaelson, "Medical Students: Healers Become Activists," *The Saturday Review,* August 16, 1969, pp. 41ff.; Ehrenreich and Ehrenreich, *American Health Empire,* Chap. 17; and Lerrigo, "The Delivery of Health Care."
31. See the Special Report, "How Well Are Patients' Rights Observed?" *Hospital Practice,* Vol. 8, No. 3 (March 1973), pp. 31ff.
32. H. Richard Niebuhr, *The Responsible Self* (New York: Harper & Row, 1963), p. 126.
33. Paul L. Lehmann, *Ethics in a Christian Context* (New York: Harper & Row, 1963), p. 101.
34. Robert M. Veatch, "Models for Ethical Medicine in a Revolutionary Age," *The Hastings Center Report,* Vol. 2, No. 3 (June 1972), pp. 5ff.
35. E. Fuller Torrey, "Ethical Issues in Medicine: The Future," in Torrey (ed.), *Ethical Issues in Medicine* (Boston: Little, Brown and Company, 1968), p. 405.
36. Paul Tillich, *Love, Power, and Justice* (New York: Oxford University Press, 1960), p. 65.

93197

AUTHOR
Nelson, James B

TITLE
Human medicine...

DATE DUE	BORROWER'S NAME
03 04 6	KIMBERLY LANGLEY
	RETURNED
RETURNED	SR E I JACKSON
28	KATHRYN HEIMANN
05 15 7	RETURNED

174.2   1973
N427h
Nelson, James B
Human medicine...